Building Competitiveness in Africa's Agriculture

AGRICULTURE AND RURAL DEVELOPMENT

Seventy-five percent of the world's poor live in rural areas and most are involved in agriculture. In the 21st century, agriculture remains fundamental to economic growth, poverty alleviation, and environmental sustainability. The World Bank's Agriculture and Rural Development publication series presents recent analyses of issues that affect the role of agriculture, including livestock, fisheries, and forestry, as a source of economic development, rural livelihoods, and environmental services. The series is intended for practical application, and we hope that it will serve to inform public discussion, policy formulation, and development planning.

Titles in this series:

Agribusiness and Innovation Systems in Africa

Agricultural Land Redistribution: Toward Greater Consensus

Agriculture Investment Sourcebook

Bioenergy Development: Issues and Impacts for Poverty and Natural Resource Management

Building Competitiveness in Africa's Agriculture: A Guide to Value Chain Concepts and Applications

Changing the Face of the Waters: The Promise and Challenge of Sustainable Aquaculture

Enhancing Agricultural Innovation: How to Go Beyond the Strengthening of Research Systems

Forests Sourcebook: Practical Guidance for Sustaining Forests in Development Cooperation

Gender and Governance in Rural Services: Insights from India, Ghana, and Ethiopia

Gender in Agriculture Sourcebook

Organization and Performance of Cotton Sectors in Africa: Learning from Reform Experience

Reforming Agricultural Trade for Developing Countries, Volume 1: Key Issues for a Pro-Development Outcome of the Doha Round

Reforming Agricultural Trade for Developing Countries, Volume 2: Quantifying the Impact of Multilateral Trade Reform

Shaping the Future of Water for Agriculture: A Sourcebook for Investment in Agricultural Water Management

The Sunken Billions: The Economic Justification for Fisheries Reform

Sustainable Land Management: Challenges, Opportunities, and Trade-Offs

Sustainable Land Management Sourcebook

Sustaining Forests: A Development Strategy

Building Competitiveness in Africa's Agriculture

A GUIDE TO VALUE CHAIN CONCEPTS AND APPLICATIONS

C. Martin Webber and Patrick Labaste

THE WORLD BANK
Washington, DC

ISBN: 978-0-8213-7952-3
eISBN: 978-0-8213-7964-6
DOI: 10.1596/978-0-8213-7952-3

Library of Congress Cataloging-in-Publication Data

Webber, C. Martin.
Building competitiveness in Africa's agriculture : a guide to value chain concepts and applications / C. Martin Webber and Patrick Labaste.
      p. cm. — (Agriculture and rural development)
   Includes bibliographical references and index.
   ISBN 978-0-8213-7952-3 (pbk.) — ISBN 978-0-8213-7964-6 (electronic)
      1. Agricultural industries—Africa. 2. Agriculture—Economic aspects—Africa. I. Labaste, Patrick, 1952-
II. World Bank. III. Title.

HD9017.A2W43 2009
338.1096—dc22

                                                                                          2009019928

Cover photographs: Tea-picker in Rwanda by Günter Guni, ©iStockphoto.com / guenterguni; vegetable garden in rural Kwa-Zulu Natal, South Africa, by Trevor Samson / World Bank.
Cover design: Critical Stages, based on a template by Patricia Hord Graphik Design.

Building Competitiveness in Africa's Agriculture is available as an interactive textbook at http://www.worldbank.org/pdt. The electronic version allows communities of practice and colleagues working in sectors and regions, as well as students and teachers, to share notes and related materials for an enhanced multimedia learning and knowledge-exchange experience.

CONTENTS

ACKNOWLEDGMENTS

This Guide was prepared by J. E. Austin Associates, Inc., for the Agriculture and Rural Development Group of the Sustainable Development Network of the World Bank. The work was directed by Patrick Labaste, Sustainable Development Department of the Africa Region of the World Bank. The principal author and team leader was Martin Webber, Executive Vice President of J. E. Austin Associates, Inc.

This work was funded by the World Bank, by contributions from the Bank-Netherlands Partnership Program (BNPP), and from the All-ACP Agricultural Commodities Programme (AAACP) of the European Union.

Contributors from J. E. Austin Associates, Inc., included Marcos Arocha, Nayha Arora, Virginia Brandon, Lisa Carse, Grant Cavanaugh, Michael Ducker, David Feige, Michael Gorman, Carlton Jones, Mollie Logue, Jennifer Lynch, Alicia Miller, Kirk Nathanson, Matthew Shapiro, Jane Shearer, Justin Stokes, and Gina Tumbarello. Kevin X. Murphy, President of J. E. Austin Associates, Inc., deserves special appreciation. World Bank collaborators included Malick Antoine and Jean-Luc Bosio. Jean Michel Voisard and Martin Donarski also provided valuable guidance and comments.

The authors convened a roundtable of industry experts, who provided suggestions and experiences that enhanced this Guide. The roundtable participants included: Grahame Dixie, Richard Henry, Steve Jaffee, John Lamb, Svetlana Meades, Paul Siegel, Yolanda Strachan, and Uma Subramanian of the World Bank Group; Susan Bornstein (TechnoServe); Jeanne Downing (USAID); Paul Guenette (ACDI-VOCA); Olaf Kula (ACDI-VOCA); Frank Lusby (Action for Enterprise); and Lynn Salinger (AIRD).

Numerous individuals contributed their expertise and experience, particularly to the case studies. They shared their own stories, and their analyses and observations. Their personal experiences and generous willingness to share their stories and conclusions make this Guide a particularly rich source of ideas and information. We sincerely apologize for any omissions, which, of course, are inadvertent, in citing contributors.

ACRONYMS AND ABBREVIATIONS

AAK	Agricultural Association of Kenya
ADAR	Agribusiness Development Activity in Rwanda
AGOA	African Growth and Opportunity Act
AIA	Agro Industria Associadas
AMAP/BDS	Accelerated Microenterprise Advancement Project/Business Development Services
APEP	Agricultural Productivity Enhancement Program
BCPA	Botswana Cattle Producers Association
BDS	Business Development Services
BMC	Botswana Meat Commission
BMU	Beach Management Unit
CAADP	Comprehensive Africa Agricultural Development Programme
CFA	Communauté Financière d'Afrique
CTBI	Coffee Taxation and Benchmarking Initiative
DFID	Department for International Development
DPL	Dipped Products Ltd.
DRC	Domestic Resource Cost
EAGA	East African Growers Association
EFEG	Exotic Fruit Exporters Association of Ghana
ESSD Africa	Environmentally and Socially Sustainable Development Department, Africa Region (World Bank)
EU	European Union
EurepGAP	Euro-Retailer Produce Working Group on Good Agricultural Practices
FAO	Food and Agriculture Organization of the United Nations
FAOSTAT	FAO Statistical Database
FCFA	CFA Franc
FDI	Foreign Direct Investment
FOB	Free on board
FPEAK	Fresh Produce Exporters Association of Kenya
GAP	Good Agricultural Practices
GDP	Gross Domestic Product
GMP	Good Manufacturing Practice
GPSCA	Gabinete de Promoçao do Sector Comercial Agrário
GTZ	Gesellschaft für Technische Zusammenarbeit

HACCP	Hazard Analysis and Critical Control Point
HAG	Horticultural Association Ghana
HCDA	Horticultural Crops Development Authority
IDA	International Development Association (World Bank)
IFC	International Finance Corporation
IFPRI	International Food Policy Research Institute
INCAJU	National Cashew Institute
KARI/NHRC	Kenya Agricultural Research Institute/National Horticultural Research Centre
KEPHIS	Kenya Plant Health Inspectorate Services
KILICAFE	Association of Kilimanjaro Specialty Coffee Growers (Tanzania)
LINTCO	Lint Company of Zambia
M&E	Monitoring and evaluation
MCI	Mongolian Competitiveness Initiative
MDG	Millennium Development Goals
MT	Metric ton
NEPAD	New Partnership for Africa's Development
NGO	Nongovernmental organization
OCAB	Office Centrale des Producteurs-Exportateurs d'Ananas et de Bananes
OCIR-CAFÉ	Rwanda Coffee Development Authority
PAID	Process indicators, action indicators, investment indicators, delivered results
PCPB	Pest Control Products Board
PEARL	Partnership to Enhance Agriculture in Rwanda through Linkages
PISDAC	Pakistan Initiative for Strategic Development and Competitiveness
PoP	Point of purchase
PSD	Private Sector Development
R&D	Research and Development
RCA	Revealed comparative advantage
SADC	South African Development Community
SAGCH	Southern Africa Global Competitiveness Hub
SME	Small and medium enterprise
SMEX	Small and medium enterprise exporters
SPEED	Support for Private Enterprise Expansion and Development
SPEG	Sea Freight Pineapple Exporters of Ghana
SSA	Sub-Saharan Africa
SWOT	Strengths/weaknesses/opportunities/threats
TIP	Trade and Investment Program
TSC	Sri Lankan Spice Council
TZS	Tanzanian shilling
UBA	Union Bananiére Africaine
UFEA	Uganda Flower Exporters Association
UFPEA	Uganda Fish Processors and Exporters Association
UNBS	Uganda National Bureau of Standards
USAID	U.S. Agency for International Development
USDA	United States Department of Agriculture
WCO	World Customs Organization
ZEGA	Zambian Export Growers Association
ZPA	Zambia Privatization Agency

Introduction and Overview

For many years and until quite recently, agriculture fell out of favor with development practitioners, receiving only 4 percent of official development assistance and 4 percent of public expenditure in sub-Saharan Africa (SSA) (World Development Report [WDR] 2008). However, as exemplified by the 2008 WDR dedicated to Agriculture for Development, the development community has refocused on agriculture as an effective means of fighting poverty, and we may expect the above pattern to be reversed. The 2008 WDR notes, "[f]or the poorest people, GDP growth originating in agriculture is about four times more effective in raising incomes of extremely poor people than GDP growth originating outside the sector." This renewal of interest in agriculture has been further enhanced by the recent rise of global food prices. As more and better-funded agricultural development projects emerge in the next few years, policy professionals will require new frameworks for designing and evaluating investments in commercial agriculture. This Guide to value chain approaches provides the user with actionable methods and tools to design programs and investment projects that aim to increase the productivity and performance of sub-Saharan African agriculture.

AGRICULTURAL VALUE CHAINS AND AFRICA'S DEVELOPMENT AGENDA

Value chains are a key framework for understanding how inputs and services are brought together and then used to grow, transform, or manufacture a product; how the product then moves physically from the producer to the customer; and how value increases along the way. The value chain perspective provides an important means to understand business-to-business relationships that connect the chain, mechanisms for increasing efficiency, and ways to enable businesses to increase productivity and add value. It also provides a reference point for improvements in supporting services and the business environment. It can contribute to pro-poor initiatives and better linking of small businesses with the market. Increasingly, the value chain approach is being used to guide and drive high-impact and sustainable initiatives focused on improving productivity, competitiveness, entrepreneurship, and the growth of small and medium enterprises (SMEs).

Despite the successes of many African exporters in selling to new markets, without further improvements to their business environments and to the competitiveness of their export commodities, many SSA countries risk being trapped into producing low-skill, low-value products and services, struggling to obtain a significant value-added share in global trade. It follows that raising the productivity and increasing the efficiency of agricultural value chains are basic to the success of SSA rural economies and to the growth of incomes of their rural populations.

The Comprehensive Africa Agricultural Development Programme (CAADP), a program of the New Partnership for Africa's Development (NEPAD), is directly aimed at raising productivity and increasing the efficiency of agriculture. Through this program, the African Union has agreed to increase public investment in agriculture by a minimum of 10 percent of their national budgets and to raise agricultural productivity by at least 6 percent. According to 2008 data from IFPRI, African countries and their partners need to focus on boosting the supply response to the rise in international food prices in order to continue growing at the same rate. The CAADP will help committed member states effectively respond to the food price crisis and other pressures, enabling agriculture to contribute substantially to continued economic growth.

The development and business communities involved in the African agriculture and agribusiness sectors have recently experienced a strong resurgence of interest in promoting value chains as an approach that can help design interventions geared to add value, lower transaction costs, diversify rural economies, and contribute to increasing rural household incomes in SSA countries. Enhancing value chain competitiveness is increasingly recognized as an effective approach to generating growth and reducing the rural poverty prevalent in the region. This is a welcome development for practitioners who have long been convinced of the need to look differently at agriculture—not just as a means of survival, but as smaller or larger commercial businesses linked to domestic and global markets—and of the need to identify and tap into new sources of potential growth and value addition in the sector. Hopefully, renewed engagement will lead to a substantial increase in the flow of financial resources and technical assistance devoted to supporting market-driven, competitive agroenterprises and agricultural value chains throughout the African continent.

However, there is danger that this renewed engagement may not last, or may even backfire, if the high expectations placed on promoting value chains are not met. Because the development literature is not clear about the concepts and methods relating to value chains, there is risk that sooner or later the benefits of the value chain approach will be overshadowed by unmet expectations. That in turn could cause the approach to be discarded categorically. Although there is no single way to mitigate such risks, this Guide aims to offer practical advice and tools to businessmen, policy makers, representatives of farmer or trade organizations, and others who are engaged in SSA agroenterprise and agribusiness development. This Guide is particularly designed for those who want to know more about value chain–based approaches, and how to use them in ways that can contribute to sound operational decisions and results for enterprise and industry development, as well as for policy making with respect to doing business, stimulating investment, and enhancing trade in the context of African agriculture.

Using concrete examples, mostly from African countries, this Guide presents, reviews, and systematically illustrates a range of concepts, analytical tools, and methodologies centered on the value chain that can be used to design, prepare, implement, assess, and evaluate agribusiness development initiatives. It presents and comments on various conceptual, methodological, and practical approaches to improving the competitiveness of agricultural supply and value chains. The Guide stresses the importance of value chain–based approaches to agroenterprise and agrofood chain development in SSA. It underscores principles of market focus, partnering, collaboration and information sharing, and innovation.

The tools and case studies discussed in this Guide have been selected for their usefulness in directing and supporting market-driven, private sector initiative and action. While the Guide is designed to speak directly to the needs of the businesses and direct actors in the value chains, it also serves as a resource for those practitioners, planners, and program implementers who work closely with value chain participants who want to improve the productivity of Africa's agriculture.

OPPORTUNITIES AND THREATS ASSOCIATED WITH TRADE AND MARKET GLOBALIZATION FOR AFRICAN ECONOMIES

Fundamental changes in international commerce and finance, including reduced transport costs, advances in telecommunications technology, and lower trade barriers, have fueled a rapid increase in global integration. International flows of goods and services, capital, technology, ideas, and people offer great opportunities for African nations to boost growth and reduce poverty by stimulating productivity and efficiency, providing access to new markets, and expanding the range of consumer choice. Yet at the same time, globalization creates new challenges, including the need to increase the quality and sophistication of African goods and services, to make regulatory reforms designed to take full advantage of global markets, and to introduce cost-effective approaches to cope with the resulting adjustment costs and regional imbalances (Bolnick, Camoens, and Zislin 2005).

The majority of sub-Saharan Africans are low-income, and often subsistence, farmers. Sixty-five percent of Africans in SSA live in rural areas (World Bank 2007), while 75 percent of the SSA labor force works in agriculture. Sub-Saharan Africa's share of the world's agricultural exports is approximately 2 percent, and imports represent approximately 2 percent of world trade (see figure 1.1; FAO 2006).

Since 1970, trade in SSA has grown at three-quarters of the world's rate and at only about half of Asia's rate. Africa's share in world trade actually fell from 4 percent in the 1970s to 2 percent in 2005 (see figure 1.2). One of the most striking phenomena is the gradual marginalization of sub-Saharan Africa in international agricultural export markets. Even though SSA possesses 12 percent of the world's arable land, the region's share of global agricultural exports has declined gradually from almost 10 percent four decades ago to around 2 percent today (FAO 2006). On the import side, the opposite pattern emerges: sub-Saharan Africa is the only developing region that has seen its share of world agricultural imports increase rather than decrease (FAO 2005).

These patterns are manifest in assessments of Africa's trade openness[1] (measured by the trade to gross domestic product [GDP] ratio), which has also liberalized more slowly than that of any other major developing region, and SSA has supplanted Latin America as the region least open to trade (Gupta and Yang 2006).

However, the trends are not all negative. In fact, several SSA countries have recently improved their standing in

Figure 1.1 SSA's Share of World Agricultural Exports by Value, 2006

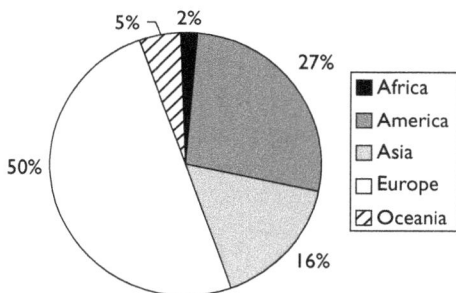

Source: FAOSTAT 2006.

Figure 1.2 Africa's Share of World Trade

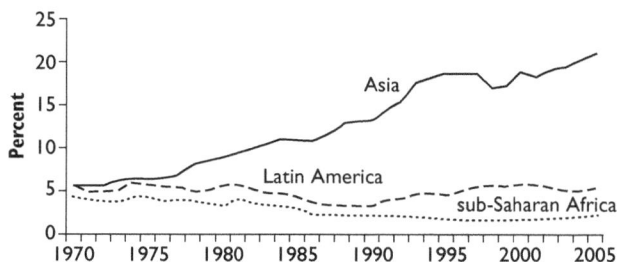

Source: Reprinted from: Gupta and Yang (2005), "Unblocking Trade."

terms of trade openness and taken advantage of new export opportunities. As a region, SSA's average trade openness in 2005, as measured by exports as a percentage of GDP, was 39 percent, an increase of 18 percent from 2002 levels (see table 1.1). Yet within Africa, levels of trade openness fluctuate depending on geographic location, resource endowment, infrastructure quality, enabling environment, and other factors.

Those blocks of countries showing notable increases in trade openness are: non-oil-producing countries (36 percent change since 2002); SSA excluding South Africa and Nigeria (33 percent change since 2002); and the countries of the Economic and Monetary Community of Central Africa (29 percent). Africa's oil-producing countries have measured a 61 percent increase in exports since 2002, but when compared to 1997–2002 levels, this is an 8 percent drop, perhaps indicating that recent growth is largely due to volatility in world oil markets (especially the drop in trade during 2002). Relative to other parts of Africa, recent trends of trade openness show poor performance by countries of the West African Economic Monetary Union (–6 percent) and those of the Common Market of Eastern and Southern Africa (6 percent).

Still, Africa's exports remain dominated by primary commodities, with fuels accounting for about 40 percent and agricultural products approximately 20 percent. SSA has seen a sharp decline in the share of agriculture in its total exports, from more than 60 percent four decades ago to around 20 percent today (FAO 2005). Only a few countries, such as Zambia and Kenya, have achieved significant diversification of their exports, while the share of manufactured goods in Africa's total exports has stagnated at about 30 percent, well below that of other developing regions. In addition, manufactured exports from African countries have a narrow base and low value added; often, they are semiprocessed, raw materials, or products that have preferential access to industrial countries.

The high commodity prices of recent years, coupled with Asia's rapid economic growth, have helped Africa expand its exports to Asia, which now imports 25 percent of all African exports. The growing economies of India and China alone account for 10 percent of Africa's exports. As these countries continue to grow and demand more natural resources, African exporters may be poised to increase revenues and expand their production in concert with the Indian and Chinese economic growth.

Even so, without further improvements to their business environments and the competitiveness of their export commodities, many SSA countries risk being competitively

Table 1.1 African Trade Growth—Export of Goods and Services (% of GDP)

Countries and Regions	Historical Average 1997–2001	2002	2003	2004	2005	Change: Historical–2005 (%)	Change: 2002–2005 (%)
Sub-Saharan Africa (SSA)	31.5	32.6	33.8	35.9	38.5	22	18
SSA excluding S. Africa and Nigeria	32.6	30.5	34.2	38.2	40.7	25	33
CFA Franc Zone	34.7	37.7	36.1	39.8	43.2	24	15
West African Economic Monetary Union	29.5	33.3	30.5	30.6	31.3	6	–6
Economic and Monetary Community of Central Africa	41.4	43.2	43.2	50.4	55.7	35	29
Common Market of Eastern and Southern Africa	30.4	31.6	31.4	31.8	33.5	10	6
Oil-producing countries	45.7	26.1	33.9	39.6	42.1	–8	61
Non-oil-producing countries	26.7	46.7	50.4	56.6	63.4	137	36

Source: Reprinted from IMF 2005.

trapped—selling low-skill, low-value products and services, with little chance to increase value-added share in global trade. Without market knowledge, particular expertise, or competitive products and services, entire economies will essentially fail to take advantage of the potentially high benefits of global markets and the increases in global trade flows. SSA economies unable to claim a more significant share of global trade will find it difficult to achieve the sustainable and accelerated growth rates that are necessary to reach the Millennium Development Goals (MDGs) and significantly reduce poverty on the continent.

These threats and opportunities hold particularly true for agriculture, the main export revenue source for many SSA countries and the largest income generator for their populations. Increasing the production of, and export revenues from, agricultural goods entails developing marketing channels and outlets. Such development is essential to national strategies to raise incomes and eradicate poverty in SSA. Increased productivity in terms of value and profitability is clearly the way to generate higher incomes in a sustainable manner—that is, without further depleting SSA's natural resource base.

COMPARISON OF AGRICULTURAL PRODUCTIVITY

One way to increase the competitiveness of an industry or product on the global market is to produce more efficiently. Increases in efficiency are captured by measuring the agriculture value added per worker, which is also a proxy for agricultural productivity.[2] For African producers to capture

more value and increase exports, they must increase productivity levels. SSA's agriculture productivity measure of US$335 value added per worker (2003–5) is the world's lowest. In comparison, at US$914, world agricultural productivity averages 3 times the SSA level, and Latin America is nearly 10 times more productive at US$3,057 per worker.

African productivity, in terms of yields, is also very low (see figure 1.3).

Such low levels of productivity hinder Africa's attempts at reducing poverty. SSA's agricultural value chains need to become more productive and competitive in the global market for agricultural goods, and its value chains need to achieve greater value within Africa, as well. Increases in competitiveness can assist those dependent on agriculture and agribusiness in increasing their incomes and asset base.

Within Africa, there are large discrepancies between countries' average levels of productivity. Countries such as Mali, South Africa, and Zambia have achieved high levels of sustained growth over the past 17 years (see table 1.2, pertaining to cereal yields). Others, such as Burundi, the Democratic Republic of the Congo, Liberia, and Zimbabwe,[3] have suffered significant decreases in agricultural productivity, which may be the result of insecurity, conflict, climate change, as well as of unsound economic policies.

Productivity in terms of net value added is a crucial measure of value chain performance. Value chains encapsulate the sequence of steps, flows, investments, actors, and interrelationships that characterize and drive the process from production to delivery of a product to the market. Raising the productivity (as well as efficiency) of agricultural value chains is key to the success of SSA's rural economies and to the incomes of SSA's rural populations.

Figure 1.3   Maize Yields and Aggregate Fruit Yields
Excluding Melons, Africa versus World

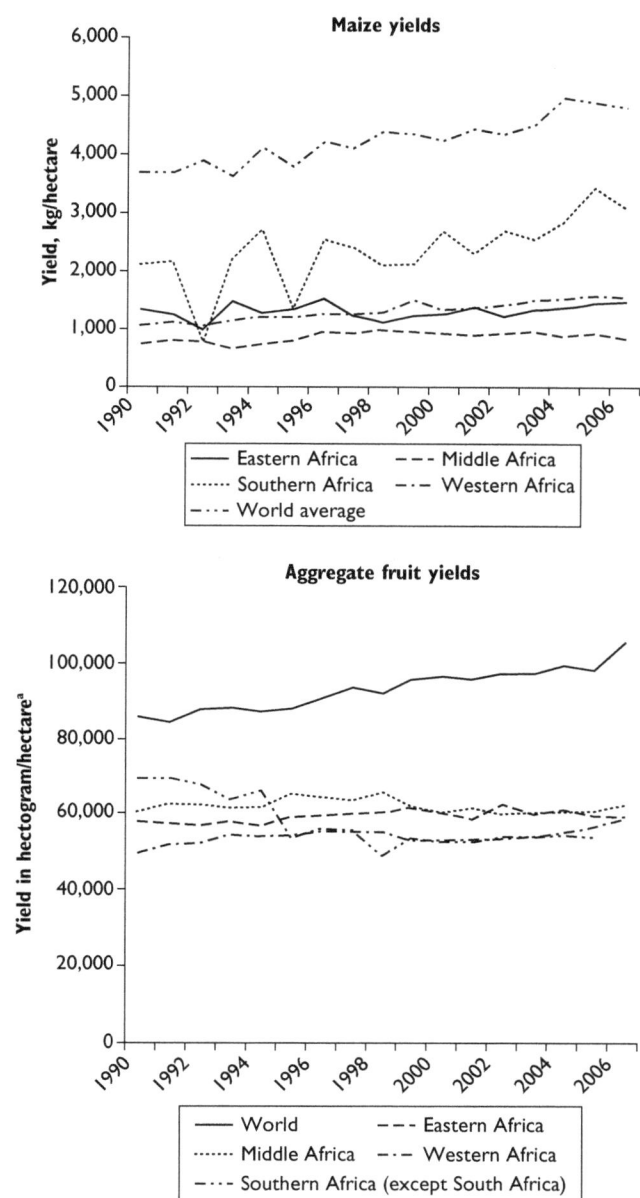

Maize yields

Legend:
— Eastern Africa   - - - Middle Africa
· · · · Southern Africa   - · - Western Africa
- · · - World average

Aggregate fruit yields

Legend:
— World   - - - Eastern Africa
· · · · Middle Africa   - · - Western Africa
- · · - Southern Africa (except South Africa)

Source: FAOSTAT data.
[a] FAO estimate.

OBJECTIVES OF THE GUIDE

Worldwide, there has been a great deal of experimentation and learning in the search for reliable strategies to achieve sustainable economic growth. Recognizing that this growth must be led by sound business strategy and operation and driven by market demand, practitioners have gradually abandoned early, state-focused models (that is, government ownership of resources and enterprises) and have since recognized that both public and private sectors have vital roles to play in the economic-growth partnership. How well those respective public and private roles are defined, and how competently each sector performs its role, are significant determinants of economic growth.

For many years, private sector development initiatives and programs have emphasized actions to increase businesses' access to training, skills development, financing, entrepreneurship, business development services, and other important elements. More contemporary focuses have included helping small and medium enterprises link with global markets and improving business environments. While these varied initiatives have all proven useful, each by itself is unlikely to generate significant changes in a country's economic performance.

Starting in the mid-1980s, as part of the push toward diversification into nontraditional agricultural export crops that occurred in the Latin America and Caribbean region with the passage of the Caribbean Basin Initiative, a great deal of useful work was done on the "deal-making" approach to high-value products, which involves helping businesses identify and penetrate new markets with path-breaking initial shipments. Often this approach was pushed in response to donor agency impatience to demonstrate visible results in the short run.

However, while buy-sell transactions are the essence of business, over time it has become clear that the transaction-based approach does not adequately respond to the desire of large buying organizations to have a consistent supply of high-quality, standards-compliant product, nor does it ensure long-term viability. Both the "category management" that drives the food industry and the quest for sustainability that drives development require a shared vision that engages all partners, planning that spans across seasons and years, as well as structured procurement/supply programs that present win-win situations and sustainable results for a particular food category.[4] So in recent years, leading practitioners have refocused on improving access to and participation in the more profitable, higher volume value chains, and the efficient supply chains on which they must rely, both as a means to achieving better category management in food enterprises as well as forging longer-term partnerships.

In the above context, the World Bank has been giving increasing emphasis in recent years to challenges associated with agricultural trade facilitation, export promotion, and global or regional competitiveness. The Bank hopes to contribute to the transformation of African agriculture into a

Table 1.2 Aggregate Cereal Yield per Hectare (kg/Ha), by Country

Country	1990	2002	2006	Change 1990–2006 (%)	Change 2002–2006 (%)
Angola	320.59	640.12	485.44	51.4	−24.2
Benin	847.85	945.13	1,125.16	32.7	19.0
Botswana	265.38	358.82	341.47	28.7	−4.8
Burkina Faso	600.22	942.68	1,126.59	87.7	19.5
Burundi	1,348.51	1,334.28	1,329.73	−1.4	−0.3
Cameroon	1,241.44	1,683.00	1,408.39	13.4	−16.3
Cape Verde	334.60	148.50	354.72	6.0	138.9
Central African Republic	806.99	1,019.68	1,074.07	33.1	5.3
Chad	559.21	670.89	749.54	34.0	11.7
Congo, Dem. Rep. of	799.85	771.98	785.42	−1.8	1.7
Congo, Rep. of	624.31	785.52	789.92	26.5	0.6
Côte d'Ivoire	884.82	1,719.47	1,776.51	100.8	3.3
Djibouti	1,666.67	1,666.67	1,500.00	−10.0	−10.0
Eritrea		164.65	405.58		146.3
Ethiopia		1,351.29	1,589.49		17.6
Gabon	1,643.33	1,282.05	1,539.79	−6.3	20.1
Gambia, The	1,003.92	960.27	1,222.62	21.8	27.3
Ghana	989.20	1,349.03	1,334.48	34.9	−1.1
Guinea	1,455.05	1,706.55	1,435.77	−1.3	−15.9
Guinea-Bissau	1,530.74	1,067.26	1,625.25	6.2	52.3
Kenya	1,561.77	1,488.47	1,674.82	7.2	12.5
Lesotho	1,038.89	1,618.22	653.52	−37.1	−59.6
Liberia	1,028.57	919.79	550.00	−46.5	−40.2
Madagascar	1,945.30	1,967.29	2,511.19	29.1	27.6
Malawi	991.55	1,045.69	1,106.78	11.6	5.8
Mali	726.38	792.38	1,067.48	47.0	34.7
Mauritania	869.85	1,010.00	782.36	−10.1	−22.5
Mozambique	473.91	809.63	902.31	90.4	11.4
Namibia	457.32	412.58	433.56	−5.2	5.1
Niger	310.28	411.48	605.23	95.1	47.1
Nigeria	1,147.92	1,255.24	1,464.11	27.5	16.6
Rwanda	1,042.65	1,028.48	1,117.79	7.2	8.7
Senegal	795.02	651.61	879.03	10.6	34.9
Sierra Leone	1,201.67	2,118.88	1,485.22	23.6	−29.9
Somalia	793.04	769.65	589.28	−25.7	−23.4
South Africa	1,876.60	2,770.70	3,142.96	67.5	13.4
Sudan	455.74	487.17	718.07	57.6	47.4
Swaziland	1,277.64	993.65	546.77	−57.2	−45.0
Tanzania	1,506.24	1,290.58	1,513.62	0.5	17.3

(Table continues on the following page.)

Table 1.2 Aggregate Cereal Yield per Hectare (kg/Ha), by Country *(continued)*					
Country	1990	2002	2006	Change 1990–2006 (%)	Change 2002–2006 (%)
Togo	746.84	1,130.97	1,135.12	52.0	0.4
Uganda	1,497.63	1,638.75	1,522.93	1.7	−7.1
Zambia	1,352.06	1,412.97	1,837.12	35.9	30.0
Zimbabwe	1,625.41	458.47	713.52	−56.1	55.6

Source: FAOSTAT data.

profitable economic endeavor by focusing on increased productivity, efficiency, and stronger linkages for farmers with more lucrative markets. In the framework of the African Action Plan, the World Bank/Sustainable Development Department of the Africa Region (AFR-SDN) has further engaged in generating and disseminating knowledge concerning the potential development of high-value agricultural supply chains as a means to increase and diversify revenues in rural areas of SSA.

This Guide to value chain approaches is part of that effort, designed to provide the user with actionable methods and tools based on value chain concepts that can help design interventions to increase the productivity and performance of SSA agriculture. A wide range of tools and approaches—traditionally considered to be relevant mostly to sophisticated private businesses as they develop their own strategies and implement their own business plans—are, in fact, proving to be useful to development planners and practitioners when it comes to designing subsector, commodity, and value chain strategies.

This Guide is intended for use by a number of audiences. Most directly, it provides planners, decision makers, and implementers with practical tools for creating effective value and supply chain development programs. It also provides public and private stakeholders with a common framework for designing strategies and prioritizing decisions on sector and subsector competitiveness. Policy makers, business leaders, members of the development community, researchers, and practitioners can use these methods and approaches to promote the development of traditional and nontraditional value chains in sub-Saharan Africa.

To introduce the individual tools, approaches, and case studies, the Guide also discusses several key topics that the tools embody or take into account. In this regard, however, the important "take-away" from this document is not the identification of common topics, but rather the insights and practical applications that value chain–based approaches provide for adding value, creating opportunities, and enabling SSA's agricultural farmers, entrepreneurs, and businesses to reach markets.

The literature and practice of development concerning value chains, both academic and applied, is very substantial (see section 3). Special mention must be made of the considerable body of work that is being developed by and with the sponsorship of international agencies. The U.S. Agency for International Development (USAID) has developed many useful materials centered on value chain analysis, and its work is well reflected in its modular value chain training program, the Value Chain Wiki (http://apps.develebridge. net/amap/index.php/Value_Chain_Development) and by its ongoing value chain work. Germany's Gesellschaft für Technische Zusammenarbeit (GTZ) has also pioneered excellent work on value chains (for example, ValueLinks), as has the United Kingdom's Department for International Development (DFID) (for example, Regoverning Markets), and several other agencies. The World Bank and International Finance Corporation (IFC) have also made available other toolkits and guides with complementary purposes and focus areas. This Guide provides a specific implementation focus on value chain applications in agriculture and agribusiness in the African context.

ORGANIZATION OF THE GUIDE

The Guide is organized as follows:

- **Section 1** introduces the Guide, its objectives, and its scope.
- **Section 2** includes the definition of value chains, a description of their structure, and background on using and analyzing value chains.
- **Section 3** reviews existing literature on value and supply chains, including current theories and applications.
- **Section 4** discusses individual tools used in value chain analysis.

This Guide begins by examining core concepts and issues related to value chains. A brief literature review then focuses on five topics of particular relevance to African agricultural value chains, which can contribute to effective implementation tools and approaches. These are:

- Trust and cooperation
- Governance
- Market power
- Innovation and knowledge
- Focus/intervention points

These topics pertain to conditions and challenges faced by value chain participants and practitioners. They resonate throughout the many cases described in this Guide.

The core of the Guide presents methodological tools and approaches that blend important value chain concepts with the topics discussed and with sound business principles. The accompanying cases illustrate the application of the tools. The tools and case studies discussed in this Guide have been selected for their usefulness in directing and supporting market-driven private sector initiative and action to implement improvements in agricultural value chains.

This Guide offers 13 value chain implementation tools, presented within the implementation cycle of a value chain program. The cycle typically consists of six stages, corresponding to different entry points for using the value chain approach, depending on the specificities of the situation and problems to solve:

1) Designing strategies and business plans (and obtaining and using information)
2) Developing robust new businesses
3) Supplying the market (aligning supply to match market opportunity)
4) Reaching the market (market positioning and market opportunities)

5) Improving the business and policy environment
6) Monitoring results in value chain development

Each tool is followed by descriptions of one or more actual cases. These cases illustrate the tool's application, and are coupled with embedded mini-cases for additional perspective. Roughly 60 percent of the examples are from Africa, while the rest come from Europe, Latin America, and Asia.

NOTES

1. The trade ratio is widely used as a measure of integration into the world economy. Caution is needed, however, in interpreting it as an indicator of policy openness or competitiveness, because countries that are large or distant from major markets tend to have low ratios regardless of whether their policy regime is open. Similarly, small countries typically have a high trade ratio even with protectionist policies. Oil exporters also may have high trade ratios despite restrictive policy regimes.

2. Value added in agriculture measures the output of the agricultural sector less the value of intermediate inputs. Agriculture comprises value-added from forestry, hunting, and fishing as well as crop cultivation and livestock production. Data are in constant 2000 U.S. dollars.

3. Between 2001 and 2002, Zimbabwe's yield fell by two-thirds. This low yield for 2002 accounts for the growth between 2002 and 2006 despite a general trend toward lower yields over the last five years.

4. For a recent discussion of sustainability in supplier-buyer relationships, see *The Ties That Bind: Making Buyer-Supplier Relationships Stick,* USAID's Business Growth Initiative, J. E. Austin Associates, Inc. https://www.businessgrowthinitiative. org/ResourceCenter/Pages/TechnicalBriefs.aspx.

Concepts and Definitions of Value Chains and Supply Chains

DEFINITION OF CONCEPTS

Chains composed of companies (or individuals) that interact to supply goods and services are variously referred to as productive chains, value chains, filières, marketing chains, supply chains, or distribution chains. These concepts vary mainly in their focus on specific products or target markets, in the activity that is emphasized, and in the way in which they have been applied. What they have in common, however, is that they all seek to capture and describe the complex interactions of firms and processes that are needed to create and deliver products to end users. Moreover, they all strive to identify opportunities for and constraints against increasing productivity.

Although it is impossible to draw clear distinctions among these often overlapping concepts, it is still worthwhile to provide some basic definitions and highlight some of the differences. Typically, "value chain" describes the full range of value-adding activities required to bring a product or service through the different phases of production, including procurement of raw materials and other inputs, assembly, physical transformation, acquisition of required services such as transport or cooling, and ultimately response to consumer demand (Kaplinsky and Morris 2002). As such, value chains include all of the vertically linked, interdependent processes that generate value for the consumer, as well as horizontal linkages to other value chains that provide intermediate goods and services. Value chains focus on value creation—typically via innovation in products or processes, as well as marketing—and also on the allocation of the incremental value.

By contrast, the term "supply chain" is used internationally to encompass every logistical and procedural activity involved in producing and delivering a final product or service, "from the supplier's supplier to the customer's customer" (Feller, Shunk, and Callarman 2006). Since the primary focus of supply chains is efficiency, the main objectives are usually to reduce "friction" (for example, delays, blockages, or imbalances), reduce outages or overstocks, lower transaction costs, and improve fulfillment and customer satisfaction.

The issue is not so much about which concept is superior or preferable, since they are complementary and their effective implementation can deliver improved business results.[1] It must be noted, though, that practitioners of the supply chain approach often fail to consider to what extent cost reduction and inefficiencies in supply chain logistics actually add value, and if so, who benefits. On the other hand, value chain proponents sometimes forget that effective value chains must rest in efficient supply chains.

"Clusters" represent collections of firms and institutions that perform many of the functions segmented and described in both the value chain and supply chain literature. Clusters themselves display horizontal and vertical links among enterprises that produce a single or closely related product or service, which in turn may combine to satisfy the demand of a particular value/supply chain. The literature on clusters stresses the benefits of enterprise agglomeration and geographic proximity, which can generate economies of scale and positive externalities such as lower costs of intermediate inputs or services, better access to skilled personnel, or greater attractiveness to external procurement agents. Improving clusters typically requires more emphasis on the local environment (both policies and institutions, public and private) and context in which it operates.

Generally the "chain" concept, whether value or supply, places less emphasis on the enabling environment, while "cluster" analysis often neglects the necessary linkages to specific target markets that exist outside the cluster.

Another related concept is the Francophone *filière* (literally "thread" in English). "Filière" is used to describe the flow of physical inputs and services in the production of a final product, and is essentially similar to the modern value chain concept in its emphasis on vertical and horizontal coordination (Kaplinsky and Morris 2002). Filière studies do not have a single unifying theoretical framework, and its practitioners have borrowed from different theories and methodologies for their analyses. The concept is often used as synonymous to commodity chain or subsector. The filière was initially used to study contract farming and vertical integration in French agriculture in the 1960s. It was, soon thereafter, applied to agriculture in developing countries, such as the model implemented to develop the cotton sectors in West and Central Africa. Over time, filière analysis focused more on how public institutions affect local production systems, and how "interprofessional associations" can help glue together direct and indirect economic actors, that is, those who handle the product of interest versus those who contribute ancillary goods or services.

All of the commodity system concepts discussed—whether chain, cluster, or filière—underscore the importance of linkages to gain value and advantages to compete in global markets. The term value chain is primarily used in this Guide, as it is inclusive and incorporates supply logistics, value addition, transactions, and market linkages. We use other terms occasionally (particularly supply chain) where we believe that the Guide's conceptual focus or a specific case warrants.

HOW VALUE CHAIN ANALYSIS HAS BEEN USED

Interest in value chains is not new. Businesses have been using value chain analysis and implementation principles for years to formulate and implement competitive strategies. Corporations use value chain analysis to answer questions such as, "Where in the value chain should my business be positioned to improve its performance?" The value chain's popularity has been reinforced by many important business strategy themes, including core competencies, comparative and competitive advantage, outsourcing, vertical and horizontal integration, and best practices.

Businesses (individually and in groups, such as clusters) have focused on value chains while searching for alternative ways to remain competitive. Value chain approaches have been used to guide product and process innovations, such as specialty or organic coffee, that final customers or receivers value. Further, there is increased awareness that procedures within a firm might not affect its own competitiveness unless other firms adopt similar or linked practices. Recognizing that partnerships and joint programs aimed at better category management and sustainability need not be a zero sum game has paved the way for businesses to use collaborative value chain concepts to identify efficiencies and competitiveness both within and among firms, acting on opportunities to build win-win relationships. Recent technological developments that permit high levels of information sharing have reinforced businesses' capacity to upgrade value chain productivity and supply chain efficiencies.

More recently, governments and donors, realizing that upgrading the performance of individual firms can best be achieved in the context of market-based rewards for improved performance, have shown significant interest in value chain analysis and implementation. In their effort to devise interventions that can help reposition entire industries, build business competitiveness, and spur economic growth, governments and donors can use value chain–based approaches as robust tools to protect threatened links, facilitate upgrading of others to generate greater returns, and to promote foreign direct investment (FDI) programs. Additionally, value chain analysis has been used to examine constraints in the enabling environment in which the chains operate. Value chains have also been used as a tool for SME development, with new methods of linking SME suppliers and service providers to the value chains of lead processors or marketers.

More importantly, value chain analysis sheds light on the size of the firms participating in each link, how they are participating or could be participating in the chain, and opportunities to facilitate or improve those linkages. This is particularly crucial in agriculture, where governments and aid agencies are confronted with the challenge of including small farmers in modern value chains so that they can benefit from the globalization of markets. The value chain concept is therefore not only relevant to deal with growth, but also with the equity dimension of the modernization of the agrifood systems.

ANALYZING AND EVALUATING VALUE CHAINS

Value chain analysis rests on a segmentation of the different activities and mapping of interactions that may generate costs or value in the production and sale of a product or service. Although it is also concerned with structure, conduct, and performance, it differs from traditional commodity system or industry analyses in some important ways:[2]

- It focuses on net value added instead of just overall revenue and gross physical output.
- It is concerned with cost build-up and value accretion, as well as the distribution of burden or benefit in both.
- It recognizes that linkages between productive activities and actors vary according to the specific product type and target market, even if the main actors are the same.
- It recognizes that economic activity is very dynamic, necessitating adjustments in strategy and tactics constantly as circumstances change.
- It recognizes that there are different kinds of value chains (buyer-dominated, supplier-dominated, balanced, or directed) depending on which actors or activities have the most leverage, information, and power.
- It looks not just at physical flows, but also informational flows.
- It seeks to better understand the constraints and opportunities within each segment, as well as the context in which the chain operates.

There are many ways to analyze or evaluate a value chain. Analysis can stem from research of secondary information, such as government or industry data, to interviews with industry participants. It can also be derived from participatory market assessments and market observations. Once the information is gathered, numerous tools and processes help interpret and inform the resulting analysis.

In general, an in-depth value chain analysis considers the following questions (SNV 2004):

- What are the target markets that the value chain of interest serves?
- What/where are the main competing value chains?
- What are the product types, forms, and presentation that each target market seeks?
- What are the pathways from source to each end-market?
- What are the value chain's comparative advantages?

- How do financial (and sometimes economic) costs rise as the product moves along the value chain?
- How does market value rise as the product moves along?
- Where is there the most potential for growth in sales or profitability?
- Who are the most important actors within the value chain and how do they behave?
- To what extent is trust and cooperation evident at each step in the chain?
- What is the share of volume and value associated with different types or cohorts of actors?
- Where are the apparent choke points or bottlenecks in the value chain?
- What is the overall size of the value chain of interest?
- How does this value chain connect to others, and what possible synergies exist?
- How has the value chain been evolving over time?
- How is the value chain governed, and who holds power or influence?
- In what ways is the value chain regulated from outside, or self-regulated?
- What is the institutional framework of the value chain (for example, producer or trade associations)?
- What factors in the enabling environment hinder or support chain growth and prosperity?
- What is the potential for improving or upgrading any of the above?

LIMITATIONS OF VALUE CHAIN ANALYSIS

As mentioned, there are many ways to analyze a value chain. For example, value creation can be disaggregated between each link in the chain, as well as within each link. Some chains are merely a directional map (such as the one in figure 4.25), which is, in itself, valuable for beginning to understand the actors and processes that intervene to create value for particular consumers. However, agencies and other sponsors that commission value chain analysis often find that the analysis as carried out is insufficient and cannot be used to guide them in making informed decisions—particularly in deciding on actions that will greatly impact value added, rather than merely reducing costs.

Indeed, many of these analyses have a common weakness: the tendency to focus excessively on cost efficiency or breakouts of cost components. While efficiency in production is increasingly becoming a necessary condition for penetrating global markets, it will not ultimately be the only factor that determines sustained participation and increased incomes for value chain participants. The following sections contain examples of some related analytical weaknesses and challenges.

Value chains are not fixed or static

It is important to recognize that value chains are not fixed in terms of composition, relationships, or market positioning, and that there is a competitive need to alter and improve the value chain in light of strategic choices that businesses can make regarding the markets in which they compete. While a value chain's purpose is to link production to the target market advantageously, it is the private sector that decides which markets and where to compete—and alters the value chain accordingly. Value chain analysis too often focuses simply on improvements within the given value chain, rather than on how value chains can be shifted to target different, more attractive markets and business strategies.

Market dynamics matter

Value chains can be helpful instruments for serving the needs of a particular market sector, but focusing on a static value chain can also mask the need to segment and customize products for different markets. The key elements of building sustainable competitiveness are a solid understanding of market dynamics and a thorough analysis of the attractiveness of potential market segments and the competition. Businesses must choose which products and which markets can be served competitively and base their goals and strategy on good market analysis.

Quality and service are also important

Similarly, excessive focus on delivering a product (especially a commodity) may hide opportunities to deliver a package of products and services that the market or customer will find desirable. Too often, a value chain analysis is not designed to help businesses and planners weigh choices about delivering product quality, information, and service.

Considering the environment in which a value chain operates

Often, value chain analysts do not properly consider the business environment in which the value chain operates. In doing so, the analysis can fail to identify potential interventions for improved business and value chain performance.

Government regulations, international standards, trade regulations, and market forces typically shape the business environment. Michael Porter's diamond for depicting the major competitiveness factors, shown in figure 2.1 below, is a useful framework for assessing a value chain's business environment (the diamond is discussed further in section 4, tool 2.)

A simple cost analysis will not do

Some value chain analyses merely depict a cost build-up per activity without mapping the actors involved or identifying the value that is captured at each link of the chain. An evaluation of a value chain based only on an analysis of cost structure at various stages in the value chain is not sufficient to assess the competitiveness position of the value chain—because it disregards the market and value addition side of the equation. In some cases, it can even result in misleading conclusions.

Creating a cost build-up, and benchmarking it against competitors, will obviously provide ideas on areas for improvement. But the analysis will probably not shed light on which activities generate more value, whether the product can be produced at a competitive price for other markets, how well the chain is integrated, or how easily information flows throughout it. More importantly, a simple cost build-up will tend to focus on interventions that improve on costs, rather than on the broader and more comprehensive value chain approach that looks at repositioning the whole chain into more lucrative markets and products.

Shifting value within a value chain, rather than creating more value

As mentioned earlier in this section, donor agencies and governments have sometimes used value chain analysis to identify and protect threatened links along chains. Additionally, some stakeholders continue to look at value chain analysis as a zero sum game focused on shifting value from one link of the chain to another. This cutthroat perspective obscures opportunities to upgrade the whole system to the benefit of all value chain participants.

IMPLICATIONS OF THE OPERATING ENVIRONMENT: BEYOND THE VALUE CHAIN

While value chain analysis is extremely useful, its weaknesses highlight the fact that many other important considerations

Figure 2.1   Competitiveness Diamond

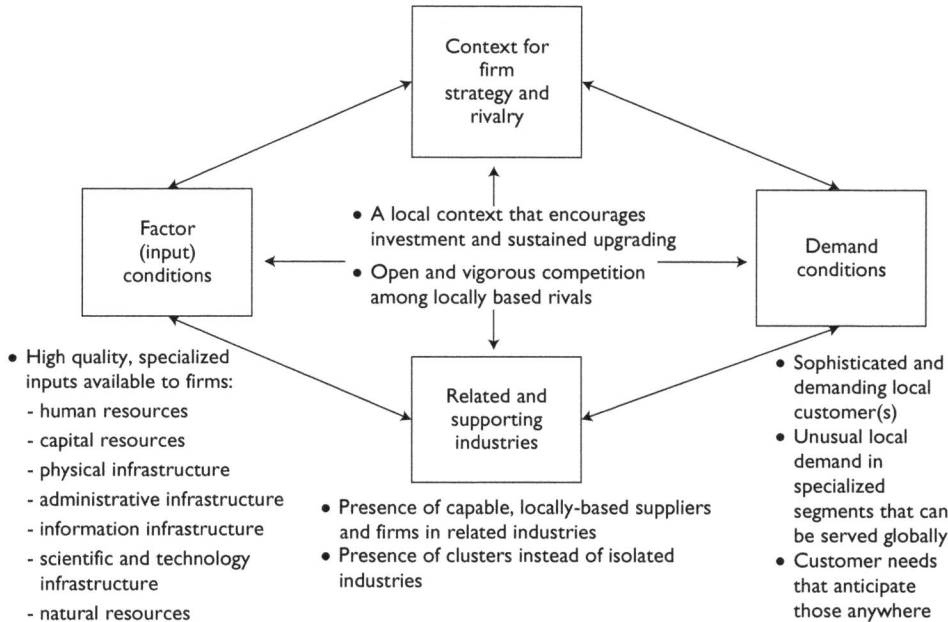

┌─────────────────────┐
│   Context for   │
│   firm   │
│   strategy and   │
│   rivalry   │
└─────────────────────┘

• A local context that encourages
  investment and sustained upgrading
• Open and vigorous competition
  among locally based rivals

┌─────────────┐   ┌─────────────┐
│   Factor   │   │   Demand   │
│   (input)   │   │ conditions │
│ conditions │   │   │
└─────────────┘   └─────────────┘

• High quality, specialized
  inputs available to firms:
  - human resources
  - capital resources
  - physical infrastructure
  - administrative infrastructure
  - information infrastructure
  - scientific and technology
    infrastructure
  - natural resources

┌─────────────┐
│ Related and │
│ supporting │
│ industries │
└─────────────┘

• Presence of capable, locally-based suppliers
  and firms in related industries
• Presence of clusters instead of isolated
  industries

• Sophisticated and
  demanding local
  customer(s)
• Unusual local
  demand in
  specialized
  segments that can
  be served globally
• Customer needs
  that anticipate
  those anywhere

Source: Michael Porter, 2009.

are necessary to increase the net value generated for the entire chain or some of its participants. It is important to understand market dynamics, competitive forces, and the operational environment that can affect the value chain's performance and growth.

Yet at the same time, there is a need to focus on fundamentals. Every target market and value chain role has key elements and drivers that are important for competing successfully. Interventions to build competitiveness should not attempt to make quick, comprehensive improvements throughout an entire value chain. Rather, a competitiveness-building strategy should target priority elements for improvement. In other words, improvements should not be made irrespective of a strategy that has set goals and objectives and is based on identified opportunities, given the value chain's relative position. It is crucial to identify success factors and driving forces in the target markets in question and subsequently benchmark these elements against top performers and competitors.

While reductions in production or transaction costs are always desirable, competitors can and will easily imitate them. Value chain interventions should therefore concentrate at least as much, if not more, on achieving: (1) products

of higher unit value; (2) more volume of products of the same value; (3) a different mix of products; and/or (4) delivery of a given set of products into more diverse markets.

Product innovations such as new varieties, new formulations, new presentations, or entirely new manufactured products are one way to add value. Process innovations such as changes in technology, production or manufacturing practices, certification, traceability, identity preservation, or branding are another major way. New business models and their business-to-business relationships are a third. All such innovations can benefit from inward as well as externally provided investment, technical support, or mentoring.

NOTES

1. In fact, Feller, Shunk, and Callarman (2006) argue precisely for the need to stop thinking of supply chains and value chains as different entities, but rather, for integration of the two.

2. Some of these differences were adapted from Kaplinsky and Morris (2002), "A Handbook for Value Chain Research," p. 46–47.

Review of Existing Literature on Value Chains and Supply Chains

This section, through a review of value chain literature, provides a summary of and commentary on the state of knowledge and available information on several main topics currently being discussed by researchers and practitioners regarding how value chain–based implementation is framed, focused, and realized. The literature review emphasizes key topics from value chain development and identifies the bases for appropriate tools used to guide decision making and action in the agricultural sector. While not specific to Africa, the topics below are highly applicable to African agricultural value chains and are woven throughout the tools and cases presented in section 4.

This section highlights a number of issues, patterns, and topics; the discussion of their contexts and relevance establishes a good background for understanding the implementation tools that follow. Although the documents reviewed here indicate the remarkable breadth of work that has been done on value chain development, they are only a small portion of the available literature. This section is not intended to comprehensively review the entirety of value chain literature; the reference documents presented and cited here were selected for their coverage of the topics most relevant to the tools and approaches presented in this Guide.

The Guide's bibliography includes a comprehensive list of the resources consulted. Those documents, specifically mentioned below, are highlighted for their usefulness in discussing topics, models, theoretical considerations, lessons learned from past program implementations, operational implications, and illustrative examples.

This literature review emphasizes five topics, currently the focus of much consideration, that are of particular relevance to African agricultural value chains and that can contribute to effective implementation tools and approaches:

- Trust and cooperation
- Governance
- Market power
- Innovation and knowledge
- Focus/intervention points

These topics pertain to conditions and challenges faced by value chain participants and practitioners and can help answer questions such as:

- Why do certain firms find it in their interest to cooperate or develop win-win relationships?
- Why do certain firms have the most market power and the ability to determine price to their advantage?
- What is a strategy for maintaining market share?
- How does a supply or value chain get pulled by market demand?
- How is innovation allowed to flow among members of a chain?

These common topics were extracted or developed from various works. A partial list (and their emphasis) is shown in table 3.1 We particularly note:

- *A Handbook for Value Chain Research*, Kaplinksy and Morris, International Development Research Center.

- *Global Commodity Chain Analysis and the French Filière Approach: Comparison and Critique*, Raikes, Jensen, Ponte Royal Dutch Veterinarian and Agricultural University.
- *Globalization and the Small Firm: A Value Chain Approach to Economic Growth and Poverty Reduction*, Downing, Field, Kula, United States Agency for International Development.
- *Governance in Global Value Chains*, Humphrey and Schmitz, Institute of Development Studies at the University of Sussex.
- *Implementing Sustainable Private Sector Development: Striving for Tangible Results for the Poor: The 2006 Reader*, Miehlbradt, McVay, Tanburn, International Labor Organization of the United Nations.
- *Info-Cadena: Instruments to Foster Value Chains*, Springer-Heinze, German Agency for Technical Cooperation (GTZ).
- *Integrating SMEs in Global Value Chains: Toward Partnership for Development*, Kapinsky, Readman, United National Industrial Development Organization.
- *AMAP BDS Knowledge and Practice Task Order: Lexicon General*, Dunn, United States Agency for International Development.
- *Commodity Chains and Global Capitalism*, Gereffi, Korzeniewicz, 1994.
- *ValueLinks Manual*, GTZ.
- *Regoverning Markets: Small Scale Producers in Global Agrifood Markets*, UK Department for International Development.

For references specifically focusing on sub-Saharan African agricultural value chains, we turned most frequently to commodity-specific or program implementation reports. These reports were useful for African perspectives and for understanding key geographic aspects of value chain program implementation. Some of the most pertinent reports that provided African perspectives were:

- "Successes and Challenges in Promoting Africa's Horticultural Exports," by Gabre-Madhin and Minot, World Bank, 2003.
- "Partnerships for Agribusiness Development, Agricultural Trade, and Market Access: A Concept Note for NEPAD," by TechnoServe, November 2004.
- "The Market for Non-Traditional Agricultural Exports," by Hallam, Liu, Lavers, Pilkauskas, Rapsomanikis and Claro, Commodities and Trade Division, FAO, 2005.
- "Etude sur la Compétitivité des Filières Agricoles dans l'Espace UEMOA," Union Economique et Monétaire Ouest Africaine (UEMOA).

- "Exporting Out of Africa: The Kenya Horticulture Success Story," by Jaffee and Okello, World Bank.
- "Globalization of the Agro-Food System: Success and Challenges for Promoting Africa's Horticultural Exports," by Gabre-Madhin and Minot, International Food Policy Research Institute, 2004.
- "Guide to Commodity-Based Export Diversification and Competitiveness Strategies for African Countries," by Stryker and Salinger, Associates for International Resource Development.
- "High Value Agricultural Products for Smallholder Markets in Sub-Saharan Africa: Trends, Opportunities, and Research Priorities," by Temu and Temu, ICTA.
- Programme de Développement des Marchés Agricoles—AgMarkets Sénégal, GEOMAR International Inc.
- "The European Horticulture Market: Opportunities for Sub-Saharan African Exporters," edited by Patrick Labaste, 2005.

In table 3.1, each document's technical focus is distinguished according to focus on private sector development (PSD), value chain, and agribusiness. Documents with an Africa focus are indicated specifically.

Undoubtedly, academics, international organizations, bilateral development institutions, and nonprofit organizations have done a great deal of work related to these common topics. There is broad agreement on the importance of these identified topics and concepts. But the nomenclature is still ambiguous and not universally accepted. Attempts have been made to define and provide a lexicon, but inconsistencies persist. The concepts and definitions used in this Guide result from experience, generally accepted expert terminology, and, in some cases, ad-hoc definitions that will be made explicit.

CREATING TRUST

At the heart of value chain development is the effort to strengthen mutually beneficial linkages among firms so that they work together to take advantage of market opportunities, that is, to create and build trust among value chain participants. Nearly all of the documents on value chain development contain this notion of the importance of interfirm cooperation and creating economies of scale through increased coordination.

Most value chain–based initiatives work with a range of business types to strengthen both vertical linkages (between firms that buy from and sell to one another) and horizontal linkages (between firms that serve the same functions in the value chain). These interfirm connections are especially

Table 3.1 Key Documents Utilized in the Literature Review

Value chain or agribusiness resource document	Geographic focus	Technical focus	Relevant value chain topic covered					Author(s)	Affiliated or donor organization
			Trust	Governance	Market power	Innovation and knowledge	Intervention		
Addressing Marketing and Processing Constraints That Inhibit Agrifood Exports: A Guide for Policy Analysis and Planners	General	Agribusiness		✓	✓			Westlake	FAO
Agri-Supply Chain Management: To Stimulate Cross-Border Trade in Developing Countries and Emerging Economies	General	Agribusiness	✓	✓				Roekel, Willems, and Wageningen	World Bank
AMAP BDS Knowledge and Practice Task Order: Lexicon	General	VC	✓	✓	✓	✓	✓	Dunn	USAID
Commodities, Diversification, and Poverty Reduction	General	Agribusiness	✓	✓	✓			Humphrey	FAO
Commodity Chains and Global Capitalism	General	VC	✓	✓	✓			Gereffi, Korzeniewicz	USAID
Competitive Strategies for Agriculture-Related MSEs: From Seeds to Supermarket Shelves	General	Agribusiness		✓			✓		
Compilation of Insights on the Online Debate, Value Chains in Rural Development (VCRD): The Role of Donors in Value Chain Interventions	General	VC		✓			✓	Roduner, Gerrits	SDC
"Customized Competitiveness" Strategies for Horticultural Exporters: Central America Focus with Lessons from and for Other Regions	General	Agribusiness			✓			Reardon	USAID, MSU
Etude sur la Compétitivité des Filières Agricoles dans l'Espace UEMOA	Africa	VC		✓	✓		✓	Faivre Dupaigre, Baris, Liagre	ECOWAS
Exporting Out of Africa: The Kenya Horticulture Success Story	Africa	Agribusiness		✓	✓			English, Jaffee, Okello	World Bank
Globalization and the Small Firm: A Value Chain Approach to Economic Growth and Poverty Reduction	General	VC	✓	✓	✓		✓	Downing, Field, Kula	USAID
Globalization of the Agro-food System: Success and Challenges for Promoting Africa's Horticultural Exports	Africa	Agribusiness		✓				Gabre-Madhin, Minot	IFPRI
Governance in Global Value Chains	General	VC		✓	✓			Humphrey and Schmitz	IDS
The Governance of Global Value Chains	General	VC	✓	✓	✓	✓		Gereffi, Humphrey, Sturgeon	Rockefeller Foundation

(Table continues on the following page.)

Table 3.1 Key Documents Utilized in the Literature Review *(continued)*

Value chain or agribusiness resource document	Geographic focus	Technical focus	Relevant value chain topic covered					Author (s)	Affiliated or donor organization
			Trust	Governance	Market power	Innovation and knowledge	Intervention		
Guide to Commodity-based Export Diversification and Competitiveness Strategies for African Countries	Africa	Agribusiness		✓				Stryker, Salinger	AIRD
A Handbook for Value Chain Research	General	VC	✓	✓	✓	✓	✓	Kaplinksy and Morris	IDRC
High Value Agricultural Products for Smallholder Markets in Sub-Saharan Africa: Trends, Opportunities and Research Priorities	Africa	Agribusiness			✓			Temu and Temu	ICTA
Implementing Sustainable Private Sector Development: Striving for Tangible Results for the Poor: The 2006 Reader	General	PSD	✓				✓	Miehlbradt, McVay, Tanburn	ILO
Integrating SMEs in Global Value Chains: Towards Partnership for Development	General	VC	✓			✓	✓	Kapinsky, Readman	UNIDO
Participatory Market Chain Approach	General	VC	✓	✓				Bernet, Devaux, Ortiz, Thiele	—
Promotion of Commercially Viable Solutions to Subsector and Business Constraints	General	Agribusiness					✓	Lusby, Panlibuton	USAID
Strategies for Diversification and Adding Value to Food Exports: A Value Chain Perspective	General	VC		✓				Humphrey and Oetero	UNCTD
Successes and Challenges in Promoting Africa's Horticultural Exports	Africa	Agribusiness	✓	✓	✓	✓		Gabre-Madhin, Minot	World Bank
Trade, Micro and Small Enterprises, and Global Value Chains: microREPORT #25	General	VC		✓	✓		✓	Barber and Goldmark	USAID
Upgrading Global Value Chains	General	VC		✓	✓	✓		Humphrey	ILO
Value Chain Analysis for Policy-Makers and Practitioners	General	VC		✓	✓		✓	Schmitz	ILO, Inst. Dev. Studies
Value Chains and Their Significance for Addressing the Rural Finance Challenge	General	VC		✓	✓		✓	Akin, Fries	USAID

Note: VC = Value Chain. — = not available.

important to consider when examining how agile a value chain can be regarding market developments, or how able it is to link to markets. Positive outcomes undoubtedly result when there is a strong market drive for linkages, strong investment from many businesses in the chain, and a market system in place to replicate improved models and practices (ILO 2006).

More specifically, interfirm cooperation refers to the joint action between two or more firms in a value chain. It includes horizontal and vertical linkages between firms and can be formal or informal. Examples include information sharing, bulk purchasing of inputs, contract farming, and industry branding campaigns. Unfortunately, value chain participants frequently do not work cooperatively, and market conditions sometimes propel firms to adapt cutthroat measures while competing for highly segmented market rents.

Too often, many participants in a value chain choose not to collaborate among themselves due to lack of leadership, mistrust of competitors, weak information, or lack of scale. Without a strategic direction for the value chain and effective management of its economies, a cutthroat and zero-sum mentality can take hold among value chain participants, who then ignore or cannot see the benefits of cooperation, including the mechanisms that foster it. Competition is, of course, useful, but that usefulness is limited if it blinds the participants to productive collaboration and incentives. For example, if a lead exporting firm or monopoly is able to concentrate its buying power, it can rely on multiple suppliers for inputs and ignore price incentives for service and quality. Given its situation, the lead firm might restrictively determine the price, erect barriers to entry, and prevent the dissemination of information or opportunities to innovate.

A situation that prevents collaboration (beyond simply transactional relationships) can leave producers/suppliers competing among themselves for less lucrative rents and with little opportunity to capture more value. In such low-trust value chains, the lead firm(s) may perpetuate its short-term advantage by switching (or threatening to switch) suppliers in constant pursuit of cost advantages.

In this respect, the level of development of the value chain is important. In many instances in SSA, value chains lack the required ingredients for trust building merely because of their lack of effective performance, which in turn leads actors to opt for opportunistic and risk mitigation behaviors.

Characteristics of value chain relationships that have the largest effect on the level of trust between participants include (Kaplinsky and Morris 2002):

- Length of trading relationship
- Ordering procedures

- Contractual relationship
- Inspection
- Degree of dependence
- Technical assistance
- Communication
- Price determination
- Credit extended
- Outsourcing payment terms

The literature frequently emphasizes the idea that building trust by rewarding collective action among stakeholder participants is crucial for upgrading a value chain. Indeed, working within value chains requires establishing relationships in order for participants to gain the "win-win" perspective. When trust, learning, and benefits are shared among firms (vertically and/or horizontally), there is a greater likelihood of generating collective efficiency and scale. Increased trust has also proven to lead to greater specialization by the value chain, as well as eventual outsourcing that provides cost advantages (adapted from Moran [2001]). For instance, less time and money need to be invested to monitor performance when suppliers can be trusted to meet quality, quantity, and time requirements. High-trust situations enable lead firms within the value chain to assist each other in achieving common objectives.

Value chain development initiatives have orchestrated stakeholder meetings by providing neutral outsiders to help build trust among the participants. Oftentimes, removing the zero-sum mentality among value chain participants requires more objective assistance and successful early initiatives to trigger change. An outside and neutral facilitator can drive home the concept of participating in a mutually beneficial commercial relationship, but it remains necessary that the value chain participants drive the entire process.

More recently, observers have questioned the sustainability and utility of non-profit-motivated organizations and government agencies acting as market advisors to value chain participants. Their argument states that, for sustainability purposes, market conditions, rather than government agents or nonprofit professionals, should determine the role that participants take and the relationships that are formed. There is substance to this criticism, but depending on the focus of the development intervention, a facilitative role of a neutral broker may be very often critical in order to stimulate or create markets in underserviced areas, or where market demand has not yet been recognized (ILO 2006). However, the general consensus among practitioners is that a good exit strategy must accompany such approaches from the very beginning, or else distortions or dependencies will result.

GOVERNANCE: WHAT TYPE OF POWER RELATIONSHIP EXISTS, AND IS INFORMATION SHARED?

"Governance" is a description of the dynamic distribution of power, learning, and leadership in standards and strategy-setting among a value chain's firms. While the term can have many meanings, in this instance we use it to describe the sharing of information and systematic standards promoted by the "governing" entity in a value chain.

Governance can be characterized along a continuum of four types of relationships that center on information and the use of market power (Dunn 2005):

- **Market relationship**: Arms-length transactions in which there are many buyers and many suppliers. Repeat transactions are possible, but little information is exchanged between firms, interactions are limited, and no technical assistance is provided.
- **Balanced relationship**: Both buyers and suppliers have alternatives, that is, a supplier has various buyers. There are extensive information flows in both directions, with the buyer often defining the product (that is, design and technical specifications). Both sides have capabilities that are hard to substitute, and both are committed to solving problems through negotiation rather than threat or exit.
- **Direct relationship**: Main buyer takes a large percentage of supplier's output, defines the product (that is, design and technical specifications), and monitors the supplier's performance. The buyer provides technical assistance and knows more about the costs and capabilities of the supplier than the supplier does about the buyer. The supplier's exit options are more restricted than those of the buyer.
- **Hierarchical relationship**: Vertical integration of value-added functions within a single firm. The supplier is owned by the buyer or vice versa, with the junior firm having limited autonomy to make decisions at the local level.

Governance ensures that interactions between firms along a value chain exhibit some level of organization rather than simply being random. Value chains are governed when the parameters requiring product, process, and logistic qualification that are set have consequences up or down the value chain, encompassing bundles of activities, actors, roles, and functions (Kaplinsky and Morris 2002). Of course, one objective of value chain development is to engender informed, incentive-producing governance targeted at achieving high-value results.

In many sub-Saharan Africa cases, certain key actors—the lead firms or "governors of value chains"—have the capability and power to define and set the parameters of contracts and subcontracts in their supply chains. For example, they can define chainwide product and process standards, quantities, and conditions of delivery. This power may be based on ownership of well-established brand names, proprietary technology, or exclusive information about different product markets, which enable the firm to act as a system integrator (Altenburg 2006).

The governing entity is often a lead firm that is closer to the market or business environment that the value chain inhabits. Leadership or being a "lead" firm implies success, efficiency, a competitive composure, or direct information. As such, working with lead firms is often the most efficient and effective way for a development program or market partner to reach a large number of chain participants. The advantages are an easy entry point, a possibly guaranteed market or reliable supplier, leveraged technical expertise, and marketing connections. The disadvantages are that the lead firms too often seek exclusive producers, resist replication, and limit competition, while small value chain participants risk becoming too dependent on one lead firm (ILO 2006).

In economics, a competitive lead firm is said to arise in a contestable market. Contestable markets are ones in which monopoly/monopsony-type market distortions do not arise despite dominance of the value chain by few (or even one) firm(s). These firms do not exercise their ability to manipulate prices because low barriers to entry guarantee that new firms will quickly enter and return the market to equilibrium prices. Hence, the threat of competition is sufficient to induce competitive pricing. In the context of African value chains, contestable markets are particularly important in the West African cotton sector, where the pricing power of monopolistic, often parastatal firms, is ostensibly checked by the threat of competition.

MARKET OR BARGAINING POWER (BUYER VERSUS PRODUCER)

All approaches to value or supply chains identify the crucial impact of power relations among different actors. Power relations determine how economic gains and risks are distributed among value chain actors (see figure 3.1) and to what extent dominant firms may set and enforce standards

Figure 3.1   Power Relations in Value Chains

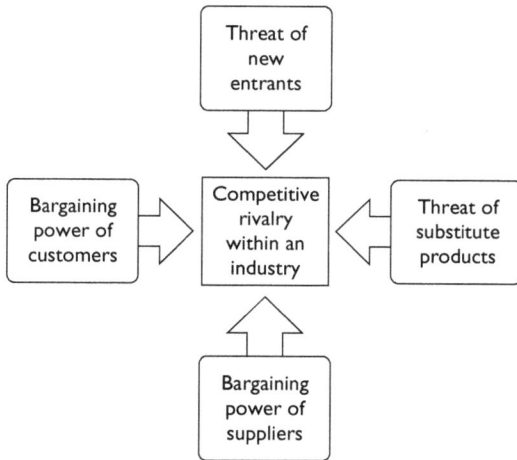

Source: Michael Porter, 2007.

with the aim of raising entry barriers for competitors and achieving market foreclosure. The concept of "governance of value chains" implies that "there are key actors in the chain who take responsibility for the inter-firm division of labor, and for the capacities of particular participants to upgrade their activities" (Kaplinsky 2000).

"Market power" refers to the idea that one firm in the market may be able to exert significant influence over the goods and services traded or the price at which they are sold. Governance plays a large part in determining and explaining various firms' market power. However, commercial competence, market forces, and technical capabilities also determine the market power of value chain participants.

A commercial transaction's price is determined by the bargaining power of the transacting entities. In economics, bargaining power refers to the ability to set prices or wages, usually arising from some sort of monopoly, monopoly-like position, or non-equilibrium situation in a market. The economic actor with greater bargaining power has the greater decision-making freedom. Typically, value chains feature two types of bargaining power relationships: buyer-driven and producer-driven.

Buyer-driven value chains refer to a market context where producers have few options for selling their goods or services. These chains typically have low barriers to entry at the producer level, or they may have locational/logistics limitations to whom the producer can sell (for example, "captive" tea producers for a tea estate or cotton producers for a ginner). This type of market condition is referred to as a "buyer's market" (if not a monopolistic one).

International brand name and retailing companies ("buyers"), therefore, define the rules of the game in particular industries and appropriate the largest share of the gains from those industries' production. In the developing world, buyer-driven value chains are often characteristic of labor-intensive industries like agriculture, clothing, and furniture. The typically low barriers to entry on the production side of buyer-driven value chains mean that a multitude of suppliers compete for very low rents. Essentially, the buyer has an advantage because these numerous producers compete to offer goods and services at the lowest cost. Quality and other standards tend to be imposed by the buyer or appear as entry requirements to the buyer's geographic marketplace (for example, GlobalGAP, formerly EurepGAP).

Producer-driven value chains are often characterized by knowledge intensity, relatively higher levels of technology or skills, scarcity, high levels of marketing, or capital-intensive production practices. These high-level factors, scarcities, and differentiations produce barriers to entry for competition. These barriers to entry include the large amounts of capital needed for investment and, therefore, entry, limiting the number of producers. Similarly, environmental factors, such as location, can present physical barriers. The products of producer-driven value chains often require high research and development (R&D) expenditures or have been branded with costly marketing efforts in order to increase barriers to entry and protect market shares.

Examples of producer-driven value chains are perhaps most readily seen in complex technology industries, such as the commercial airline, automobile, or computer industries. But they are also often present in agricultural sectors when freshness standards and protected varieties are important, when there is high product differentiation, when packaging and logistics are complicated, or when R&D and other knowledge elements in production or processing are critical. In such situations, the producer can capture a higher profit because sales are high margin and based on factors such as quality management or differentiation, rather than on strictly cost-based competition. Examples from the agricultural sector include: bananas produced by the leading multinationals, organic products like cotton, branded products like processed and packaged agricultural products, quality-differentiated products like specialty coffees, or high-value processed products like essential oils.

Power and governance in value chains are common topics in the literature, but their relation to the prospects of upgrading value chains in developing countries is inconclusive. The literature seems to recognize that, in reality, value chains are not purely buyer driven or producer driven, and that they can and do change. Indeed, the creation of competitive advantage by elements of the value chain is a means to alter the power balance among actors within the chain, or in relation to competing chains.

INNOVATION, INFORMATION, INFORMATION SHARING, AND KNOWLEDGE

In competitive markets, innovation helps maintain or grow market share or profits and can be a route to competitiveness and the development of competitive advantage. Innovative production and processing can create cost efficiencies and improved services that translate into higher margins or more competitive pricing. Innovations in logistics can also provide cost efficiencies, as well as improved service. In terms of value chain development, innovation must be viewed as necessary for overall chain competitiveness by capturing more value or upgrading the value chain. The production factor of "know-how" is one core factor regarding the upgrading of value chains (Porter 1998a). A value chain's access to information (for example, regarding market trends) can itself be a competitive advantage.

The way that knowledge is transferred is determined by the information flows or linkages between firms within a value chain. Targeted transfer of knowledge by the lead firms, using backward linkages, is usually seen in the development of product specifications (for example, quality, preferences, or certifications) and other expectations (for example, price, quantity, or time) that are communicated by the lead firm to its suppliers. This relationship is often part of an "embedded services" relationship between buyer and producer. In such relationships, firms or producers pay for the services of technical assistance or innovation in the price they get for their products.

In general, learning processes among firms are most effective where they are located close to one another and are therefore able to benefit from a high level of communication, networking, and other exchanges of information. If the rate of innovation is lower than that of competitors (whether firms or competing value chains), this may result in declining market share and value added; in extreme cases it may also involve negative growth. Thus, innovation has to be placed in a relative context—pace compared to competitors—that can be referred to as upgrading.

Upgrading refers to the innovation that increases firm and/or value chain competitiveness. According to the Accelerated Microenterprise Advancement Project (AMAP)/Business Development Services (BDS) lexicon developed by USAID, there are five categories of upgrading (Dunn 2005).

1. **Process upgrading**: Increasing efficiency (that is, more output for same level of inputs or same output for lower level of inputs), achieving standards and certifications (for example, organic, HACCP, and ISO).
2. **Product upgrading**: Improving product quality, new product development, new varieties, or line extension.
3. **Functional upgrading**: Operating at a new level in the value chain.
4. **Intrasectoral upgrading**: Operating in a new market channel within the same value chain.
5. **Intersectoral upgrading**: Producing a completely different product in a completely different value chain.

The concept of upgrading explicitly recognizes relative endowments and, hence, the existence of value. Upgrading approaches emphasizes issues of knowledge creation, transfer, and appropriation. Critical questions are raised regarding the manner in which knowledge flows along value chains, firms acquire information and upgrade processes, firms "unlearn" certain capabilities as they specialize, types of knowledge are transferred by technology proprietors, and firms disclose their core competencies. However, this field requires substantial further research.

INTERVENTION ENTRY POINTS AND INITIAL FOCUS

By "entry point" we refer to the elements of the value chain structure, relationships, market linkages, or strategic or operational objectives that provide effective leverage points for working with or influencing the value chain actors. Many documents, including many project reports, describe elements of value chain operation or strategy around which an initiative can take root, and methods that various types of development shareholders use to work with value chains. The choice of an initiative's entry points, partners, tools, and approaches strongly depends on the characteristics of the value chain, its participants, the business environment, and many other factors.

It should be axiomatic that interventions be based on well-considered needs or strategies of the value chain and its participants, rather than a "solution looking for a value chain."

CONCLUSION

As mentioned, we have selected topics for emphasis that are highly pertinent to upgrading and improving value chain targeting, linkage, and operation and that are the current focus of much innovative thinking and practice. These topics are particularly applicable to Africa's agricultural value chains.

These topics resonate throughout the many cases described in the following section of the Guide. The Guide's tools and approaches make use of the thematic principles that this section has highlighted, as well as several other intervention ideas.

Improving value chain competitiveness in Africa presents challenges, but is, of course, subject to the same worldwide trends, competitive forces, and business principles that are common to value chains in the global economy. The specifics of any value chain initiative are nonetheless highly contextual.

The second portion of this Guide discusses methodological tools and approaches that incorporate important value chain concepts with the topics discussed and with sound business principles. The accompanying cases, mostly from Africa but also from the Americas, Asia, and Europe, illustrate the application of the tools.

SECTION 4

Discussion of Individual Tools

INTRODUCTION AND OVERVIEW

This section presents 13 value chain implementation tools. They are presented in six themes within a program implementation cycle. Figure 4.1 illustrates how the focus of each tool and theme relates to a program implementation cycle. The themes, and a brief explanation of the tools that fall within them, are shown below:

THEME ONE: DESIGNING STRATEGIES AND BUSINESS PLANS—OBTAINING AND USING INFORMATION

Tool 1: Choosing Priority Sectors for Value Chain Interventions
Helps practitioners consider: Which are the priority value chains? Which ones should be supported? Why does comparative advantage matter, and how can it be assessed? How should public, private, and collective perspectives and interests be harnessed?

Tool 2: Designing Informed Strategies across the Value Chain
Offers analytical methods for understanding the value chain and integrating the information into sound strategy along various points of the chain.

Tool 3: Conducting Benchmarking and Gap Assessments of Value Chains
Describes how to measure and compare a value chain's performance (whether in relation to itself, similar value chains, or to best practices) as a means of gaining insight into appropriate strategic choices.

THEME TWO: DEVELOPING ROBUST NEW BUSINESSES

Tool 4: Upgrading and Deepening the Value Chain
Describes ways to add efficiency, improve product quality, and add new operations to increase value added within the value chain.

Tool 5: Identifying Business Models for Replication
Focuses on opportunities to implement sound business models repeatedly within a value chain. The ability to replicate these business models is useful in increasing value-added volumes, intermediation, and access to services and inputs.

THEME THREE: SUPPLYING THE MARKET— ALIGNING SUPPLY TO MATCH MARKET OPPORTUNITY

Tool 6: Capturing Value through Forward and Backward Integration
Explains how vertical integration can help businesses ensure supply or otherwise control inputs, capture more value, achieve economies of scale, and/or ensure access to information.

Tool 7: Horizontal Collaboration—Creating and Taking Advantage of Economies of Scale
Provides approaches to create economies of scale that help to increase production, ensure quality, improve access inputs, and achieve more market power.

THEME FOUR: REACHING THE MARKET— MARKET POSITIONING AND MARKET OPPORTUNITIES

Tool 8: Positioning Products and Value Chains for Greater Value and Competitiveness
Describes how competitiveness positioning considerations can enable businesses to choose wisely, market value chain business models, and provide strategic direction to many value chain actions to improve competitiveness.

Tool 9: Applying Standards and Certifications to Achieve Greater Quality
Describes how meeting (and exceeding) the quality and performance standards of desired markets can help achieve entry, market share, and higher unit values for a value chain's products.

THEME FIVE: IMPROVING THE BUSINESS AND POLICY ENVIRONMENT

Tool 10: Identifying needed support services for the value chain
Discusses how improving the depth and breadth of services offered to a value chain can help member firms to be commercially sustainable and improve operations.

Tool 11: Improving the Operating Environment by Promoting Public-Private Dialogue
Describes how value chains can improve their operating environments by engaging the public sector and other actors in effective public-private dialogue.

Tool 12: Achieving Synergies through Clustering
Demonstrates how cluster-strengthening and cluster-development initiatives can help value chain participants achieve results that an emphasis solely on core value chains may not be capable of generating.

THEME SIX: MONITORING RESULTS IN VALUE CHAIN DEVELOPMENT

Tool 13: Monitoring achievements in value chain performance
Explains how monitoring and evaluation methods can help value chain participants track implementation progress, evaluate value chain performance, and identify the impacts of initiatives.

Each of the tools presents value chain–based actions that can form part of a competitiveness-focused agriculture development initiative. Figure 4.1 presents a sequencing in which these tools will typically be employed over the life of a project.

The tools were selected to provide a broad range of interventions across and within the value chain and its operating environment. The thoughtful reader will recognize that many other tools are available and could be described, or that any one of the included tools could be considered in much greater depth. Several of these could easily command their own volumes—for example:

- Market-based approaches (segmentation, marketing, and promotion)
- Logistics as a tool
- Managing the distribution chain
- Branding (that is, connecting differentiation with standards and with service qualities)
- Workforce and skills competitiveness
- Jumpstarting value chains

However, this Guide provides a highly functional entry point to the field of value chain analysis and is well illustrated by examples specific to African agribusiness.

While the Guide's emphasis is on implementation, actions are likely to be most effective when underpinned by sound information and analysis. Therefore, we begin with three largely analytical tools relating to choosing priority sectors, designing informed strategies, and conducting benchmarking and gap assessment.

The base of practical analysis provided by these three tools is an important input or prerequisite for many of the implementation tools.

Each tool is followed by descriptions of one or more actual cases that illustrate the tool's application. Embedded mini-cases offer additional illumination.[1] Most of the examples are from Africa, others are from Europe, Latin America, and Asia. We return to the same cases as appropriate when describing different tools, which serve to highlight the multiple dimensions of a single value chain and the rich set of opportunities value chain initiatives can offer.

Figure 4.1   Value Chain Program Implementation Cycle

The value chain framework: A program implementation cycle showing the sequences in which various tools can be employed over the course of a project[a]

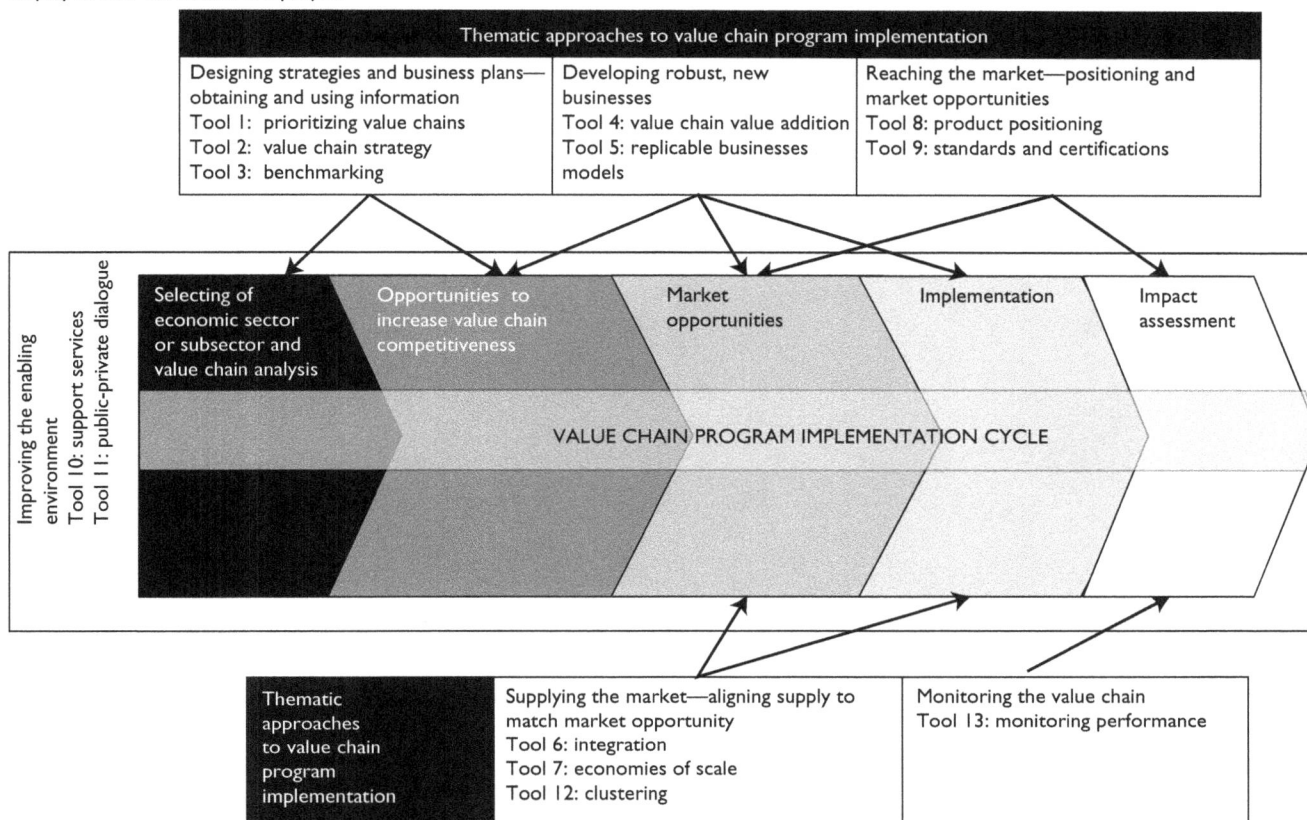

Thematic approaches to value chain program implementation		
Designing strategies and business plans— obtaining and using information Tool 1: prioritizing value chains Tool 2: value chain strategy Tool 3: benchmarking	Developing robust, new businesses Tool 4: value chain value addition Tool 5: replicable businesses models	Reaching the market—positioning and market opportunities Tool 8: product positioning Tool 9: standards and certifications

Improving the enabling environment
Tool 10: support services
Tool 11: public-private dialogue

Selecting of economic sector or subsector and value chain analysis

Opportunities to increase value chain competitiveness

Market opportunities

Implementation

Impact assessment

VALUE CHAIN PROGRAM IMPLEMENTATION CYCLE

Thematic approaches to value chain program implementation	Supplying the market—aligning supply to match market opportunity Tool 6: integration Tool 7: economies of scale Tool 12: clustering	Monitoring the value chain Tool 13: monitoring performance

[a] The value chain implementation cycle is adapted in part from Action for Enterprise's Value Chain Approach and J.E. Austin's Associates, Inc.'s productivity and value enhancement model (see figure 4.3).

Source: J. E. Austin Associates, Inc.

NOTE

1. Since these are actual, "living" cases, they will evolve from the time of this writing. Some may have even experienced reversals in their competitiveness progress. The evolution of any specific story does not diminish the case's relevance, since its inclusion in this Guide is to illustrate approaches and methodologies that are found within the described events, and not just to document success stories.

Choosing Priority Sectors for Value Chain Interventions

This tool describes how investors, governments, donors, and other organizations can prioritize among the value chains when considering investment possibilities. The process can help businesses and domestic or foreign investors to determine where they can invest most profitably and can help planners in the public sector and development partner organizations to select which value chains to support.

In most cases, the process will start with an initial list of potential value chains based on a general definition of product category and target market(s), followed by various types of market analyses, an evaluation of the operational and strategic opportunities and their potential impact, and a willingness assessment of the chains' leaders and other stakeholders to work toward improving their collective competitiveness.

This process does not necessarily need to be carried out in a linear fashion. In fact, involving various stakeholders in the early stages of the analysis is an excellent means of gauging (and building) their willingness to invest time and resources in the resulting initiatives.

In the case of governments and donors, the process assumes that the program has not prescribed beforehand which value chains it must support. Such preselection should be avoided. Selecting before testing can distort incentives and project dynamics among stakeholders, effectively limiting the project's prospects for a meaningful impact.

The discussion within this tool is not intended as an exhaustive list of criteria upon which value chains can be prioritized. It should be considered a guide for businesses, planners, and practitioners to identify which value chains offer the best opportunities to invest profitably, encourage economic growth, and enhance competitiveness. Each business or practitioner can add criteria depending on their particular focus. Additional typical criteria include involvement of small and medium enterprises, variability of returns, gender considerations, and environmental impact. A multicriteria

approach is, in fact, a commendable approach to filtering alternatives.

INITIAL LIST

To begin, it is helpful to compile a list of combinations of product category, target market, and resulting value and supply chains that could become more competitive and thus enhance economic growth, exports, and/or incomes of intended beneficiary groups. Narrowly speaking, and often perhaps too simplistically, competitiveness in such cases is simply interpreted as being able to sustainably export at a profit, or to compete favorably against imports (in a way that increases productivity and, hence, the incomes of affected populations).

There are many sources from which an initial list of products can be compiled. These include consultation with experts, previous assessments, products in industry sectors that have been identified as national priorities, and sectors being supported by other initiatives.

In addition to these sources, quantitative tools that rely on the concept of comparative advantage are often used to refine and prioritize the potential list of products and value chains. The comparative advantage concept focuses on the relative efficiency of producing different goods in the home country or region compared with the rest of the world. It must be emphasized, though, that the fact that a product possesses comparative advantage does not necessarily mean that it can be produced and sold at a profit under prevailing economic conditions. Many other elements need to be in place—including appropriate marketing links and input supply channels, financing mechanisms, uniform product quality, and many other demand requirements. In other words, comparative advantages can be built into competitive advantages.

To identify products or chains with a comparative advantage, practitioners have often used the revealed comparative advantage (RCA) index. The RCA denotes relative efficiency indirectly, based on trading patterns that emerge from actual market transactions. RCAs identify the extent to which an exporting country captures world market share in a particular area relative to the degree at which it captures export market share for all traded goods.[1] An RCA greater than 1.0 indicates a comparative advantage for that item, while an RCA lower than 1.0 identifies a comparative disadvantage.

The RCA is, however, imperfect because it embodies not only the fundamental economic factors affecting relative efficiency but also government policies and institutions that may distort markets. The usefulness of RCA indexes is also limited because they indicate past performance but do not take into account current market dynamics and likely future trends and conditions in those markets. Nor does the traditional RCA take sufficiently into account the key role of transport availability and cost for many exportable products. As long as these imperfections and limitations are recognized, RCAs can be helpful as analysis tools, since data are generally available in the trade record to gauge comparative advantage.

An alternative measure of comparative advantage is the Domestic Resource Cost (DRC) coefficient, which compares the cost of domestic production with world prices. The DRC measures the dollar cost in domestic resources of earning or saving a net dollar of foreign exchange. Therefore, values below 1.0 indicate a comparative advantage and values above 1.0 a disadvantage. To the extent that a country persists in producing commodities whose DRCs are greater than one, its resources are being poorly utilized. The country would have little chance of increasing exports of those items or increasing domestic production to substitute for imports, since they are inherently noncompetitive on world markets. Therefore, policies that encourage the production of products without a comparative advantage tend to drag down the country's agricultural growth rate and opportunities for employment creation.

Perhaps more importantly, DRCs can be compiled in such a way that disaggregates cost data by productive stages along the chain. Presenting data in this manner illustrates how income is distributed among the different links in the value creation process and allows for the analysis of other weaknesses and inefficiencies in each link. Tool 2 demonstrates how to use and benefit from this information.

A drawback of DRCs is that the data required to calculate them are often not readily available for many commodities. The calculation of DRCs requires data on domestic prices, international prices, government subsidies, and taxes for the specific commodities being evaluated, as well as the shadow price of foreign exchange. In addition, these indicators require information about the proportion of tradable and nontradable inputs used to produce one unit of each particular good. Given these requirements, it is difficult to assemble such detailed data for all but a few commodities in a limited number of countries. DRCs, though, are often the preferred indicators of comparative advantage when the focus of attention is restricted to a few commodities and/or trading areas. However, since DRCs are estimated on the basis of certain production conditions, their results most likely do not apply countrywide (Norton and Balcazar 2003). And once again, transport costs and availability are not formally reflected, yet can be quite important.

Box 4.1 demonstrates how an initial list was chosen for a project in Senegal.

The RCA and DRC approaches provide useful but incomplete information and guidance. Thus, they must be tested using a sensitivity analysis—testing different assumptions to see how and to what extent the outcomes change—and considered in the light of other important decision criteria. Among these criteria are market strength, domestic capacity, and level of commitment.

MARKET ANALYSIS

Market analysis to examine the nature of demand—its size, tendencies, segments and potential niches due to seasonality and other factors, price tendencies, customer preferences, current competitors, market access, and other requirements—is particularly important in prioritizing product/value chains. A market analysis allows the investor, business, or planner to identify whether attractive opportunities to improve and upgrade a given value chain exist, using market conditions as the benchmark of what needs to be achieved.

DOMESTIC CAPACITY AND ECONOMIC IMPACT

Once an initial list of potential product/value chains has been vetted by confirming market opportunities, program implementers can evaluate the capacity to respond competitively to those opportunities, as well as the extent to which upgrading and change are needed to be able to produce according to market requirements and customer preferences. This evaluation involves the analysis of institutions, technology, service providers, policies, and other production conditions, in addition to the investments needed to take advantage of the identified opportunities. An assessment of capacity also provides guidance as to important program intervention points, where the opportunities available within the target value chain can be leveraged or unleashed.

Before a detailed analysis can be performed to determine the most appropriate subsectors on which to focus interventions, planners must generate a list of possible subsectors from which to choose. The selection of items for the list can be conducted informally—for example, brainstorming the obvious sectors in a country or basing the list on the most widely grown crops. Or the process can be more rigorous such as in Senegal, where a more deliberate approach was taken to identify the list of possible target subsectors.

Senegal's Projet Croissance Economique is a five-year program supported by USAID[a] that began in 2005. The aim of the project is to help Senegal stimulate accelerated growth, competitiveness, and trade. Its initial work has focused on improving the value chains of a number of products produced in Senegal in order to achieve greater production and productivity, higher prices, and increased exports. The project's approach is to ensure that Senegalese stakeholders are engaged at every juncture along the production process so that improvements are sustainable.

At the start of the project, the government of Senegal, donors, and a consulting firm collaborated to create an initial long list of possible value chains on which to focus interventions. This initial list included many subsectors, but through a sequential refinement process, the list was shortened to six subsectors. This process involved five stages:

1) **Mandatory sectors:** If the government prioritized development of a subsector, it was automatically given strong consideration. These priority subsectors were identified based on government policies that emphasized the subsectors because they were considered vital to the country, had high value added, or were import substitutes. Using these criteria, cotton and horticulture-related products were priorities.

2) **High economic impact sectors:** Next, subsectors with extensive economic impact on the country were given priority. The team looked for subsectors with perceived competitive advantage, perceptions of high impact on rural incomes and employment, or export market potential, including sectors potentially benefiting from the U.S. African Growth and Opportunity Act (AGOA). Cashews, mangoes, dairy, and bissap (hibiscus tea) were identified through these criteria.

3) **Sectors with private sector appeal:** Finally, the team looked at subsectors that were of interest to private enterprise, were already a focus of the private sector, or that had a high likelihood of attracting private domestic and foreign direct investment. Banana production for export was already targeted by private sector investors, and export of neem seed to the United States (where it can be used as a raw material for organic agriculture inputs) was promoted by a foreign investor, so those subsectors were also considered priorities.

4) **Applying additional criteria:** Supplementing the criteria highlighted above were cross-cutting themes like poverty reduction, women's empowerment, and employment creation. The final short list that was created included six subsectors: mangoes, cashews, bissap, fonio (a small millet), woven textiles, and fisheries.

5) **Value chain analysis and feasibility analysis:** Next, a value chain analysis and feasibility analysis were conducted to verify soundness and opportunities, to determine which three of the initial six subsectors would be selected for the interventions, and to guide the nature of the particular value chain emphasis within each sector. Cashews, bissap, and mangoes were the initial choices.

This project is now in its fourth year. As it has progressed, changes in market opportunities have caused the list of selected subsectors to be expanded to include bananas, gum Arabic, neem, and dairy.

Source: Carlton Jones and Martin Webber, J. E. Austin Associates, Inc.
[a] Implemented by a consortium including International Resources Group and involving J. E. Austin Associates, Inc.

Further, given the market analysis and the opportunities identified, practitioners are able to construct scenarios of the economic impact (profits, jobs, increased exports, and wages) that the proposed changes would have.

TESTING COMMITMENT

It is essential to take into account the commitment of the chain's leadership and stakeholders when deciding which value chains to prioritize. Stakeholders must be willing to invest time and resources to achieve the identified opportunities for upgrading. Their motivation will rest on many factors, including their understanding of the likely returns, the time and level of investment required, perceived risk, and the leadership of opinion leaders and champions. It is generally a good idea to include stakeholders in the process as early as possible and conduct workshops to discuss the current conditions of the product/value chain. Their commitment to the process can be gauged by their repeated attendance, expressed enthusiasm, and commitment to resources. Their level of responsiveness will help practitioners prioritize value chains.

A STEP-BY-STEP SUMMARY OF TOOL 1: CHOOSING PRIORITY SECTORS FOR VALUE CHAIN INTERVENTIONS

- Start the prioritization process by compiling an initial list of products/chains whose competitiveness could further be enhanced. Sources for an initial list include experts, sector reviews, previous assessments, national priorities, and sectors supported by other initiatives.

- Add to or refine the list using quantitative tools, such as revealed comparative advantage and domestic resource cost coefficients, to assess comparative advantage.
- Conduct market analysis to identify if attractive opportunities to improve and upgrade a given value chain exist.
- Evaluate the capacity to respond competitively to those opportunities. Construct scenarios of the economic impact that the proposed changes could achieve using multiple assumptions about profits, jobs, increased exports, and wages among other variables.
- Make the stakeholders part of the process as early as possible, especially through workshops to discuss the current conditions of the product/value chain and to test their willingness and commitment to the process.

NOTE

1. The formula for calculating the RCA index of a given product (p) is $RCA_p = (x_p/X_p)/(x_t/X_t)$; where X_p are total world exports of product (p), x_t stands for total country exports, and X_t for the world total of all kinds of exports.

Prioritizing Value Chains by Using Comparative Analysis—Value Chain Selection in Mozambique

Carlton Jones and Martin Webber
J. E. Austin Associates, Inc.

INTRODUCTION

In the early 2000s, Mozambique was set to receive International Development Association (IDA) loan funds from the World Bank for a targeted agricultural program. In preparation, the parties agreed to carry out a study to identify the agricultural sectors with the greatest comparative advantage, as a method to prioritize from among a wide range of possible sectors. This case study uses the first tool to decide which specific value chains in Mozambique are the best candidates for intervention. It illustrates how the DRC can help decision makers select among value chain options.

POINTS TO CONSIDER

When reviewing this case, it is important to consider the following points:

- What are the steps involved in comparative analysis?
- Which method of comparative analysis was employed, and why?
- How do differing assumptions change the outcome of the analysis?
- How does information from the analysis shape future interventions?
- What limitations are there in a DRC-type analysis? How can the analysis be supplemented?

BACKGROUND

Mozambique is a largely rural country located on the southeastern coast of sub-Saharan Africa. After gaining independence from Portugal in 1975, Mozambique adopted a socialist economic system and later plunged into a civil war that lasted over 16 years. Peace was established in the early 1990s, providing a foundation for economic recovery.

More than 75 percent of the population relies on agriculture for their livelihoods, although less than 20 percent of the arable land is cultivated, and yields of all major cash crops are low. Seventy percent of the population lives on less than US$1 per day, and one-third suffers from chronic hunger.

Table 4.1 presents the major Mozambican commodities (2005).

In 2005, an agricultural economist was commissioned to perform an analysis for a targeted agricultural program to be implemented with loan funds from the World Bank, which culminated in a report entitled "Economic Analysis of Comparative Advantage for Major Agricultural Cash Crops in Mozambique."[1]

CREATING AN INITIAL LIST

Before the comparative study could be conducted, a list was generated that included possible sectors for intervention.

Table 4.1   Mozambican Commodities by Price, 2005

Rank	Commodity	Production price (Int $1,000)	Production volume (mt)
1	Cassava	443,169	6,150,000
2	Maize	168,490	1,450,000
3	Indigenous cattle meat	78,296	37,856
4	Pulses	54,382	205,000
5	Groundnuts in shell	53,156	110,000
6	Rice, paddy	42,815	201,000
7	Indigenous chicken meat	40,472	34,698
8	Sorghum	38,305	314,000
9	Cashews	38,108	58,000
10	Coconuts	23,967	265,000
11	Tobacco leaves	21,879	12,000
12	Vegetables, fresh	19,703	105,000
13	Fruit, fresh	18,344	115,000
14	Cow milk, whole, fresh	16,049	60,350
15	Indigenous pig meat	12,977	12,815
16	Bananas	12,826	90,000
17	Hen eggs	12,156	14,000
18	Potatoes	11,604	80,000
19	Tea	11,366	10,500
20	Oilseeds	8,789	30,000

Source: FAOSTAT data.

The original list was prepared by World Bank staff and focused on sectors linked to domestic priority crops.

The list was vetted by the Office of Commercial Agricultural Sector Promotion within GPSCA (Gabinete de Promoção do Sector Comercial Agrário), a department of the Mozambique Ministry of Agriculture. GPSCA felt that potatoes and paprika were very relevant in the Tete Province. The World Bank and GPSCA agreed to remove tobacco and flowers from the list and replace them with these sectors (see table 4.2).

Table 4.2   Original and Revised Sectors for Intervention in Mozambique

Original list	Revised list
Cashews	Cashews
Rice	Rice
Tobacco	Potatoes
Flowers	Paprika
Cotton	Cotton
Export fruits, (bananas and grapefruit)	Export fruits, (bananas and grapefruit)
Sugar	Sugar

Source: J. E. Austin Associates, Inc.

THE ANALYSIS

As previously described, there are two principal means to determine the comparative advantage of an agricultural sector: RCA and DRC. Of the two, the RCA method is the easier to use because it relies on trading patterns that emerge from actual market transactions to indirectly indicate relative efficiency; the data required are typically readily available. However, the RCA method requires data on international market transactions that were not available for Mozambique. Also, the RCA method paints a picture of past performance but does little to take into account future trends.

DRC and RCA are helpful tools, but they alone should not determine which value chain is selected for intervention. These tools should be used in conjunction with other analyses and scenarios that when combined make the best case for desired and successful outcomes.

The parties decided to employ the DRC method (see figure 4.2).

DRC is highly dependent on selected cost and other assumptions that, when changed, can affect outcomes. For example, real outcomes may vary in cases where unpredictable

Figure 4.2   Mozambican Cashew Domestic Value Chain

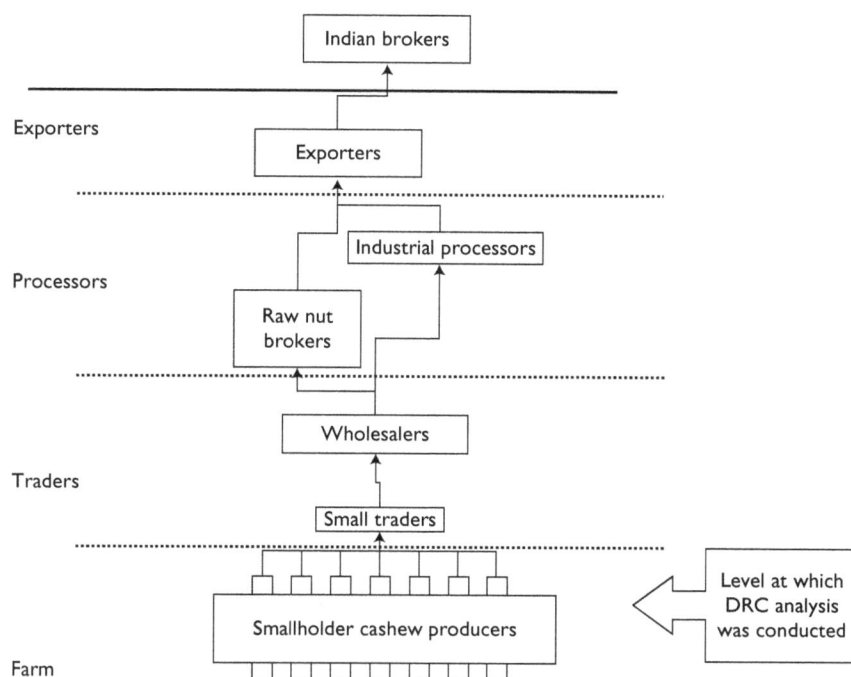

Source: J. E. Austin Associates, Inc.

costs determine value chain profitability. In such instances, flexible cost assumptions allow stakeholders to glean the correlation between outcomes and actual costs. Assumptions regarding other variables, such as location, access to inputs, or extension and training, will similarly affect the accuracy of DRC estimates.

Note: The value and limitations of this particular DRC analysis came into focus more recently as investment flooded into the sugarcane subsector of Mozambique, despite its being tagged in the following findings review as fundamentally uncompetitive in the study region. This subsequent investment highlights the fact that a given DRC is specific to a region and a moment in time. DRCs do not tell us about competitiveness on a national level, which was the driver of that later investment, nor do they tell us how the competitiveness of one region will change over time.

FINDINGS

The results of the sector comparison are below. Note that DRC values below 1.0 indicate a comparative advantage, and values over 1.0 indicate that resources are being poorly utilized:

- **Cashews:** The cashew sector possessed the highest comparative advantage, with a DRC coefficient well below 1.0, at 0.10. Local processing contributes two-thirds of

total value added to the product, so local processing is desirable for exporting raw nuts. Cashews also provide a significant profit (32.8 percent) to producers.

- **Rice:** At present, neither of the local rice varieties (Chokwe and Zambezia) are financially or economically profitable, but with technical assistance and credit access schemes, this could be changed. The Chokwe and Zambezia DRCs are both higher than 1.0; with interventions they could achieve coefficient below this value.

- **Potatoes:** Although they command low prices, potatoes are profitable and have a comparative advantage thanks to low production costs. The potato DRC is 0.36, but with interventions to improve yields via better inputs, it could be improved slightly.

- **Paprika:** This crop is somewhat profitable for farmers, but better pesticide and fertilizer interventions could increase profitability. Yields could be increased with the further extension of credit schemes that allow for more input purchases. Paprika profits are lower than those of tobacco and potatoes, which are the two competing crops in the region. However, paprika has a comparative advantage at the farm and export levels. Its DRC is .58.

- **Cotton:** In comparison to other agricultural crops, cotton is not profitable due to relatively high family labor requirements. However, in some cases, cotton is slightly profitable, and is the only option for growing a cash crop. This profitability is very fragile, however, as it depends on world prices for cotton, which fluctuate. Cotton's DRC is .76.

- **Export fruits (bananas and grapefruit):** Grapefruit is highly profitable in economic and financial terms. Bananas, on the other hand, are barely profitable in financial terms and generate an economic advantage only when taxes are eliminated. Grapefruit's DRC is .15, banana's is .40.
- **Sugar:** Sugar is not economically profitable but possesses a slight financial profitability because of domestic subsidization. Sugar has the highest DRC at 17.04. It is hoped that, through existing interventions, it can be lowered to .99 by the year 2012.

Of the seven sectors and eight cash crops studied, cashews possessed the lowest DRC (.10), with the grapefruit following close behind (.15).

The study noted that several sectors (rice, potatoes, paprika, and bananas) could have different profitability and DRC levels if technical assistance or different sets of inputs were available. This highlights how DRC can be a useful tool, but should not be the only determinant for sector selection. DRC use should be weighed in light of the assumptions used to complete the analysis. Even though cashews have the lowest DRC, it could be determined through further analysis that, for example, the relative cost of intervention for another product might make that other crop a preferable fulcrum for interventions.

OUTCOMES

The Mozambican Ministry of Agriculture refers extensively to this report for planning and analysis. The report also serves as a useful reference for further exploratory research.

CONCLUSIONS AND FUTURE STEPS

Markets with the best comparative advantage were identified based on well-considered cost and other assumptions.

However, the user or interpreter of DRC analysis should bear in mind the importance of recognizing that when assumptions are changed, the relative desirability of outcomes may change as well. DRC analysis provides important insights and a basis for comparing the profitability of value chains but should not be the sole tool used for sector selection. Complementary analytical tools should be employed to ensure that differing outcomes are identified and considered. For instance, DRC does not take into account market opportunities. Combining a market assessment with DRC analysis facilitates more informed decisions on agricultural interventions.

As the World Bank continues supporting agricultural projects in Mozambique, more DRC analyses can be conducted to ensure the data sets remain current, especially with respect to labor costs. Recommendations for future analysis include working with the Ministry of Agriculture's Policy Analysis Department to validate and/or update production costs and prices used in the previous comparative analysis report. It will also be worthwhile to extend the analysis to other cash-producing agricultural sectors such as livestock, fiber, and fuel crops and to conduct regional level studies to show impact in areas where agricultural projects are underway (Gergely 2005).

NOTE

1. The analysis was conducted and the report was prepared by Nicolas Gergely.

A Structured Value Chain–Based Approach to Designing a Strategy of Agricultural Competitiveness and Diversification in Mali

Carlton Jones and Martin Webber
J. E. Austin Associates, Inc.

INTRODUCTION

In 2005, the government of Mali, with the support of a US$46.4 million loan from the World Bank, launched the Agricultural Competitiveness and Diversification Project (PCDA) in hopes of diversifying the country's agricultural income into markets with clear competitive advantages for Mali. The project team identified target sectors for support by comparing Mali's agricultural sector using a series of analytical tools with a broad range of data. Through this process, the team identified value chains for export markets, which provide a basis for import substitution, improve livelihoods for Malian small growers, and contribute to Mali's GDP.

POINTS TO CONSIDER

When reviewing this case, consider the following questions:

- How did the PCDA team's approach to sector selection differ from other analytical approaches?
- If time and resource are factors, which steps are necessary and which can be set aside?

APPROACH TO VALUE CHAIN ANALYSIS AND SELECTION

The government of Mali and the World Bank enlisted the Geomar International Group,[1] a Canadian-based global consulting firm, to assist with the project's sector review component, which used five modules to assess Malian agricultural competitiveness. Each module built on the previous and helped practitioners progress from a comprehensive list of sectors to those with true marketability, competitive advantage, and comparative advantage. This process also took into account the demand in existing end-markets, identification of new potential end-markets, regional climate and growing factors, production capacity, access to finance, and infrastructure, and other determinants.

Module 1: Defining Mali's broad portfolio of agricultural value chains

Step 1:1   Create a comprehensive list of agricultural value chains in the country, including informal ones.

Step 1:2   Categorize each value chain using criteria that defines its particular storage and/or delivery needs, such as perishable, semiperishable, durable, transformed, semitransformed, or processed.

Step 1:3   Classify each value chain based on potential end-markets, such as export markets for consumption or processing, regional markets for consumption, or local markets for consumption.

Step1:4   Summarize the structure of the various value chains by organizing the categories defined earlier, incorporating upstream-downstream relationships and key factors of value addition.

Module 2: Analyzing market demand and market entry conditions

Step 2:1 Create a market demand data sheet for every value chain listed in module 1, providing a comprehensive snapshot of that chain's viability and market opportunities.

Step 2:2 Chart opportunities in each end-market for all identified classifications. For example, identify European markets for perishable product/value chains intended for export markets, including value and quantity. Do the same for other end-markets and sector classifications.

Module 3: Analyzing the competitiveness of potential Malian offerings

Step 3:1 Determine the production potential for each sector using information from the first two modules. Add data on number of producers, production, farm yields, unit price, and revenue.

Step 3:2 Analyze regional potential based on comparative advantages. Map the key production regions to determine target areas for select agricultural products, highlighting geographic advantages (for example, access to water or growing seasons); constraints (for example, distance from main markets, distance from Bamako for transport, pollution, or poor climate); and producible crop sectors.

Step 3:3 Create subregional identification sheets that present annual rainfall, temperature, sun exposure, and humidity for each subregion to determine the suitability of crop selection.

Step 3:4 Illustrate the growing months and seasonal market demands for all products to show areas of opportunity for producers based on their production cycles and periods of crop availability.

Step 3:5 Conduct an analysis that shows constraints and subsequent interventions that would improve value chain competitiveness.

Module 4: Defining priority sectors

Step 4:1 Prioritize value chain criteria by triangulating the interests of various stakeholders. Rank the priorities for each value chain based on production sophistication, number of solvent operators that could be integrated into the strategy, strategy duration, social impact, market appropriateness, existing professional organizations, and existing programs.

Step 4:2 Create a matrix that identifies priority sectors. Put priority levels from the final stage of step 4:1 in columns, and categorize the rows based on various end-markets. Insert sectors into their respective boxes, thus identifying the sectors with the highest probability for success and impact. The matrix can be used to balance strategies for a variety of sectors.

Step 4:3 Organize the priority sectors by area using the regional analysis conducted in module 3 that shows which value chains should be implemented in which regions of the country. This table also provides an at-a-glance view of the crops that can be grown in several regions.

Step 4:4 Create a reference index showing growth and economic impacts for certain priority value chains, highlighting all indicators used during the previous modules of the analysis.

Module 5: Competitiveness planning: putting the analysis into action

Step 5:1 Determine which approach will improve the competitiveness of the sectors in question. In this instance, the team recommended that Mali's competitive strategy include short-, medium-, and long-term objectives, each with pragmatic and obtainable interventions.

Step 5:2 Address the issues with solutions, taking into consideration the constraints highlighted in module 3 and their associated investment needs. For example, "Improve technical skills and human productivity by introducing new technologies and training facilities."

Step 5:3 Wrap the entire strategy together by providing implementation guidelines and a framework that encompasses standard, specific activities that fall under four stages: provisioning, production, logistics, and marketing. Overlap these stages with cross-cutting activities.

LOOKING AHEAD

The value chain strategy that the team recommended to Mali is currently being implemented. About 10 value chain competitiveness strategies and action plans have been developed and are being implemented. In committing to these strategies and actions, Malians will have invested in a strategy that takes into account the many elements of value chain analysis that have often been overlooked in previous strategies. This, in itself, will prove to be beneficial in increasing the institutional knowledge, not only for the government, but also for all stakeholders taking part in the implementation of PCDA.

NOTE

1. Geomar International Group was acquired by SNC-Lavalin in 2006.

Designing Informed Strategies across the Value Chain

A strategy is an integrated set of choices about the markets a firm or set of firms should serve; how to compete in each market; and how to allocate resources to the most valuable production, marketing, and support activities. In increasingly integrated regional and global markets, firms don't merely compete against firms—value chains compete against value chains. Increasing productivity and competitiveness requires a comprehensive strategy. In vertically integrated industries, firm strategy and value chain strategy are synonymous. However, in fragmented supply chains, buyers, suppliers, and intermediaries must work together to increase their productivity and to raise the value of the end product.

This section outlines a selection of fundamental analytical tools for understanding the quality and efficiency of a cascading series of activities that increases value added.[1] A vast set of tools exist that can be used to describe, analyze, and evaluate the value chain. Several are highlighted here to demonstrate the types of analysis and information that typically guide the strategies and actions to enhance the productivity of a value chain (see figure 4.3). Since the analytical tools outlined below are point-in-time assessments, they should be updated on a frequent basis to ensure that any changes in the market dynamics or performance of the business are quickly integrated into a new strategy.

ENHANCING VALUE CHAIN PRODUCTIVITY

Competitiveness is determined by the productivity (value per unit of input) with which a firm or value chain uses its human, capital, and natural resources. Productivity depends on the value, uniqueness, and quality of a product, in addition to the efficiency with which it is produced. Productivity can be strategic, as well as operational, in nature. The overall productivity of a value chain can be segmented into various components, each of which can be analyzed and addressed in concrete, tangible ways to increase the overall return to businesses within the

Figure 4.3   Enhancing Productivity and Value across the Value Chain

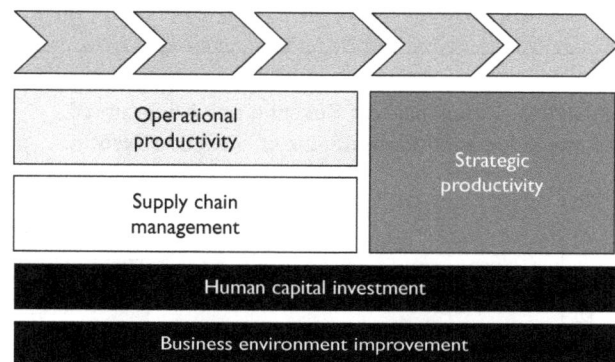

Source: J. E. Austin Associates, Inc.

chain.[2] The graphic above and the more detailed explanations below outline a framework and key questions that can be used for analysis and evaluation in guiding the development of a comprehensive, integrated value chain strategy.

Assessing the overall status of the value chain

An awareness of the distribution and flow of profits in the value chain is fundamental to understanding the relationships among and behaviors of each segment, as well as the opportunities for increasing productivity and profit across the chain of activities. Information should be collected at each segment of the chain: for instance, the number of enterprises; number of employees; unit labor costs; unit input costs; unit sales, marketing, and distribution costs; annual volume sold; annual sales revenue; unit price; and net profit.

Figure 4.4 illustrates a standard value chain, or value system analysis and graph. This analysis is the quantitative building block for understanding the cascade of value-added activities in a particular industry. By summarizing the price build-up for each activity in the chain, the graph tracks the distribution

At each segment of the chain, the following information should be collected:

- Number of enterprises
- Number of employees
- Unit labor costs
- Unit input costs
- Unit sales, marketing, and distribution costs
- Annual volume sold
- Annual sales revenue
- Unit price
- Net profit

Source: J. E. Austin Associates, Inc.

Figure 4.4 Mongolia: Net Revenue per Kilogram of Cashmere for Each Component of the Value System

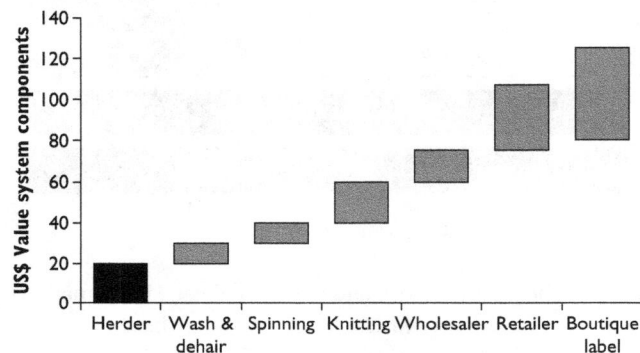

Source: Nathan Associates Inc. and J. E. Austin Associates, Inc., for USAID.

of net revenue for one unit of a good from raw material to point of sale. It is important to note that this graph does not incorporate costs at each activity, and so does not give any insight into the market economics and profitability of each activity. It is useful when mapping the roles of each segment and the incremental value that the market assigns each role based on additional inputs and services to the product.

The example in figure 4.4 depicts the build-up of the net revenue of one kilogram of Mongolian cashmere from herder to retailer. Over 60 percent of the value of the end product is captured by the knitting, wholesaling, and retailing activities.

SWOT analysis

Complementing the value system analysis above, a SWOT (strengths, weaknesses, opportunities, and threats) analysis is

the general, qualitative starting point for any competitiveness strategy or other analysis for decision-making purposes (see figure 4.5). While the SWOT analysis is not a very precise tool, it is a good way to provide a general characterization of the current state of the industry, identify issues, and generate discussion. It is particularly useful as a neutral facilitation tool to focus an initial discussion on the perceived state of the value chain or to perform initial brainstorming on the potential opportunities and risks.

SWOT analysis is simple and can be used at differing levels of focus (examining a single firm, a segment of the chain, or the chain overall). It is also a good way of identifying areas to examine in greater detail. Thus, it is an excellent analytical starting point.

It is important to identify the right focus for the SWOT analysis and to keep the discussion on point. SWOT analysis is not an effective tool for identifying alternate strategies, nor is it terribly rigorous. It is, therefore, most valuable when supported by other forms of analysis rather than as a standalone tool.

Once a broad overview of the structure and characteristics of the value chain has been established, a more in-depth understanding of the drivers of productivity is required to uncover the highest-value strategies to raise productivity in the value chain.

Using the competitiveness diamond

The Competitiveness Diamond[3] is a more rigorous analytical tool for evaluating an industry or value chain. The Competitiveness Diamond framework has been validated by numerous analytical and case studies and is now used by industries and governments worldwide to assess industry cluster competitiveness and to develop strategies for improving competitiveness. It is structured around four pillars:

1. Factor (input) conditions: skilled labor, infrastructure, and others
2. Demand conditions: size and type of accessible demand
3. Related and supporting industries: presence of supplier and supporting industries
4. Context for firm strategy and rivalry: conditions for conducting business

Within each sector and across the economy, these four pillars interact to form a foundation for building a competitive system of firms. For developing economies like those in Africa, building a competitive value chain starts with understanding the demand for products and services in key markets and then organizing and investing in the factor inputs

Figure 4.5   Pakistan Dairy SWOT Analysis

Strengths

- Large population and high per capita consumption of dairy products, ahead of other regional markets in Asia.
- A high ratio of agricultural land to agricultural population.
- Large aggregate supply and breed potential of indigenous cattle/buffalo.
- Regular culling of less productive/ unproductive animals.
- Internationally cost-competitive farm types already exist in Pakistan.
- Willingness of processors to develop infrastructure linking them to the farmer because of consumer preferences against reconstituted milk.
- Larger and smaller processors are willing to invest given the right support.
- Central geographic location with easy access to large, potential regional markets.

Opportunities

- Consumption can be increased with the right emphasis on nutritional value, quality, and price. Capitalize on traditional nutritional value placed on milk and related products.
- Exploit potential to improve animal yield through better feed availability and breeding. Potential to maintain/establish feasible, larger farms. Interest in investing in larger model farms.
- Induce productivity and quality specific farmer cooperation around collection and possibly milking, and support efficient collection at larger scales.
- Develop extension services model based on NRSP to promote farmer cooperation.
- Encourage large farm types as well as give incentives to subsistence farmer to invest in productivity.
- Emergence of commercial dairy farms on a large scale.
- Large aggregate production of milk. Develop rural and urban markets to sell milk and dairy products from adjacent milk pockets.
- Joint ventures based on large potential and access to regional markets.
- Government interest and willingness to contribute.
- Build on consensus to develop and implement quality standards.
- Consolidation and improvement in retail segment in large cities.

Weaknesses

- Consumers are price sensitive and ignorant of quality requirements.
- Significant cost variation in milk production across sizes and types of farms.
- Poor quality of milk.
- Middlemen operating without regulations leading to significant value destruction.
- The existence of the bandi system (under which the middleman predetermines the producer's sale price for the entire year at the rate most beneficial to him).
- Low animal productiviy, no breed management, and little productivity support services to farmers.
- Farmers not organized, general lack of able management structures in sector.
- Poor quality of animal health care and breeding services. Support structure and industry are not well developed to support animal productivity.
- Seasonality leading to fluctuations and uncertainty in feed supply and quality.
- Underdeveloped cold chain to consumers.
- Poor physical infrastructure.
- Small-scale and fragmented animal holdings.
- Lack of remunerative producer price for milk.
- Low utilization of installed capacity of dairy plants.
- Lack of a well-defined national policy for dairy development.

Threats

- Farmer cooperation around collection and central milking is expensive and difficult to manage.
- Lack of breed management at the macro level and low potential of indigenous animals.
- Unregulated imports of dairy products and additives.
- Vested interests in perpetuating the dependence on imports of dairy commodities. manage.

Source: J. E. Austin Associates, Inc.

(supply) to best meet the needs of those markets. Only by accessing and understanding the specific needs of the market can the commercial sector utilize its resources in the most efficient way that creates the most value for both the producer and the customer. As a more in-depth understanding of the market is developed and the supply is upgraded accordingly, the value chain then must concentrate on upgrading its suppliers and supporting industries and working with the government to improve its business environment.

In contrast to the SWOT analysis, the Competitiveness Diamond is an analytical tool that poses very specific questions to the economic leadership about a specific industry. It can also be used as a framework for evaluating an overall regional or national economy. Figure 4.6 outlines many of the key questions to be posed when conducting a diamond analysis.

Once the competitiveness of a value chain has been understood, value chain analysis must then delve more deeply to highlight the underlying drivers of competitiveness: strategic productivity, operational productivity, supply chain management, human capital, and the business environment. Only at this level of assessment is it possible to uncover the investment and actions required to increase the performance of the chain in regional and international markets.

Assessing strategic productivity

The primary means of increasing value chain productivity is by choosing appropriate markets and products and by adding new product features and service components that enable companies to increase the value of their product and, hence, its price. This "strategic" or "market price–related" productivity can be as important as "operational" productivity in determining competitiveness. In practice, understanding the strategic position of a firm or value chain in key markets helps to orient and focus investment on the highest value activities. By (re)positioning products in new markets or to new customers or by adding additional value (real and perceived), companies increase their sales and profits per unit of capital and labor. Positioning is further discussed in tool 8.

When evaluating a value chain's strategic productivity, the key questions to consider are:

- Which product segments are currently being offered by the companies in the chain? Do they represent the full range of segments that could be offered? Do they represent the highest-value segments in the industry?
- Which markets are currently being served by the companies in the chain? Do they represent the highest-value markets?

- Of the spectrum of potential customers in each key market for the chain, which customers is the chain best positioned to target?

A number of analytical tools can be employed in answering the questions above:

- Market segmentation and assessment
- Customer profiling
- Customer benefit analysis (product attribute gap analysis based on customer perceptions)
- Mapping the consumption chain (from sale to point of consumption)

Assessing operational productivity

A second way to improve value chain productivity is through operational productivity, improved technology, manufacturing, and service processes within specific segments of the value chain. Operational productivity focuses on the efficiency of each appropriate segment of activities on its own. By introducing new technology that improves processes and management systems, key players in the value chain can lower their costs and raise the productivity of their businesses, and the value chain overall.

The following questions are useful in evaluating the operational productivity of a specific segment of the value chain and developing strategies to enhance it:

- How do our costs compare to the price for the product in different markets (that is, which markets are profitable to serve based on the current cost structure)? Are we excluded from competitively serving key markets because of our cost structure?
- How do the costs of the value chain compare to other competing value chains?
- What are the key trade-offs between cost and quality for the product?
- Who is in control of the cost drivers?
- What are the opportunities for lowering costs without compromising quality?

Analytical tools that can assist in determining the answers include:

- Per unit economic cost-driver analysis (fixed versus variable costs within each activity)
- Cost-trend analysis (historical and projected changes in cost drivers)
- Per unit activity-cost benchmarking

Figure 4.6   Competitiveness Diamond Analysis—Key Questions

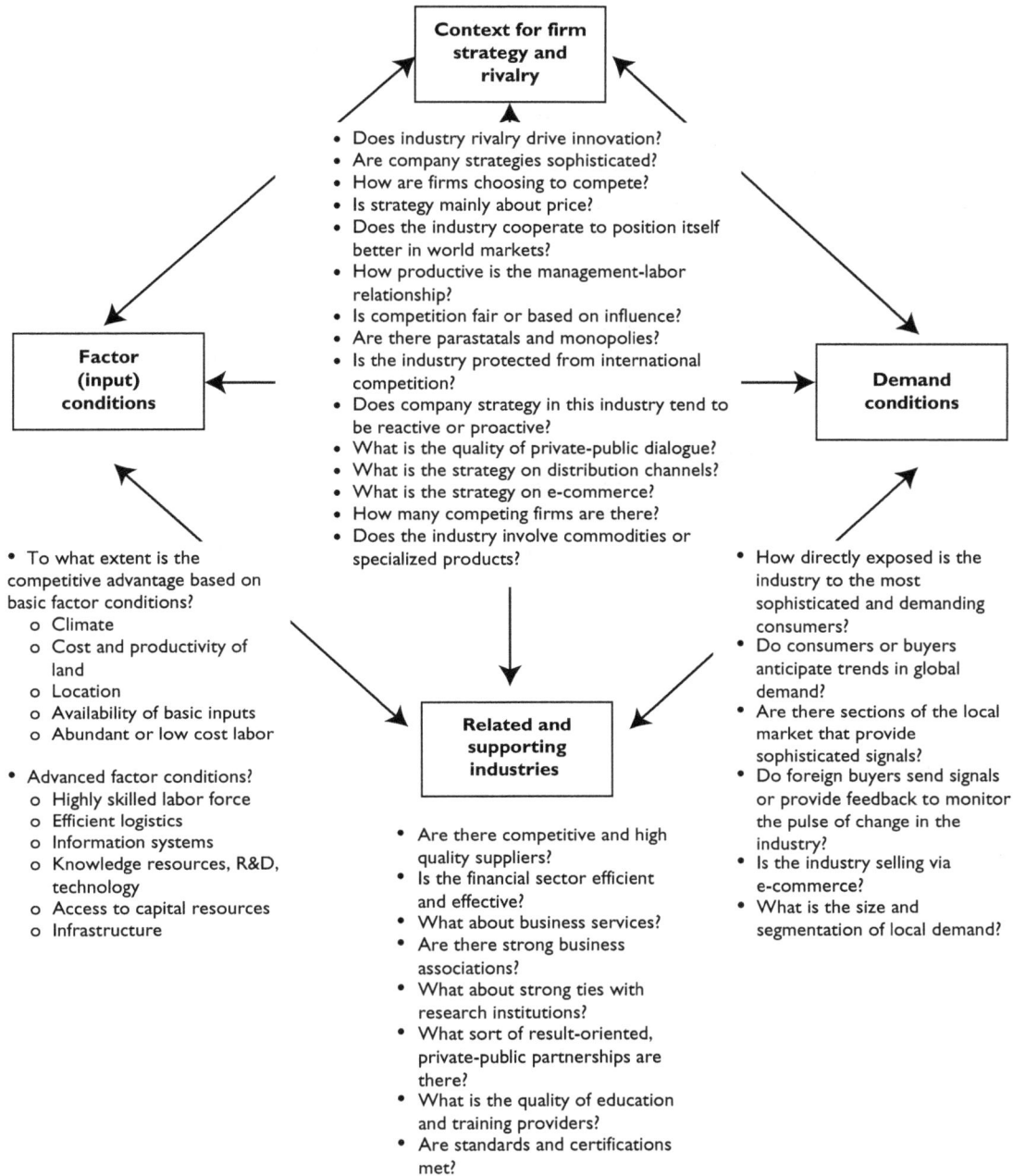

Context for firm strategy and rivalry

- Does industry rivalry drive innovation?
- Are company strategies sophisticated?
- How are firms choosing to compete?
- Is strategy mainly about price?
- Does the industry cooperate to position itself better in world markets?
- How productive is the management-labor relationship?
- Is competition fair or based on influence?
- Are there parastatals and monopolies?
- Is the industry protected from international competition?
- Does company strategy in this industry tend to be reactive or proactive?
- What is the quality of private-public dialogue?
- What is the strategy on distribution channels?
- What is the strategy on e-commerce?
- How many competing firms are there?
- Does the industry involve commodities or specialized products?

Factor (input) conditions

- To what extent is the competitive advantage based on basic factor conditions?
  - o Climate
  - o Cost and productivity of land
  - o Location
  - o Availability of basic inputs
  - o Abundant or low cost labor

- Advanced factor conditions?
  - o Highly skilled labor force
  - o Efficient logistics
  - o Information systems
  - o Knowledge resources, R&D, technology
  - o Access to capital resources
  - o Infrastructure

Related and supporting industries

- Are there competitive and high quality suppliers?
- Is the financial sector efficient and effective?
- What about business services?
- Are there strong business associations?
- What about strong ties with research institutions?
- What sort of result-oriented, private-public partnerships are there?
- What is the quality of education and training providers?
- Are standards and certifications met?

Demand conditions

- How directly exposed is the industry to the most sophisticated and demanding consumers?
- Do consumers or buyers anticipate trends in global demand?
- Are there sections of the local market that provide sophisticated signals?
- Do foreign buyers send signals or provide feedback to monitor the pulse of change in the industry?
- Is the industry selling via e-commerce?
- What is the size and segmentation of local demand?

Source: Michael Porter, adapted by J. E. Austin Associates, Inc.

Assessing the quality of supply chain management

Focusing on supply chain management in terms of costs of raw materials, transportation logistics, communications, and information technology—aspects of the chain that have generated great efficiencies in manufacturing, retailing, and other industries—is a third way to fully understand the underlying drivers of competitiveness. Supply chain management is different from operational productivity. It focuses on the flow of goods and information along the chain of activities, the efficiencies of these flows, the transactions that facilitate value added, and the economic relationships that underlie each set of transactions.

Questions to consider when evaluating the supply chain include:

- Is the relationship among buyers and suppliers in the value chain cooperative or adversarial?
- How effective is the flow of information along the value chain (market trends, changes in price, external cost pressures)? How aware are the producers of the downstream market dynamics of the industry (market trends, demand conditions, pricing)?
- How sensitive is the overall cost structure to the cost of raw materials?
- How do logistics services affect the cost of raw materials and intermediary products?
- What is the availability of supporting services (financial, logistics, administrative) across activities in the value chain?
- How long does it take for a product to go from initial production to end-market? How does this compare with competing value chains?

Analytical tools that can assist in determining the answers include:

- Supply chain analysis:
  - Distribution of players across chain activities
  - Farm-to-market mapping: number of transactions and time required
- Benchmarking other supply chains
- Mapping of support services across the supply chain
- Mapping of information flows along the chain
- Supplier assessments

Assessing human resources across the value chain

The next driver of value chain productivity is the quality of human resources available for the chain to tap.[4] Thus, a fourth way to improve productivity is by investing in human resources. This may involve enhancing motivation, management, and training at the firm level, both by upgrading the overall education system and through utilizing specialized institutes.

Improving the overall quality of the workforce is often seen as the mandate of government and the educational institutions, outside of the direct control of industry. Similarly, specific technical and management skills are viewed as the concern of specific firms or industries. Neither perception is

accurate. Upgrading the technical and management skills of an entire value chain requires close cooperation of the firms along the chain and the supporting government and academic institutions.

The following questions can be considered when assessing the level of human resources across the spectrum of activities in a value chain:

- What incentives are present to encourage firms to invest in the technical and management skills of their employees?
- Do firms have difficulty retaining trained talent?
- What supporting educational services are available to firms locally to increase the skill levels of their staff? (industry certifications, IT training, technology application)
- How well do the academic institutions know the needs of industry? Is the curriculum aligned with the specific skill requirements of the industry?
- Are there industry standards for industry skill levels? Do the academic institutions teach to these standards?
- How do the skill levels of the value chain's workforce compare to competitors along key skills categories?

Analytical tools that can assist in determining the answers include:

- Industry workforce assessments to evaluate the demand- and supply-side conditions for labor in the industry and across the labor market in general.
- Skills segmentation, classification, and benchmarking analyses for the value chain against competitors.
- Bridge analyses[5] to assess the strength of linkages between industry and academic institutions.

Assessing the business environment

The quality of the business environment ultimately serves a gate-keeping function, and often a negative one. Productivity increases are achieved at the firm and value chain levels by improving the quality of business strategy and operations—for example, by forming new partnerships with international firms in their value chains that provide access to markets, technology, finance, and know-how. Interventions designed to enhance productivity will differ by value chain and will require a different balance across the four components (strategic productivity, operational productivity, supply chain management, and human resources) discussed above. However, a factor common across all value chains and components is that the business environment contributes importantly to the ability of firms to succeed in enhancing productivity. These "business environment" factors, also called the microeconomic foundations of growth, are perhaps especially important in the context of Africa,[6] they include: the level of bureaucracy and red tape; the extent to which the rule of law is enforced and commercial courts are functional; the quality of infrastructure; the level of financial sector modernization and regulation; levels of trade access; and the ability of the country to attract foreign investment and to ensure the proper functioning of land markets (through reliable registries) and labor markets (through policies that encourage job creation, labor flexibility, and overall productivity).

Numerous methodologies and analytical tools exist to evaluate the business environment of a particular value chain.[7] In most cases, the analytical tools are targeted at a specific area of the business environment. The following are a few general tools that can be used:

- Regulatory impact analysis
- Mapping of the time and cost of bureaucratic processes
- Per unit costing of rent-seeking activities across the value chain
- Total annual costing of weaknesses in infrastructure relevant to the industry

Means by which businesses can participate in improving the business environment are described in tools 10 and 11.

A STEP-BY-STEP SUMMARY OF TOOL 2: DESIGNING INFORMED STRATEGIES ACROSS THE VALUE CHAIN

- Conduct a value chain product unit financial analysis and SWOT analysis. First, understand the distribution and flow of resources and profits along the chain. Collect key data at each segment of the value chain, and graph the unit costs, unit revenue, and unit profit for each step. To complement the financial and operational data, conduct a SWOT analysis in a participatory manner with value chain leadership to qualitatively characterize the state of the value chain.
- Conduct a Competitiveness Diamond analysis. For the value chain, assess the strengths and weaknesses of each of the four pillars of the competitiveness diamond: 1) demand conditions; 2) factor inputs; 3) context for firm strategy and rivalry; and 4) related and supporting industries.
- Assess strategic productivity of the value chain. Use analytical tools such as market segmentation and assessment, customer profiling, customer benefit analysis, and

consumption chain mapping to understand the current strategic positioning of the value chain, as well as potential markets and product offerings.

- Assess operational productivity of the value chain. A variety of tools are available to analyze the operational productivity and performance of the value chain including per unit economic cost-driver analysis (fixed versus variable costs within each activity), cost-trend analysis, and per unit activity-cost benchmarking.
- Assess the quality of supply chain management. To gauge the efficiency in the flow of goods along the chain, the following tools can be useful: farm-to-market mapping (number of transactions and time) and distribution of players across the chain, supply chain benchmarking, mapping of supporting services, mapping of information flow along the chain, and supplier assessments.
- Assess the human resources across the value chain. To assess the quality of the value chain workforce, the following tools can be used: Demand- and supply-side analyses of the labor market for the value chain, skills segmentation and benchmarking analyses with competitor value chains (including labor productivity, number of skilled graduates), or the 10 bridges analysis[8] of the linkages between industry and academia.
- Assess the business environment. Numerous tools are already well developed to assess the business environment of a value chain. Among the most tested are regulatory impact analyses, mapping of time and cost of bureaucratic processes at each stage of the value chain, per unit costing of rent-seeking activities along each segment of the value chain, and total annual cost of weaknesses in infrastructure.

NOTES

1. This value chain productivity framework was developed by J. E. Austin Associates, Inc., for use in developing and implementing industry strategic agendas with public and private sector leaders.

2. Productivity is the efficiency by which a firm uses its natural resources, labor, and financial resources. It is measured in terms of output per unit hour of labor, capital-output ratios, and total factor productivity. These drive returns to labor and capital, which in turn drive wage levels and overall prosperity.

3. Often referred to as the "Porter Diamond," the diamond and many of its applications were developed by Michael Porter of the Harvard Business School.

4. Many tools and methodologies have already been developed to evaluate and address this area. A detailed consideration

of workforce issues is largely beyond the scope of this Guide. Perhaps they can be addressed more fully in a subsequent volume. For more detailed information on workforce development, readers are directed to the extensive body of literature available publicly on the World Bank Web site.

5. Derived from J. E. Austin Associates, Inc.'s "10 Bridges Approach," a methodology for building workforce competitiveness through university-industry collaborations.

6. Dr. Michael Porter, the thought leader of business competitiveness, weights his "Business Competitiveness Index" in the influential World Economic Forum Global Competitiveness Report with 80 percent on the national business environment and 20 percent on "the quality of business strategy and operations."

7. Annual reports on the conditions of the business environment in specific countries, such as the World Bank Doing Business and the Global Competitiveness Report, provide useful examples as they use many of the survey and analytical tools at the economy level.

8. Analytical tool developed by J. E. Austin Associates, Inc.

Understanding the Value Chain and Integrating Information into Strategy— Nigerian Domestic Catfish

Michael Gorman and Martin Webber
J. E. Austin Associates, Inc.

INTRODUCTION

Despite government support for major investments in some 40 additional public fish farms and hatcheries, aquaculture expansion has been a slow process in Nigeria, because private sector fish farmers have faced major constraints, including lack of supporting feed and seed companies. Dixie and Ohen (2006) conducted a market study to better understand these private sector constraints and opportunities.

Nigeria is the fifth largest aquaculture producer in the world. In Nigeria, domestic fish is a preferred protein that rivals red meat in consumer demand. Domestic demand for fresh catfish has grown as Nigerian incomes increase. Nigeria has become one of the largest importers of fish in the developing world, bringing in some 600,000 metric tons (mt) annually. There is a growing awareness of aquaculture in Nigeria, with more than 100 private commercial fish farms currently in production.

At the New Partnership for Africa's Development (NEPAD) 2005 "Fish for All Summit," Nigeria's president Olusegun Obasanjo stated that, "if Africa's per capita consumption of fish is just to be kept at its present level, though grossly low and unacceptable, then fish production must be increased by over 250 percent by 2015. This unhealthy situation calls for urgent action and indeed poses a great challenge to all of us." President Obasanjo further remarked in his closing address that although fishing brings Africa export earnings of US$2.7 billion annually, "these benefits are at risk as the exploitation of African natural fish stocks is reaching its limits, and aquaculture production has not realized its full potential" (EurekNews and BBC News).

THE TOOL: MARKET ASSESSMENTS

Value chain participants must consult the market when determining how to increase profits, reach new markets, innovate, and increase productivity. There are seven widely accepted means of developing market analysis that contribute to identifying opportunities to capture more value. They are detailed in the Market Assessment Methods box below (Engelmann and Swisscontact 2005).

In Nigeria, a market survey was used to gather quantitative and qualitative information about buyers, sellers, volumes, prices, market trends, market share, and market segments, along with qualitative information on competitors. The rationale behind this approach was that surveys can accurately represent the opportunities and demand characteristics of the markets studied. Value chain participants can use surveys to identify broad problems in a market, such as lack of knowledge about a particular service, limited understanding of its benefits, or failure to assign appropriate value to outside assistance. This type of information is useful for establishing new products or services within the value chain.

The following methods are derived from Engelmann and Swisscontact (2005).

- Secondary research refers to the use of data that have already been collected, analyzed, and made available for other purposes. Value chain participants may find such research useful for identifying sectors experiencing growth, as well as for understanding government regulations and policy.
- Group discussions permit value chain participants to explore issues in general terms, then seek more specific information by using focus group discussions.
- In-depth interviews provide qualitative and quantitative information on the value chain and are particularly useful for different participants of value chains to understand their complementary relationships.
- Market observation can be used by value chain participants to obtain qualitative and quantitative data from local markets on transactions, interactions, processes, and embedded services. Observations are also a simple tool to cross-check information obtained from other sources.
- Interactive workshops or meetings can be used to validate and deepen previously gathered information. They can generate ideas for addressing constraints or opportunities in the market. In addition, these workshops may lead to a common approach in solving market problems among all of the value chain participants.
- Product concept testing aims to gauge the demand for a service or product that the value chain does not yet produce and about which the value chain customers have no knowledge.
- Market and consumer surveys are useful (as evidenced by the Nigerian case study) to obtain an accurate picture of serviceable aspects of the market for the product or service.

Figure 4.7   Map of Nigeria

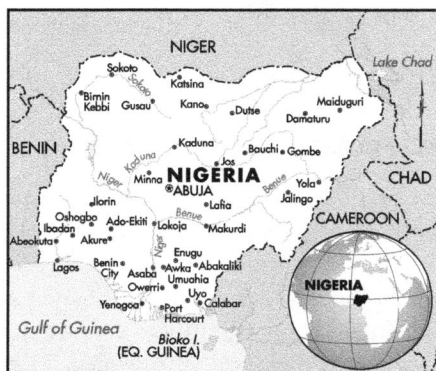

Source: World Bank.

BACKGROUND

Africa produced 7.31 million tons of fish and seafood in 2002 (Dixie and Ohen 2006). On the continent, aquaculture development has been most notable in Egypt, where a combination of tradition, market demand, available and well-managed water resources, marketable species, and private sector initiative resulted in dramatic growth during the 1990s. The top three African producer nations were Egypt (accounting for 85.6 percent of the total), Nigeria (6.5 percent), and

Madagascar (1.8 percent). Egypt's aquaculture growth and development has been the most significant because it has increased production levels from 85,000 tons in 1997 to 376,000 tons in 2002, a 35 percent average annual growth rate.

By 2006, farmed catfish accounted for approximately 50 percent of Nigeria's domestic annual fish production. The catfish industry provides approximately US$75 million in revenues at the farm gate and accounts for nearly US$180 million in consumer spending. The sector contributes to the employment of nearly 25,000 people, with the majority (over two-thirds) employed as restaurant workers. Aquaculture and Nigerian farm-raised catfish have also been identified as a growing source of income for Nigerian farmers.

To ensure success, any new investments or expansion of production must be driven by market demand and consumer preferences. This case study features the information gathered from a domestic market assessment for the farmed and fresh catfish value chain conducted by Dixie and Ohen (2006) to demonstrate the value of market information in determining future investments and/or interventions in a value chain.

THE NIGERIAN CATFISH VALUE CHAIN

The domestic market demand for fresh and smoked Nigerian catfish is outstripping the supply. Tastes and preferences for catfish have been increasing due in large part to the availability, cost, consumer preference for white meat, perceived health benefits over substitute products, and some popular catfish dishes served by restaurants (Dixie and Ohen 2006).

Production

According to Dixie and Ohen (2006), the value of Nigerian catfish produced and sold by aquaculture farmers is about US$75 million, which assumes a production level of about 30,000 tons of catfish per year. At the retail level, this tonnage rises in value to about US$120 million. Restaurant operators capture an additional US$60 million dollars on catfish, for a total of US$180 million in sectorwide consumer spending. Estimates indicate that approximately 70 percent of fresh fish in Nigeria is sold in restaurants, especially in *bukas*.[1] The major cost of production for farmers is European catfish feed, which amounts to approximately US$39 million. Nigeria currently relies on imports because a sizeable fish-feed industry has yet to develop. The majority of domestic feed supplies are farm made, with only a few animal feed millers providing domestic commercial feed pellets (Moehl, Halwart, and Brummet 2005).

Supply

Farmed catfish are almost universally sold at the farm to primary wholesalers, retailers, or buka owners. As indicated in figure 4.8, primary wholesalers have been chiefly responsible for developing the trade from the major fish farms in Nigeria. Traditionally, these wholesalers transport live catfish to secondary wholesalers who sell to other retailers, restaurants, or consumers. It is worth noting that, in the major production areas, retailers and restaurants are increasingly buying directly at the farm, thus cutting out middlemen and vertically integrating. A new trend in the industry is that the majority of fresh catfish, especially larger fish, are now sold directly to bukas, restaurants, and hotels.

Demand

Dixie and Ohen (2006) cite Nigerian consumers' requirements and demands with respect to catfish and catfish products that are fairly common across regions and markets. As indicated in figure 4.9, key consumer motivations for consuming catfish were 1) availability, 2) taste/smell, and 3) familiarity. Over 90 percent of consumers said that they were increasing their purchases of catfish, and 15 percent identified bird flu as affecting their purchases. Comments were made about the health benefits of white meat (for example, catfish), and a significant number made reference to a

Figure 4.8 Nigerian Domestic Catfish Farming Value Chain

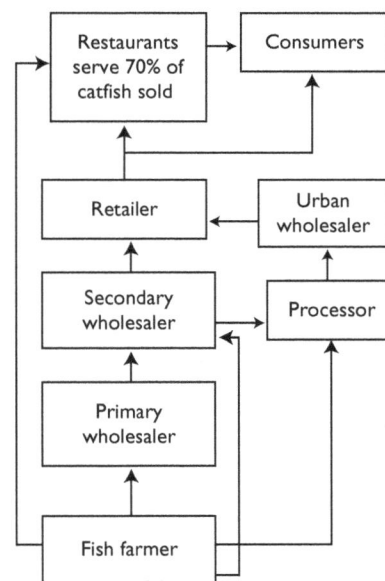

Source: J. E. Austin Associates, Inc.

Figure 4.9 Consumers' Reasons for Purchasing Live Catfish

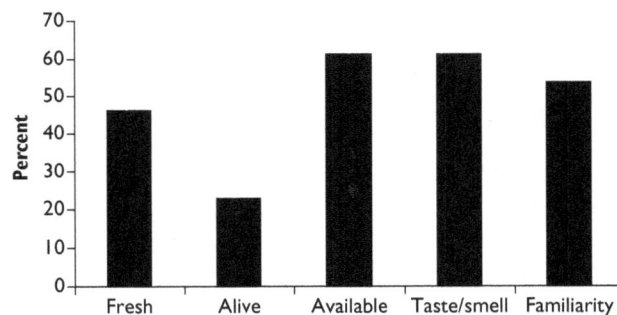

Source: Dixie and Ohen (2006).

perception that after a certain age (normally about 35), red meat should be given up entirely. Nearly 80 percent said that they would use catfish to prepare pepper soup—by far, the most popular use—and about 40 percent said it would go into other soups or stew dishes.

Opportunity

According to traders and retailers, product losses (fish death, quality loss) and finance are the most common challenges cited by fresh catfish traders and retailers. Fresh and living catfish command a retail price twice that of frozen fish. Traders and retailers do not use proper storage facilities, do not change the water sufficiently, and often leave the fish in the sun for long periods—all leading to product loss and lower quality, which translate to lower revenues. Traders indicate that limited finance constrains the ability to develop and invest in business operations or expansion. Secondary issues are problems with debt recovery, market location, electricity (mainly for refrigeration), skin damage to the fish (which reduces the sale price), and transport costs.

Nigerian catfish farmers report that the marketing of fresh catfish is becoming more difficult because of increasing competition. Some farmers in the southeast also recognize that the difficulties in selling fish result from a general lack of organization (for example, farms all try to sell fish on the same day). To control marketing problems, farmers say that they would like to have direct contact with traders further down the marketing chain. Farmers have indicated that information sharing within the value chain is sparse and that there is frustration that primary wholesalers shield their sources of supply from secondary wholesalers and retailers. In addition, in some locations, retailers feel that they have to pay higher prices than necessary because they are unable to buy direct, or at least need better information about the selling prices at the farm.

The Nigerian catfish market projections provided by the surveyors imply that the undersupply of farmed catfish may amount to some 5,000 mt per year, which could be rapidly addressed by expanding production. The urban markets, where farmed fish is primarily sold, will grow by about 3 percent annually purely through population growth.

Once these sources of demand have been met, additional supplies will have to be absorbed by stimulating sales through lower retail prices, the addition of value-added operations, or exports. Fish farmers and their value chain colleagues will have to take a much more proactive approach to learning about the market and initiating sales and marketing activities. This is likely to involve conducting their own market research and establishing closer contacts with retailers, traders, restaurants, and processors. These will be new activities for producers.

Interventions in the Nigerian fresh catfish value chain

The survey results point to many possible value chain initiatives. Unmet and clearly increasing market demand should be addressed by increasing supply from producers

Figure 4.10 Consumers' Views of What Factors Would Increase Their Consumption of Catfish

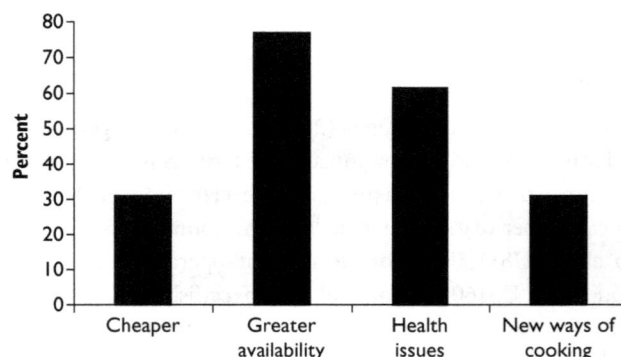

Source: Dixie and Ohen (2006).

("Value Chain Possible Action #1" in figure 4.11), taking advantage of the opportunities to vertically integrate operations ("Value Chain Possible Action #2"), and developing more sophisticated marketing and distribution systems in order to capture more value ("Value Chain Possible Action #3"). There is also ample opportunity for producers to band together and gain a competitive advantage through economies of scale. Costly inputs can be purchased at significant savings with effective cost-share agreements and in larger quantities. Also, associations of producers or the firms linked to them can combine to act in groups to attain the scale and market power necessary to create permanent marketing links and secure contracts to provide restaurants with guaranteed supply and quality.

These new distribution systems will have an opportunity to increase the marketing of catfish and improve the safe transport of products. The market assessment conducted by Dixie and Ohen (2006) confirms that consumers prefer catfish based on its purported health qualities, its cost, and its availability, as well as enthusiasm for its taste and preparation in popular dishes and as a complementary product to beer. There is an opportunity to capitalize on these preferences in marketing initiatives while simultaneously expanding the market supply.

Currently, losses during transportation are estimated to be between 10 to 15 percent of value, with practices varying widely across the sector. With better organization, appropriate postharvest methods suited to Nigerian conditions can be propagated to the retail, trading, and restaurant sectors. Producers or wholesalers should seek technical expertise and assistance to lower these loss rates and improve the quality of the catfish that they distribute.

Figure 4.11   Nigerian Catfish Farming Value
Chain—Possible Actions

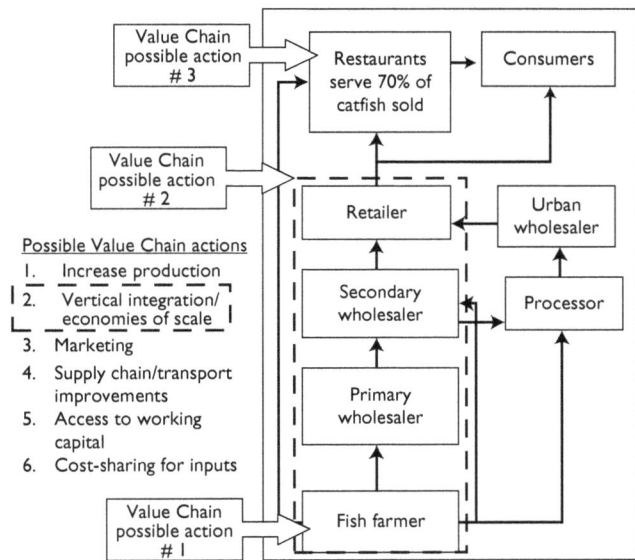

Source: J. E. Austin Associates, Inc. 2007 adapted from Dixie and Ohen 2006.

Financing is still not widely available for restaurants and bukas to increase their working capital and expand their businesses. With growing demand and falling prices, there is an opportunity to provide financing to promising end-market businesses that may pull the value chain toward higher growth vectors.

CONCLUSION

The market assessment survey has furnished important information that allows the value chain actors to identify

Figure 4.12   Projected Development of the Value Chain
for Fresh Catfish, 2005–15

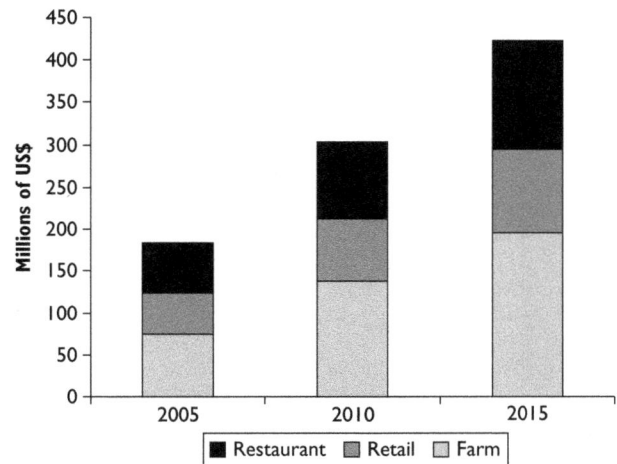

Source: Dixie and Ohen (2006).

growth opportunities and priority interventions. The Nigerian domestic catfish market is clearly rich with opportunity for increasing sales (see figure 4.12); there are numerous constraints and other issues that can be addressed, and there is room for value chain collaboration centered on production, investment in transport and infrastructure, marketing, commercialization, and vertical integration.

NOTE

1. The word "buka" refers to a "canteen or eating house" in the Hausa language.

Conducting Benchmarking and Gap Assessments of Value Chains

BENCHMARKING BACKGROUND

At both the company and value chain levels, benchmarking is crucial. Benchmarking compares the performance of a company or value chain to itself at different points in time, to another value chain in the country, or to a value chain in another country in order to establish the current baseline position and provide comparative data to guide decisions and actions. Usually quantitative indicators are used, such as total gross domestic product (GDP), time to market, pricing data, and others. Qualitative data can also be used, although such information is harder to measure clearly and objectively.

Benchmarking allows practitioners and stakeholders to understand the performance of particular value chains in comparison to competitors, and especially to global best performers. Knowing what competitors do differently, and whether these differences are important drivers of value chain performance, gives clues as to beneficial changes that could be made to improve performance of the value chain.

Benchmarking can be used by all members of the value chain to build a common understanding and vision as the basis for prioritizing objectives and decisions. Members can benchmark against each other to determine whether their performance is up to par and pinpoint areas of improvement. They can also benchmark the entire value chain against other value chains in the same industry or other global value chains.

THE BENCHMARKING TOOL

It is possible to benchmark almost anything, so, too often, stakeholders do not adequately narrow down their field of focus when benchmarking. A scope that is too broad does not allow for real drivers of performance to be analyzed. Therefore, it is necessary to first refine the scope and select appropriate comparators. Those conducting the benchmarking must keep in mind that the results should lead to clear courses of action. Therefore, if the comparators that

are selected are not appropriate, the results will not be useful and may even be misleading.

In assessing a value chain's competitiveness, several key aspects can be usefully examined. First, it is important to benchmark overall value chain performance, meaning how well the actors in the value chain deliver products to the final consumer in comparison to other value chains and other countries. Once the overall value chain is analyzed, it can be broken down into key performance components, such as yields, transport efficiency, market access, unit price, and many others. These key components and the underlying processes can then be individually benchmarked to identify relative strengths and weaknesses. Industry experts can identify important, detailed performance and competitiveness indicators; once these indicators are quantified, comparisons between different industries and countries can be made. The experts and the value chain leadership can then analyze how the better performance is being achieved.

Once benchmarking is completed and differences in performance have been identified and analyzed, the next step is to determine courses of action. In order to spur action by stakeholders, the results of the benchmarking exercise can be disseminated so that stakeholders understand their position and become a part of the action process. The information should generate dialogue to increase participants' insights into the need for intervention and achieving consensus on decisions and actions.

What benchmarking does

1. *Establishes a baseline of current performance.* Once the benchmarking exercise has been completed, a company, an industry, or a country understands its position relative to its comparators.
2. *Identifies areas and targets for improvement.* If benchmarking against best practices, then differences in performance along the entire value chain can be identified.

Shortcomings can be examined and steps can be taken to improve performance.

3. *Pinpoints potential critical factors for success.* Areas for improvement can be prioritized.

Steps to effective benchmarking

The benchmarking process is straightforward in nature. It generally includes the following steps:

- Determine what indicators and measures to benchmark
- Determine the benchmarking target groups
- Gather and analyze the data
- Convert benchmark data into action through:
  - □ Managed discussion
  - □ Prioritization and design
  - □ Implementation

Many widely available indexes measure elements of one country's competitiveness relative to other countries. Examples involve the World Economic Forum's Global Competitiveness Report, the World Bank Doing Business Report, the World Development Indicators, and a variety of standard economic indicators available through governments, universities, and international organizations. Although the data they provide can be general in nature, such data are a useful guide for specific discussions and action planning later in the benchmarking process.

In addition to the "broad strokes," decision makers and industry leaders need to understand the more detailed basis for the value chain's performance, the structure of the value chain, availability of services, and the value chain's operating environment. This targeted benchmarking is done in several steps, outlined below.

Determine what to benchmark

First, the value chain's performance must be accurately and objectively measured in the performance and operational areas most relevant to its competitiveness (for example, availability of inputs, time to export in national ports, and local transportation costs). Items that should be benchmarked will vary from value chain to value chain based on priorities determined by the value chain's strategy. It is important to select actionable items for a benchmarking exercise. It is not sufficient just to know that some process or step in the value chain is slow or costly. Selected indicators need to point to why the process is slow or exactly where costs are added (see box 4.2). This should be measured

---

Box 4.2   Ugandan Benchmarking Constraints in the Coffee Industry

Uganda, a major coffee producer, has only recently begun a concerted campaign to add value to their production. Grown in many areas of the country, Uganda's coffee is generally transported to Kampala and sent to Port Mombassa for shipment overseas.

In 2003, amidst a national decentralization initiative, coffee growers and processors were faced with increasing numbers of procedures as individual districts imposed levies on investments and shipments within and between the districts. Procedures were not combined or streamlined—indeed, the increasing fragmentation led to the need to devote substantial time to petty transactions and, reportedly, an increased incidence of "facilitation payments." These circumstances were echoed in other sectors, such as fish and wood products.

Reports indicated that once a shipment reached Kampala, it was not uncommon for the container to take a period of 20 days to reach Mombassa—but only two or fewer days are required for actual transport time. What accounted for the remaining 18 days? Lengthy and nonstreamlined border procedures accounted for some of the time, but most was taken up with multiple inspections and customs procedures. Reports also implied that numerous informal taxes were being levied. The impact on the industry in terms of product quality, losses, and the risk of missed deliveries was significant.

Ugandan stakeholders benchmarked this situation against those in other countries to see if these delays and costs were normal. Information from coffee exporters in Colombia, Costa Rica, and Vietnam indicated that instead of 20 days, the norms for delivery to port were between 1 and 7 days.

This information helped the industry and government to recognize the impact of a poor system of regulation and implementation and to focus attention on putting a streamlined system in place.

Author: Lisa Carse, J. E. Austin Associates, Inc., interviews.

---

at steps all along the value chain and in the services provided to the chain. It is important that the entire value chain be included so as to identify bottlenecks and added costs that may not be readily apparent.

The rationale for using data, and the data points themselves, can be gathered from industry and trade publications, local government sources, and through surveys. Surveying relevant firms and industry groups, and participants along the entire value chain, can provide a qualitative component that enhances understanding of the processes being measured and costs being tracked. How to conduct value chain performance gap analysis is discussed later in this section. The greater the level of specificity in the benchmarking activities, the more likely it is that the results will lead to practical applications.

Determine the benchmarking target(s)

Benchmarkers must determine comparator value chains (target comparators) and specific performance indicators that will provide the best basis for comparison. The target comparators should be value chains operating in other countries, or possibly in different regions of the same country. Once the home value chain data are obtained, the benchmarkers can turn their attention to the targets.

Including a knowledgeable outsider can facilitate the process, provide additional perspective, strengthen the objectivity of the data, and speed identification of key elements to benchmark. In choosing benchmarking targets, it is important not only to consider countries and industries that demonstrate global best practices, but also regional competitors or those countries that are operating successfully in a competitive space that the home value chain would like to occupy (positioning, see tool 8). The purpose of the benchmarking exercise within the context of the goals and strategy of the nation and/or value chain will determine which comparator indicators are examined; the key point is that the indicator should have high relevance as a standard or driver of performance. Objectives of the benchmarking might include:

- Operational improvements
- Reduced transaction costs
- More advantageous market positioning

Collecting the data—where is the benchmarking information?

A surprising number of public sources will provide useful information; sometimes the benchmarkers will have to dig more deeply. Some common sources include:

- Publicly available reports
- Published sources, especially trade publications and databases
- The target comparator value chain (and participant companies and clusters)
- Industry experts, consultants, and researchers
- Suppliers, service providers, and buyers

Utilizing the data

Once the data have been gathered, participants can carry out a careful analysis and draw insightful conclusions. Many analytical tools can be used to create clear comparisons and help identify areas for targeted intervention. Creating a graphical representation, such as the "spider" in figure 4.13, can help decision makers to easily understand certain strengths and weaknesses in their value chains so that actions can quickly be targeted in the appropriate areas.

Figure 4.13 describes the extent of coordination within the supply chains of citrus fruit and tomatoes in Morocco, Spain, and Turkey (Garcia 2003). In order to achieve Eurep-GAP certification, it is important for all members of the value chain to be in close communication to ensure quality and other elements required for certification. Morocco and Turkey were benchmarked against Spain in categories that contribute to seamless coordination along the supply chain. From figure 4.13, it is apparent that Spain is the best

Figure 4.13 Coordination within the Citrus Fruit and Tomato Value Chains, Comparison among Morocco, Spain, and Turkey

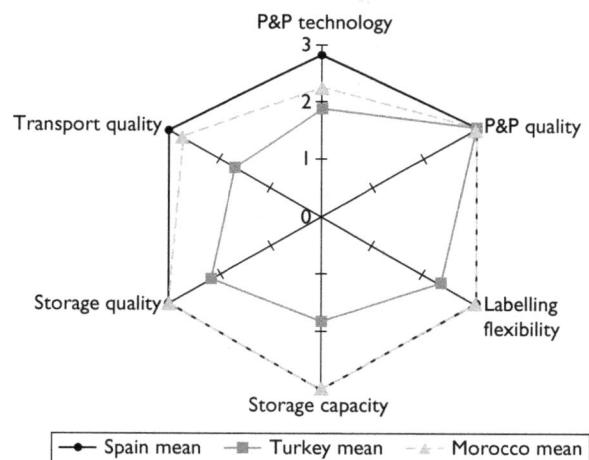

Source: Garcia Martinez et al. (2003).
Note: Higher value indicates better quality.

Box 4.3   Tanzanian Cotton—Benchmarking Costs

Cotton is a primary commodity produced in and exported by several West African countries. A field visit to Tanzania in 2004 examined Tanzanian ginning, benchmarking companies against a theoretical West African cotton company, and against actual costs in Burkina Faso and Cameroon. The theoretical costs were calculated for a West African cotton company operating at full capacity (with a volume of 50,000 tons of seed cotton) with the price of seed cotton at a level of FCFA 160 per kg, which is the actual price in Burkina Faso, Cameroon, and Mali.

Below, the price breakdown of cotton lint production is set against comparator countries, including the West Africa theoretical model.

Comparison among Tanzania, Theoretical Costs in West Africa, and Actual Costs in Burkina Faso and Cameroon

	US$[a]/kg of cotton lint			
	Tanzania	W. Africa theoretical	Actual Burkina Faso	Actual Cameroon
Collection of seed cotton	0.094	0.083	0.103	0.097
Processing costs	0.082	0.135	0.163	0.134
Financing costs (short term)	0.023	0.038	0.067	0.013
Cost from ginnery to free on board (FOB)	0.100	0.128	0.155	0.162
Subtotal	**0.299**	**0.383**	**0.488**	**0.406**
Capital costs (on investment)	0.009	0.035	0.036	0.036
Taxes	0.042			
Overhead and contingencies	0.009	0.052	0.034	0.053
Dagris[b] fee			0.012	0.012
Total intermediary costs	0.358	0.470	0.569	0.507
Purchase cost of seed cotton	0.833	0.755	0.755	0.755
CDF levy (passbook)	0.055			
Critical functions (extension, research, seeds)		0.019	0.029	0.047
Total FOB cost	**1.247**	**1.244**	**1.352**	**1.308**
Minus: value of seeds	0.079	0.038	0.038	0.050
Net FOB cost	**1.168**	**1.206**	**1.315**	**1.259**

Tanzania has a cost advantage over the theoretical figure and the actual prices from Burkina Faso and Cameroon. Knowing this allows Tanzania to develop an industry growth strategy to take advantage of its favorable cost position. Tanzania's net FOB costs are 13 percent lower than Burkina Faso's and 8.5 percent lower than Cameroon's.

Source: Lisa Carse, J. E. Austin Associates, Inc., based on Tschirley, David, Colin Poulton, and Patrick Labaste, ed., 2009, "Organization and Performance of Cotton Sectors in Africa." World Bank, Washington, DC.
[a] The comparison, in U.S. dollars, is based on the actual exchange rate (US$1 = FCFA504 and TZS1,200) at the time of writing the report in 2004.
[b] Dagris is a company involved in cotton marketing chains that holds shares in cotton enterprises in several African countries.

performer, followed by Morocco and Turkey. Turkey falls short of Spain in every category, while Morocco actually matches Spain's score in several categories. Illustrating this information in this type of graph helps value chain participants to weigh their options for which improvements to address first. In this case, Turkey needs to make improvements in every category, while Morocco can choose whether to focus on areas in which it falls far short of Spain (for example, through improvements in market orientation, production flexibility, vertical integration, vertical coordination, and IT systems), or attempt to gain a competitive advantage by outperforming Spain in areas where it is already close to achieving that goal (for example, through improvements in segregation or traceability systems).

Gap analysis is a basic tool that is useful in understanding differences among comparator value chains and in helping value chain participants to identify the areas where interventions and reforms should take place. This analytical tool, when presented graphically as a comparison of elements of value chains (or clusters—see tool 12 for comparison of the content of cluster maps) can provide strong visual impact in understanding and communicating a value chain's relative strengths and weaknesses.

Gap analysis can also be presented in a table format, as shown in table 4.3, using data gathered in a benchmarking exercise conducted for the cigar industry in the Dominican Republic.

Gap analysis can also be based on the perceptions of value chain leaders through an exercise that quantifies what members of the value chain already know. In the example below, members of the value chain use a qualitative benchmarking exercise to begin to identify both the specific areas in which they believe the chain lags behind its competitors and ideal models or industry trends. This "quick and dirty" approach to gap analysis is based more on leaders' perceptions (correct or incorrect) than on hard data. But it is a

useful means of quickly starting a benchmarking dialogue and a good strategist/facilitator can use the method and discussion to encourage the value chain participants to look more deeply into the assumptions and conclusions.

In the example illustrated in table 4.4, value chain A is the country of interest, while value chain B is the best practices target or global industry standard. The participants identify the indicators that they believe are the current drivers of their industry's global competitiveness. Members of the value chain in country A then give themselves scores for how well the chain performs on each indicator. This score is compared to the best practices score, and the gap between the two scores is recorded.

Once the participants recognize the gaps and understand the reasons for them, they will be able to make choices for a prioritized strategy change. The gap analysis and the proposed action prioritization can be used as an effective basis for public-private dialogue along with value chain and firm-level decision making (for example, see the cases in tools 2 and 8). However, because it is unlikely that value chain actors will be able to effectively manage everything at once, decision makers will need to weigh the feasibility of possible initiatives, their implementation capacity, and the relative payoff of each intervention in determining priorities. Value chain stakeholders will initially need to target high impact gaps and objectives or ones that establish a platform for follow-on steps and successes.

Table 4.3	Gap Analysis of the Dominican Cigar Industry versus Cuban Cigars		
Critical success factors	**Dominican cigars**	**Cuban cigars**	**Follow-on questions**
Sales volume	120 million sold	80 million sold	At what price point? What are industry profits?
Flavor	#2 in blind taste tests	#1 in blind taste tests	What are the key determinants of flavor?
Packaging	Imported wrapper	Local wrapper	How important is the wrapper to consumer choice? How does the wrapper affect production costs?
Research and development (R&D) capacity	Weak (but improving)	Strong	What institutions are needed to develop R&D capacity?
Distribution channels	Mostly sells to Davidoff	Controls European distribution channels	What kinds of distribution channels are most in line with the business and growth model? How can these be developed?
Final market	Over-reliance on U.S. embargo of Cuba	Strong European penetration	Where are current customers? Future/potential consumer bases?
Industry management	Dynamic enterprises	State-owned enterprises	What are managerial weaknesses? How can they be improved?
Marketing	Rising image as a "cigar country"	Strong "Cuban" brand	How can sellers develop an effective and differentiated branding strategy?

Source: J. E. Austin Associates, Inc., based on interviews.

Table 4.4   Illustrative Gap Analysis

Driving forces of industry	Country A	Country B	Gap
Health qualities	1	5	4
Branding and promotion	2	5	3
Convenience of packaging and availability	4	5	1
Guarantee of quality and standards	3	5	3
Logistics	2	5	3

Source: J. E. Austin Associates, Inc.
Note: Rating: 5 = excellent; 4 = good; 3 = average; 2 = below average; 1 = weak or poor.

A STEP-BY-STEP SUMMARY OF TOOL 3: CONDUCTING BENCHMARKING AND GAP ASSESSMENTS OF VALUE CHAINS

- Determine which value chain performance indicators and measures to benchmark. Identify the elements that are important. The indicators should point to where costs, time, quality, service, and value are added along the value chain to help identify bottlenecks, unnecessary costs, and upgrading opportunities.
- Determine the benchmarking target groups (comparators). Value chains and companies that represent global best practices, as well as regional value chains, should be compared against to identify areas of operational improvement, ways to reduce transaction costs, quality and service improvements, availability and quality of supporting services, and ways to improve competitiveness strategies.
- Identify data sources. There may be many sources, including studies and research, industry reports, trade publications, and other available material. Knowledgeable experts (within the industry and within comparator value chains and organizations), buyers, and service providers can be consulted. First-hand visits to observe operations may be warranted.
- Gather and analyze the data. A variety of tools are available to analyze and communicate benchmark data. These tools include, but are not limited to, gap analysis, spider graphs, diamond analysis, and illustrative tables.
- Convert benchmark data into strategy and action. Accurate data from benchmarking exercises provide the private sector, practitioners, and policy makers with relevant indicators highlighting the strengths and weaknesses of any value chain. These data can then be used as a springboard for discussions among stakeholders about which areas of a value chain should be priorities for intervention.

Ugandan Floriculture—Benchmarking and Gap Analysis

Lisa Corse and Martin Webber
J. E. Austin Associates, Inc.

INTRODUCTION

Benchmarking and gap analysis serve to establish the levels of performance of comparator industries, value chains, or firms. In 2002, the World Bank's "Regional Study on Agricultural Trade Facilitation/Non-Traditional Export Promotion in SSA: Uganda Horti-Floriculture Sector Technical Note 2" benchmarked the cost structure and other elements of Uganda's floriculture industry against those of Kenya, a country with similar natural attributes, ranked number one in African floriculture exports to the Dutch auctions. Therefore, Uganda's floriculture sector was not only benchmarked against its main regional competitor, it was also benchmarked against Africa's best performer in terms of total export value. The benchmarking was used to inform a gap analysis—the identification of areas of weakness relative to comparators—and create a strategy for future growth based on Uganda's competitive position.

BACKGROUND AND INDUSTRY DESCRIPTION

Uganda, a landlocked country in East Africa, has achieved considerable diversification from traditional agricultural crops such as coffee, tea, and cotton, to nontraditional exports including fish, tobacco, cut flowers, and a wide variety of vegetables. The push toward diversification of the economy was particularly important in response to falling prices for traditional goods.

Floriculture was first developed in Uganda around 1993, so it is a relatively new industry for the country. Floriculture specifically describes the cultivation of flowers and cuttings, which currently includes the majority of Uganda's horticulture production. The World Bank's 2002 assistance in studying the Ugandan floriculture sector was intended to help the industry and the government of Uganda assess growth potential and design a strategy for its development.

The value of Uganda's horticulture exports, comprising flowers, plant cuttings, fresh fruits and vegetables, vanilla, cocoa, and papain, nearly quadrupled from US$10.7 million in 1995 to US$40.7 million in 2002 (see table 4.5). Floriculture exports represented the largest share of Uganda's exports in the horticulture sector. However, experts estimated that Uganda was producing far below its potential.

In 2002, commercial floriculture was a major nontraditional agricultural export sector, valued at US$21 million freight on board (FOB). There were 20 commercial farms in production with a total acreage of 122 hectares. Export volume had increased from 721 tons in 1995 to 3,820 tons in 2002.

The Ugandan floriculture industry mainly produces sweetheart roses and chrysanthemum cuttings. Almost all exports are destined for Europe, with the Netherlands receiving the largest share. While most of the flowers produced in Uganda are sold through the Dutch flower auction (table 4.6), small quantities are also sent directly to Belgium, Germany, and the United Kingdom. In 1998, Uganda ranked eleventh among the suppliers of roses at the Dutch auction market; by 2002, it had moved up to sixth place (see table 4.6).

Producers in the floriculture industry in Uganda are large commercial farms that are vertically integrated and sell directly to importers in Europe. The value chain at the producer level is consolidated mainly because of the large amount of capital that must be invested in growing flowers suitable for export and putting a working cold chain in place (figure 4.15).

Figure 4.14   Map of Uganda

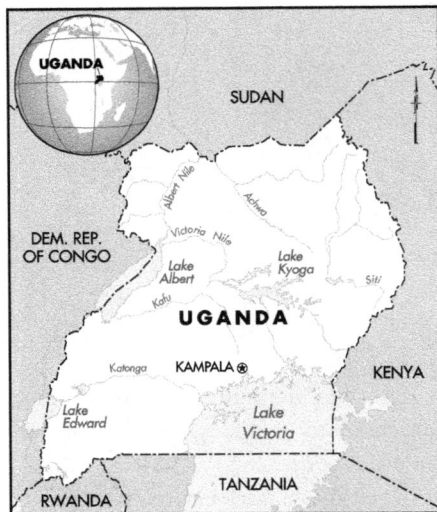

Source: World Bank.

The 2002 assessment included analyses of the Ugandan floriculture value chain and production cost structure, which were then benchmarked against those of Kenya. The value chain analysis for roses showed that, due to strong competition and exchangeability of suppliers, profit margins are very small in the flower value chain (see figure 4.16). Producers receive around 40 percent of each euro spent by a consumer on flowers. At the next step of the value chain, the exporter keeps another 40 percent of the final consumer price, although the exporter pays the associated airfreight costs. When flowers reach the Netherlands, an importing agent unpacks the flowers, rehydrates them, and palletizes them for sale to the Dutch flower auction, which adds a 5 percent fee. Wholesalers and other retailers then add another 15 percent before the final consumer pays the corresponding final price.

USING BENCHMARKING: VALUE CHAIN ANALYSIS

To help assess Uganda's competitiveness in floriculture, the World Bank benchmarked part of the Ugandan producers' value chain and production cost structure against those of Kenyan producers. Kenya was selected because it is located in the same geographic region (although with slight a difference in climatic conditions, especially the altitude for growing similar products) and is a competitor

Figure 4.15   Ugandan Floriculture Value Chain and Cluster Map

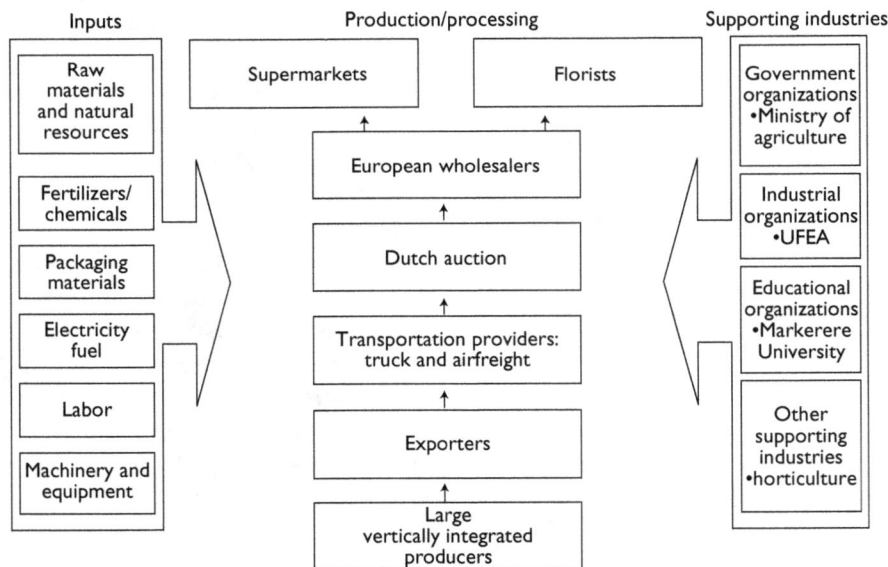

Source: J. E. Austin Associates, Inc., from Uganda Horti-Floriculture Sector Technical Note 2, 2004.

Table 4.5 Growth Performance of Ugandan Horticultural Exports, 1995–2002

Product	Value of exports (US$ Thousands FOB) 1995	Value of exports (US$ Thousands FOB) 2002	Total growth (%) 1995–2002	Annual growth (%) 1999–2000	Annual growth (%) 2000–2001	Annual growth (%) 2001–2002	Average annual growth 2000–2002
Roses	2.3	14.1	513.04	−8.34	26.32	22.40	13.46
Plant cuttings	—	7.03	—	28.21	24.44	25.54	26.06
Fresh produce	0.63	4.24	573.02	0.96	1.27	32.50	11.57
Vanilla	0.24	9.43	3829.17	34.67	183.17	64.86	94.23
Cocoa	0.64	4.97	676.56	−27.86	33.66	84.07	29.96
Papain	4.46	0.71	−84.08	−76.67	−26.53	−1.39	−34.86
Other	2.4	0.2	−91.67	−28.57	20.00	−66.67	−25.08
Total	10.67	40.68					

Source: de Vette and Gabre-Madhin 2004.

Table 4.6 Rose Sales at the Dutch Auction, 2002

Rank	Country	Value € mil.	Stems € mil.	Average price € ct /stem
1	Kenya	148.5	1,027.9	14.4
2	Israel	133.1	866.4	15.4
3	Zimbabwe	67.2	474.0	14.2
4	Ecuador	21.7	75.4	28.8
5	Spain	15.5	168.4	9.2
6	Uganda	12.8	136.6	9.4
7	France	10.0	63.5	15.7
8	Zambia	10.0	79.1	12.6
9	South Africa	9.1	31.1	29.3
10	Tanzania	7.0	55.1	12.7
	Others	46.8	299.1	15.6
	Total	481.7	3,276.6	14.7

Source: Verenigde van Bloemenveilingen Nederland (VBN), from Uganda Horti-Floriculture Sector Technical Note 2.

across many industries. Table 4.7 benchmarks Uganda's sweetheart rose production cost structure with that of Kenya's; this is illustrated in figure 4.17 (See table 4.8 and figure 4.18 for a comparison of the cost structure for cuttings production.)

Uganda produced more stems than Kenya, but Kenya's stems commanded a slightly higher price. Uganda was at a disadvantage in terms of the costs for airfreight, fertilizers and chemicals, and electricity and fuel. Net profit in Kenya was lower than in Uganda, despite Kenya's premium of half a cent per stem.

Understanding Uganda's cost position relative to its competitors allows for the development of a strategy. For example, in this case, if Uganda could lower its airfreight costs, and the costs of inputs, such as fertilizers, chemicals, and electricity, through efficiency gains, it could sell more flowers at a slightly lower price than Kenya.

In benchmarking the cost structure for cuttings, the most apparent conclusion is that Uganda does not have much comparative advantage in relation to Kenya. Again, airfreight costs and input costs are higher in Uganda, but net margin is still slightly greater in Uganda.

Figure 4.16   Value Chain Analysis for Flowers from Uganda

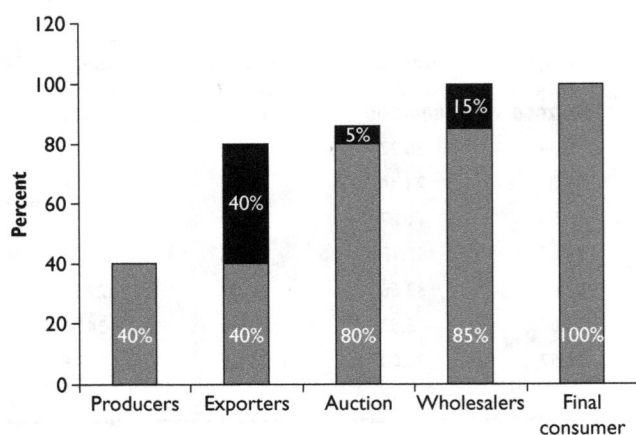

Source: World Bank Uganda Horti-Floriculture Sector Technical Note 2 (2004).

USING BENCHMARKING: CLUSTER STRUCTURE

The assessment also benchmarked the structure of Uganda's floriculture cluster against those of Kenya and the Netherlands (see tool 12 for more information on clustering). The cluster assessment included important elements that are part of a value chain analysis, but also looked at the linked impact on cluster participants of driving forces and critical success factors. In table 4.9, Uganda is seen to be the weakest of the three countries. The Netherlands was included as a best practice case, against which Kenya performs moderately well. However, both Uganda and Kenya lack the specialized equipment and services needed to reach their potential. Prices for inputs in Uganda are about 10 to 20 percent higher than in Kenya. Also, several flights per day directly link Kenya to Europe and can be used for exporting flowers. Uganda has fewer direct flights to Europe, and exporters must often ship through Nairobi rather than directly to Europe. Both countries sell their flowers on the Dutch auction.

Table 4.7   Sweetheart Rose Production Cost Structure per Hectare: Uganda versus Kenya (*in USD*)

Description	Uganda	Kenya	Difference (Uganda minus Kenya)
Production (stems)	3,750,000	3,250,000	500,000
Average price per stem	0.088	0.094	−0.006
Gross sales	330,000	303,875	26,125
Airfreight costs	71,205	63,503	7,702
Handling costs (NL)	9,821	9,408	414
Handling costs (local)	1,473	2,352	−879
Auction/agent fees	52,800	48,620	4,180
Total marketing costs	135,300	123,883	11,417
Net sales	**194,700**	**179,992**	**14,708**
Packing material	6,250	5,559	691
Fertilizers/chemicals	30,000	25,500	4,500
Electricity fuel	15,000	11,250	3,750
Labor	12,775	16,425	−3,650
Staff/management	20,000	25,000	−5,000
General production costs	5,000	5,000	0
Royalty fee	15,400	15,400	0
Repairs and maintenance	4,000	4,000	0
Operational costs	108,425	108,134	291
Gross margin	86,275	71,858	14,417
Depreciation investments	30,000	30,000	0
Interest loans	18,000	18,000	0
Net margin	**38,275**	**23,858**	**14,417**

Source: World Bank Uganda Horti-Floriculture Sector Technical Note 2 (2004).

Figure 4.17   Components of Total Cost of Sweetheart Roses in Uganda and Kenya

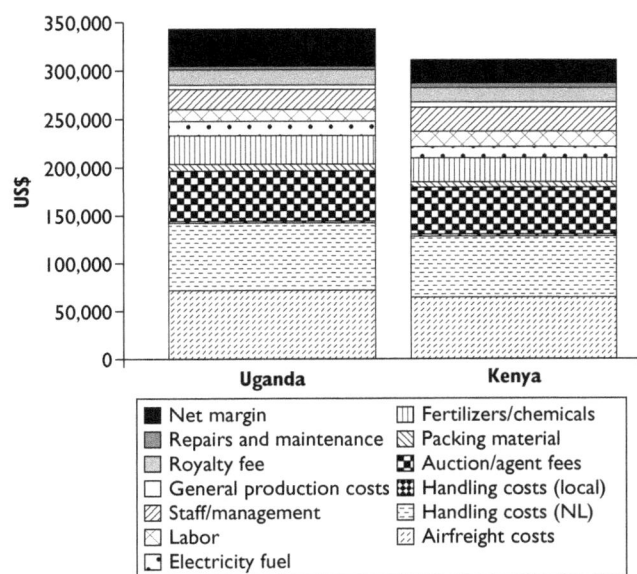

Sources: J. E. Austin Associates, Inc.; World Bank Uganda Horti-Floriculture Sector Technical Note 2 (2004).

OUTCOMES

Based on the results and findings of the benchmarking exercise, floriculture industry leaders worked together to develop the *Ugandan Floriculture Competitiveness Plan: 2005–2010*. Elements of the strategies presented in the plan build upon the benchmarking exercise. The benchmarking exercise highlighted shortcomings in several areas, including product diversification, research and development, and transport costs. The plan looks to improve the Ugandan floriculture industry's performance through the accomplishment of five key targets and associated substrategies:[1]

1. Increase export volumes and values
   ○ Expand in existing markets with existing products
   ○ Open new markets with existing products
   ○ Establish a Europe-based unpacking distribution facility
   ○ Diversify and expand product offerings

2. Increase internal and foreign direct investment
   ○ Clarify strategic industry status
   ○ Develop and implement a floriculture investment incentives package
   ○ Develop an upland expansion plan
   ○ Develop financial support mechanisms for the industry
   ○ Develop and carry out investment promotion program

3. Improve technology and practices
   ○ Set up and maintain an effective cold chain management system
   ○ Facilitate expansion of fresh management services
   ○ Establish the Floriculture Training Development Center
   ○ Develop and install a product expansion program

4. Develop and launch a quality, branding, and marketing campaign
   ○ Strengthen Uganda's position as a quality service provider
   ○ Standardize export packaging
   ○ Develop and launch a floricultural branding program
   ○ Develop and implement a marketing program

5. Position the Uganda Flower Exporters Association (UFEA) for sustainability
   ○ Prepare and implement industry development support program
   ○ Produce revenue generation and sustainability plan

Today, the volume and value of exported cut flowers continues to grow, reaching 7,596 mt and US$34.72 million in 2006 (see figure 4.19). UFEA supports the industry through research, training, and market promotion. Producers are also focusing on quality assurance, standards, and certification, with several farms already applying for EurepGAP certification. A majority of the Ugandan growers have received MPS-ABC certification, indicating that they meet standards for EurepGAP's international environmental program focusing on pesticide use, recycling, and energy and water use. Therefore, Uganda is not only competing on the basis of lower costs, it has also moved toward competing on value, as seen by improvements made in quality and standards certifications.

Most flowers are now shipped directly to Europe, rather than via Nairobi. Approximately 50 percent of the flowers are sold on the Dutch auction, with the other 50 percent sold directly to wholesalers and retail outlets in Europe.[2] Uganda has also begun shipping small quantities of cut flowers to the United States, which represents a new market opportunity for African flowers. In terms of product diversification, Uganda's competitiveness plan focuses on continuing to expand exports of sweetheart roses. However, one grower has established a farm at higher elevations to attempt growing larger-headed, higher-value roses.

Table 4.8   Cost Structure for Cuttings Production per Hectare: Uganda versus Kenya (in USD)

Description	Uganda	Kenya	Difference (Uganda minus Kenya)
Production	30,000,000	27,500,000	2,500,000
Average price	0.017	0.018	-0.001
Gross sales	495,000	484,000	11,000
Airfreight costs	79,750	74,250	5,500
Handling costs (NL)	11,000	11,000	0
Handling costs (local)	1,650	2,750	−1,100
Auction/agent fees	0	0	0
Total marketing costs	92,400	88,000	4,400
Net sales	**402,600**	**396,000**	**6,600**
Packing material	28,000	25,667	2,333
Fertilizers/chemicals	40,000	34,000	6,000
Electricity fuel	30,000	22,500	7,500
Labor	38,325	49,275	−10,950
Staff/management	60,000	60,000	0
General production costs	20,000	20,000	0
Planting material	52,500	52,500	0
Repairs and maintenance	6,000	6,000	0
Operational costs	274,825	269,942	4,883
Gross margin	127,775	126,058	1,717
Depreciation investments	40,000	40,000	0
Interest loans	24,000	24,000	0
Net margin	**63,775**	**62,058**	**1,717**

Source: World Bank Uganda Horti-Floriculture Sector Technical Note 2 (2004), VEK.

Figure 4.18   Components of Total Cost of Cuttings in Uganda and Kenya

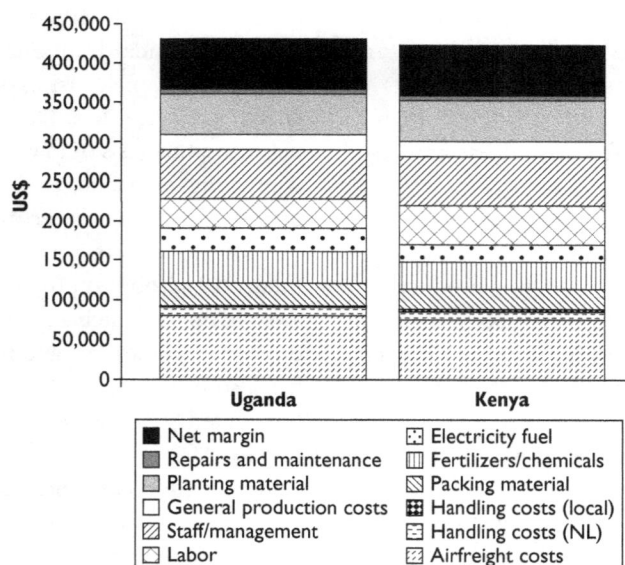

Sources: J. E. Austin Associates, Inc.; World Bank Uganda Horti-Floriculture Sector Technical Note 2 (2004), VEK.

Table 4.9 Driving Forces and a Comparison between Uganda, Kenya, and the Netherlands

		Uganda	Kenya	Netherlands
Driving forces	Society	+	+	++
	Entrepreneur	+	+	++
	Government	+/-	+/-	+
	Horticulture sector	+/-	+	++
Critical success factors				
Minimum set	Land and climate	+	+	+
	Labor	+	+	—
	Local infrastructure	+	+	+
	Agricultural input supply	-	+	++
	Water	++	+/-	+/-
	Access to the market	+/-	+	++
	Loans and credits	-	+/-	++
Additional set	Producer associations	+	+/-	++
	Skilled management	-	+	++
	Cargo handling facilities	++	+	++
	Promotion organizations	-	+/-	+
	Horticulture education	-	+/-	+
	Research and training	-	+/-	+
	Extension service	-	-	+
Sector network				
Services and production of inputs and materials	Seeds and plant material	—	+/-	++
	Soil and water testing facilities	-	+/-	++
	Growing medium	-	-	++
	Packing material	-	+	++
	Consultancy services	—	-	++
	Bookkeeping and accounting	—	-	++
	Certification institute	—	-	+
	Selection and breeding	—	-	++
	Greenhouse construction	—	-	++
	Greenhouse equipment	—	-	++
	Greenhouse covering material	—	-	++
	Fertilizers and chemicals	—	-	+
	Specialized transport	—	-	++
	Biological crop protection	—	—	++

Source: World Bank Uganda Horti-Floriculture Sector Technical Note 2 (2004).

Figure 4.19   Uganda's Flower Exports, 1994–2006

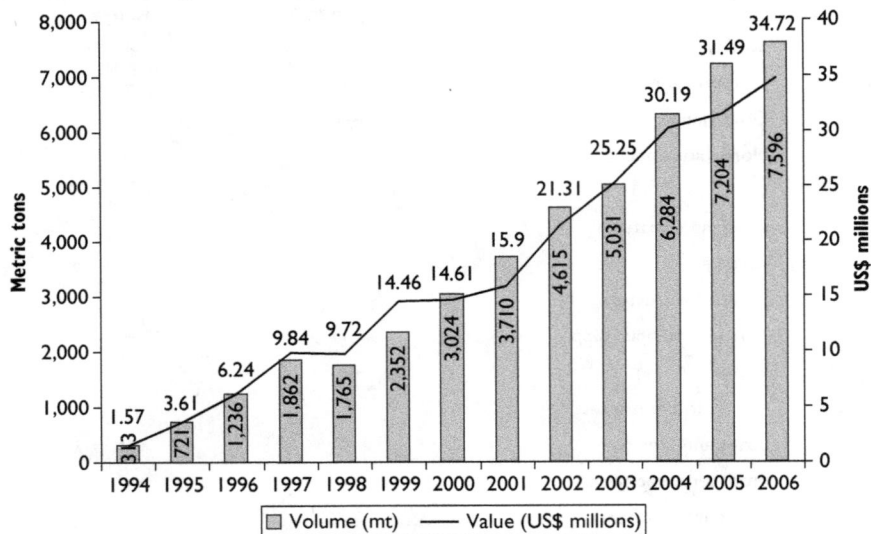

Source: Reprinted from USAID APEP Program.

NOTES

1. Building Uganda's Global Competitiveness in Agribusiness—The Uganda Floriculture Competitiveness Plan: 2005–2010. USAID.

2. Author interview with Christine Kiwanuka, USAID APEP Program.

Upgrading and Deepening the Value Chain

Increasing the competitiveness of the value chain by moving it in a new direction—toward a new market, market segment, or customer; toward increased efficiency within the value chain; or toward adding operations within the value chain, for example—is referred to as upgrading. Actions that upgrade or increase the competitiveness of a value chain can take many forms and include improving product quality, adding more operations to the value chain, bringing value chain operations into a country from overseas, capturing a new market channel, and entering a separate value chain (new market) with a similar product.[1]

In deepening the value chain, firms address gaps including unmet market demand and value, opportunities for vertical or horizontal integration, greater specialization, and the expansion of services to other value chain members.

The gap analysis (described in tool 3) methodology provides a means to identify additional operations that may usefully be added to the value chain. It also provides guidance on how best to prioritize opportunities and adjust or expand operations.

Adding value is often incremental, but it can often be accelerated by FDI and joint ventures—especially with previous buyers. As well as increasing specialization, adding value also frequently means bringing operations in-country that were previously conducted abroad.

DEEPENING THROUGH ADDING OPERATIONS

Actions to deepen the value chain must be driven by market opportunities and demands. The addition of operations requires sound market analysis, strategic planning, and good communication among value chain participants. The value chain must prioritize the possible opportunities that it identifies and then act as a unit to add them. In Mongolia, a competitiveness initiative was able to work with the meat industry in order to identify possible operations to incorporate (see box 4.4).

DEEPENING THROUGH SPECIALIZATION

Opportunities for specialization rest on the size of the market for the specialized operation or service, and on the confidence that the customers of the specialized business or operation have that the work will be carried out to an appropriate quality level with needed degrees of customer service, requisite confidentiality, and on a sustained basis (that is, the specialized business will not fail and disappear). These criteria are, in many respects, the entry criteria for value chain deepening through specialized operations.

Specialization may offer the value chain the opportunity to accomplish otherwise unattainable goals. Risk and investment costs may now be shared and offset by the cost savings that result from cooperation and information sharing.

METHODS FOR DEEPENING THE VALUE CHAIN

New entrants/entrepreneurs

Entrepreneurship generates many new entrants, added operations, and captured value in every value chain. In each market, entrepreneurs arise to take advantage of market opportunities and create links with value chains. Such new business formation can be encouraged by access to business services (such as availability of finance) and by good relationships and familiarity with the needs of the other actors in the value chain.

New investment (domestic and foreign direct)

Foreign direct investment by multinational corporations is one of the most common ways that technologies are transferred to value chains in developing and emerging economies. Also, knowledgeable domestic businesses can purchase or license new technologies. Bringing quality sorting or product-packaging operations into the developing country, for example, can increase cost efficiency and

Box 4.4   Upgrading the Value Chain—Mongolian Meat Industry

The Mongolian meat industry has traditionally been oriented toward low-end exports of animal carcasses to Siberia. Through work with the Mongolian Competitiveness Initiative (MCI)[a], plans were made to integrate value-added operations such as quality checks, packaging, and marketing into the meat industry value chain. These upgrades were intended to reorient firms toward more demanding and lucrative export markets.

With USAID and U.S. Department of Agriculture (USDA) assistance, the value chain solicited a former USDA expert in meat regulatory standards to help facilitate improvements in health and sanitary standards. MCI also identified transport options and completed cost studies to confirm the feasibility of export to five Asian and two Middle Eastern markets. Lobbying various associations and government agencies, the project worked with industry to streamline government policies and standards related to agricultural export.

In figure 1, both the traditional and a new "processed" meat export value chain are detailed. In this figure, the processed meat export channel represents the opportunity to add value by incorporating additional operations within the value chain. The "Value Chain Intervention" arrows represent opportunities identified for intervening in the Mongolian meat industry to deepen the value chain.

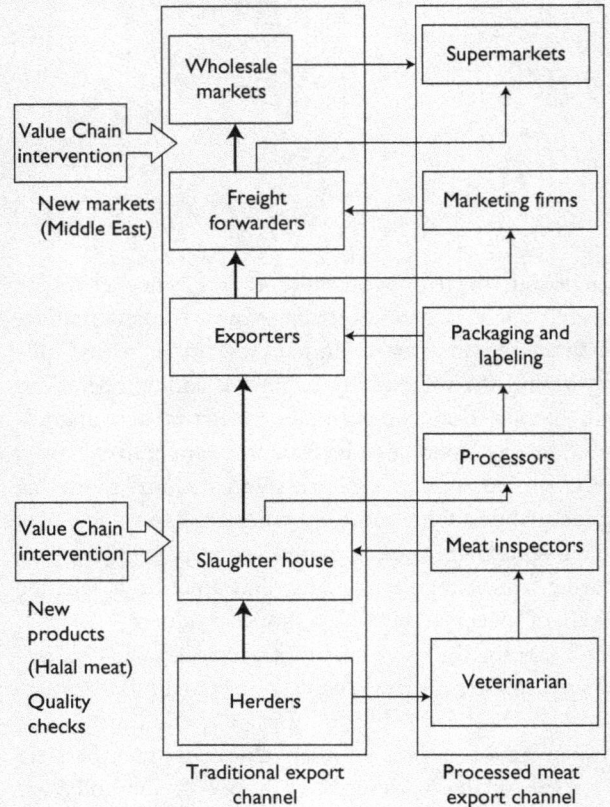

Figure 1   Mongolian Meat Export Value Chains

Source: J. E. Austin Associates, Inc.

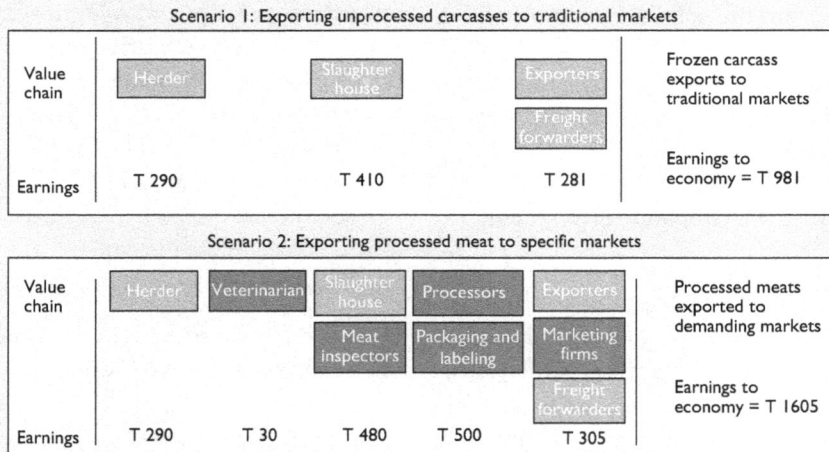

Figure 2   Deepening the Value Chain under Two Scenarios

Source: Nathan Associates, Inc., and J. E. Austin Associates, Inc., for USAID.

(Box continues on the following page.)

Box 4.4   Upgrading the Value Chain—Mongolian Meat Industry *(continued)*

Figure 2 quantifies the value that can be added by deepening the value chain. In this instance, the addition of veterinary services, meat inspection, processing, packaging, labeling, and marketing operations to the Mongolian meat value chain provides gains of nearly 40 percent in earnings from the meat industry.

Source: Michael Gorman, J. E. Austin Associates, Inc.

a The Mongolian Competitiveness Initiative was implemented by the consulting firms Nathan Associates and J. E. Austin Associates, Inc.

Box 4.5   Deepening the Value Chain: Glass Jar Production in Armenia

Armenian agricultural products include grain crops, vegetables, and fruits. The latter two are mainly exported in processed form; vegetables are most often canned, while the fruits are processed into juices, jellies, jams, compotes, leathers, and fruit fillers, which make up the majority of the produce packed in cans and jars. The lack of availability of proper quality screw-top jars and the need to import them from Europe raises costs for this type of processor/exporter. (Armenia also has important wine and brandy industries that require glass bottles.)

In 2003, Armenia had very restricted glass jar production capabilities. Existing production capacities had few molds, and, therefore, were able to produce only a limited number of standard designs. Armenia's land-locked situation and high transportation costs make the import of glass bottles and jars very expensive, which restricts opportunities for export of Armenian produce.

The fact that quality, locally manufactured screw-top jars were not available was a constraint to adding value. There are four big canners in Armenia and several smaller ones. The quality of Armenian-made glass containers and the ability to customize them (jars for juice or preserves, for example) are not satisfactory for quality- or image-conscious processors. While critical of the quality of locally made bottles, processors cited price pressure as the reason requiring them to continue to purchase locally. This greatly hampered the ambitions of producers of food and beverage products, who were unable to use Armenian-produced packaging as a differentiating factor.

Recognizing a gap in the glass container market, two companies made major investments in 2004 in glass jar manufacturing to serve the Armenian market.

The bigger investment was by Saranist, which is also trying to penetrate the Georgian market. Saranist established a new, modern glass manufacturing factory, Arm-Glass Company. The second manufacturing investment was by Glass World Company (GWC). GWC has modernized its production line through a US$30 million investment, importing advanced, high-technology equipment and installations from Western Europe. Both Saranist and GWC have long been established in Armenia—Saranist since 1990 and GWC (formerly Armkhrustal) since 1964.

Source: Michael Gorman, J. E. Austin Associates, Inc., interviews, Web sites.

---

product competitiveness while also adding value to the product value chain and the local economy.

Vertical integration

Existing firms also frequently identify opportunities to incorporate new technologies or operations into their structures. Recognizing opportunities to add value, achieve efficiencies, or improve quality—for example, by adding operations through vertical integration (by a value chain or by a firm with the value chain)—enables value chain deepening. In many parts of the world, vertical integration is achieved through acquisition of another firm along the value chain (see also tool 6).

The formation of new organizations, such as farmers associations, service-provider associations, and marketing organizations, also provides opportunities for otherwise fragmented producers or other businesses to combine their resources to add operations to a value chain.

Commercial joint ventures

Sharing the risk of incorporating new operations into the value chain or investing in a new technology is an appropriate measure in some environments. Fresh produce preparation, packaging, and logistics centers are frequently good candidates for a joint venture, for example. In another example, the tea cluster of Sri Lanka worked closely with the University of Moratuwa to jointly develop and commercialize color separator technology, which could be used to upgrade the quality of tea supplied to the local Sri Lankan auction. The cluster was able to leverage university resources to develop a new separator at one-fifth the cost of the old separators, which were imported from abroad.

CONCLUSION

Many actions can be taken to increase the competitiveness of and to add value to a product's value chain. These upgrading activities are often achieved in part by deepening the value chain through means such as adding operations to the value chain, vertical integration, bringing operations into a country's value chain, or investing in new technologies. These actions are often facilitated by the opportunities created by FDI, association-provided services, new investment, vertical integration, and public-private partnerships.

Successful value chains add value to and deepen their operations while responding to market conditions to achieve growth and increase profitability.

A STEP-BY-STEP SUMMARY OF TOOL 4: UPGRADING AND DEEPENING THE VALUE CHAIN

- Analyze market demand or value chain operations that can be serviced through upgrading or deepening.
- Review the logistics, technical capacity, and investment needs for upgrading and deepening.
- Attract FDI that will facilitate technology transfer.
- Encourage value chain actors to consider vertical integration. Partners and facilitators in this integration may include intermediate and downstream businesses, and organizations such as farmers associations, service-provider associations, and marketing organizations.
- Identify and develop facilitators for upgrading or deepening. This investment can be supported through sound business services (for example, technical capacities, access to skills, access to finance) and by good relationships and familiarity with the needs of the other actors in the value chain.
- Explore commercial opportunities for collaboration between academia and industry.

NOTE

1. "AMAP BDS Knowledge and Practice Task Order Lexicon," USAID.

Kenyan Green Beans and Other Fresh Vegetable Exports

Carlton Jones, Michael Gorman, and Martin Webber
J. E. Austin Associates, Inc.

INTRODUCTION

Possessing a perfect agricultural climate for off-season vegetable production and export to Europe, Kenya has been providing European tables with vegetables for nearly 50 years. Kenya's success has been due to market segmentation, servicing niche markets, and investing in marketing. The industry has constantly refocused its efforts on exporting higher unit-priced products. Products not fitting the profile have been dropped, and the industry has also expanded into products of greater value such as pre-packed and mixed vegetable packs. For example, mixed vegetable packs command a price of US$8.90 per kilogram (kg) versus extra fine beans at US$4.14/kg., fine beans at US$3.30/kg., and Asian vegetables at around US$2.00/kg.

TOOL: ADDING VALUE THROUGH ADDED OPERATIONS

"Deepening the value chain" refers to opportunities to add or capture more value within a particular product or industry's value chain by adding processes. Deepening can be achieved by recognizing gaps in the value chain or facilitating new linkages between value chain actors. These opportunities can be achieved through by various actions, such as adding operations to capture market demand and value, upgrading the value chain, reorienting the chain to new market opportunities, integrating different aspects of the chain, promoting specialization among chain participants, and increasing chain cost efficiencies.

BACKGROUND: KENYAN GREEN BEANS

Kenya has been exporting vegetables[1] to the United Kingdom since the 1950s. Reasons for Kenyan success have varied with the changing market forces of the highly competitive UK and European markets. Kenya's original success in exporting vegetables was based on its climatic and geographic competitive advantage. Producing temperate products year round and being well served by northbound airfreight (thanks to the Kenyan tourism market) proved lucrative for Kenyan vegetable exporters. Increasingly, Kenyan success has been due to market segmentation, investing in certification schemes, adding value to products through sophisticated packaging, servicing niche markets, and investing in marketing.

Over the years, due to effective public-private dialogue, the Kenyan government has been receptive to implementing regulatory changes, investing in education, and improving infrastructure, which have increased the competitiveness of the industry. For example, the Horticulture Crops Development Authority (HCDA) of Kenya was initially directly involved in the trading of vegetables but eventually switched to a more facilitative function; it now focuses solely on certification schemes.

Figure 4.20   Map of Kenya

Source: World Bank.

Timeline of Horticultural Development in Kenya

1957   First fresh produce to United Kingdom by air
1960s Duty-free access to UK market
1960s Investment in private farms around Lake Naivasha
1967   Horticulture Crops Development Authority (HCDA)
1970s Egerton College begins to offer degrees in horticulture
1975   Fresh Produce Exporters Association of Kenya formed
1980s HCDA passes EU trade enquiries to exporters
1987   Exports double in five years
1999   New fresh produce terminal built at Nairobi Airport

Similarly, restrictive policies regarding the sale of fresh pineapples in the 1970s and importation of planting materials in the 1980s have now been lifted as a result of close consultation with the private sector. Throughout the 1970s and 1980s, the majority of Kenyan vegetables imported into the European Community were handled by firms that serviced wholesale markets and small or medium retail outlets. In the 1980s, Kenyan exports doubled in five years due to a differential foreign exchange rate for horticultural exports, which the government set below average prices, providing further incentive for exporters to invest in the industry.

By the late 1990s, due to lobbying efforts of the Fresh Producer Exporters Association of Kenya (FPEAK), the Kenyan government partnered with the private sector to expand the Fresh Produce Terminal at the Nairobi airport, thus improving the competitiveness of fresh vegetable exports. Then, throughout the 1990s, large supermarkets began to dominate the European grocery sector, in part, by featuring signature "fresh produce" sections. As they did so, these firms increased the market demand for higher quality, more variety, and price-competitive fresh produce. To meet demand, many firms decided to vertically integrate their retail and wholesale operations, thus concentrating their power in the market and making price competition and product diversification major market forces.

In the 2000s, as the power of the supermarkets continued to drive the market, many supermarkets began to pursue market segmentation and branding strategies, which increased the demand for higher quality standards, different varieties, and organic or "safer"[2] produce. A number of exporters have invested heavily in growing their own high-quality, certified vegetables to take advantage of the increased market opportunities for high-quality produce. The effect of these trends has been a much shorter supply chain, a greater degree of vertical integration, fewer active players, and production and exporting on a much grander scale. By the early 2000s, seven of the largest food retailing chains in Europe accounted for 76 percent of fresh fruit and vegetable sales and 70 to 90 percent of fresh produce imports from Africa (FAOSTAT data).

As of 2004, the total Kenyan vegetable export trade was worth US$139 million, and the country ranked second in Africa in exporting fresh vegetables. The industry employs 45,000 to 60,000 people, of whom an estimated 60 percent are women, in commercial farms, processing, and logistics operations; another 7,000 are smallholders. Employees typically earn just under US$2 per day, while smallholders are reportedly able to earn the equivalent of US$7 per day.

THE VALUE CHAIN

In Kenya, green beans have traditionally been the most popular cash crop among smallholders due to their short growing period, which facilitates a more consistent cash income (Okado 1999). Farmers will typically plant as much as they can sell, and those with contracts or a firm commitment from an exporter may devote 100 percent of their land to the cultivation of green beans. Green bean mono-culture cultivation can yield up to four harvests per year if accompanied by application of chemical fertilizers. The two main challenges faced by smallholders are both brought by the rainy season: a higher disease incidence in the crop and poor accessibility to areas with bad roads, which prevents regular collection by exporters.

The value chain graphic (figure 4.21) illustrates the smallholder "broker" and "small to medium exporter" market channels. The broker channel is composed of approximately 20,000–50,000 microenterprises (mostly

Figure 4.21   Kenyan Green Bean Value Chain

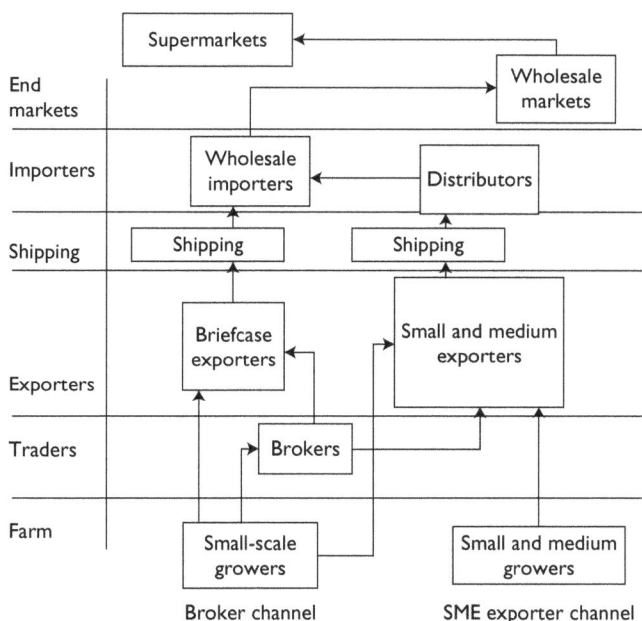

Source: J. E. Austin Associates, Inc.

households) who sell to SME exporters (SMEX) or brokers. The value chain can be characterized by its low levels of information sharing with inaccurate records of chemical usage during cultivation that denies it access to the European market. In the SMEX value chain, approximately 15–20 exporters may contract or have close working relations with their green bean suppliers (nearly 4,000 SME farmers, small outgrowers, and farmer associations). The exporters typically provide inputs to ensure the quality and quantity of products. Smallholders and small and medium producers have been increasingly pushed out of the cultivation of green beans due to market requirements and conditions.

The present market conditions in the EU supermarket sector have influenced a shift in the Kenyan green bean industry to more integrated value chains best represented by larger integrated exporters. The value chain for large integrated exporters (figure 4.22) is characterized by exporters having strong links to end-markets and producers through contractual agreements and ownership. Supply chain management is more efficient due to information sharing within the integrated value chain that eliminates costly demand shortages or oversupply. Products are traced from their origin and production practices are controlled to ensure quality and certification schemes. Increasingly, the value in these relationships is garnered from investments made in value-added operations such as packaging, labeling, certification, and product diversification.

These value-added results are clearly represented in the labor statistics for the integrated large exporter value chain. Approximately 7,000 smallholders are involved in fresh vegetable export, compared to 40,000–60,000 in the processing industry at packhouses, or as farm laborers. For example, Homegrown is Kenya's largest horticultural exporter and is an example of a highly integrated company. Ninety percent of Homegrown's crops are grown on its own farms, where it controls the storage, cooling, and logistics from the field to the packing station; it has a joint venture with an airfreight company and a dedicated importer in the United Kingdom. Homegrown works with about 600 smallholders and employs nearly 8,000 seasonal employees for its processing

Figure 4.22   Integrated Export Value Chain

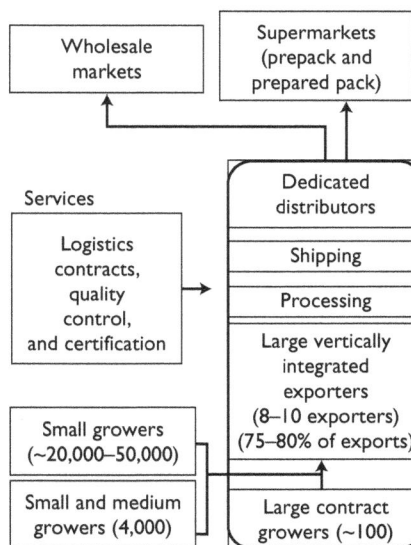

Source: J. E. Austin Associates, Inc. (2005). Analysis adapted from Irwin, Grant, Parker, and Morgan (2005).

operations. Homegrown has also recently completed a factory for prepared salads, providing the capability to pick, prepare, fully label, and transport the salads to supermarket shelves within 48 hours.

Homegrown's recent investments in product development are indicative of the value drivers for the entire fresh vegetable export industry. Driving this accelerated value growth in fresh vegetables has been the emergence of semiprocessed products that meet stringent European standards and certifications. This growth in exports consists of a broad range of products produced under very strict hygienic conditions. In Kenya, the increase in value-added processing to produce "high-care" products such as salads, prepared vegetables, and stir-fry mixes has increased export values for fresh vegetables by 250 percent (Jaffee 2003).

CONCLUSION

The Kenyan fresh vegetable export industry has grown enormously in size and value added, in large part by implementing new processes and operations. These have been initiated by private business in response to evolving market trends, recognized opportunities, and value chain pressures. The public sector has been an active partner in this growth. Further opportunities exist to increase the competitiveness of the Kenyan fresh vegetable export industry through value chain deepening, as well as through other approaches (for example, increasing the technical capacities and market understanding of serving growing markets beyond Europe, extending the exporting season, and reducing costs and losses through infrastructure) (TechnoServe 2004). The realization of each enhanced process will, in turn, provide opportunity for added services within the value chain.

NOTES

1. NEPAD TechnoServe case study.
2. "Safer" refers to produce with limited levels of chemical residue.

Identifying Business Models for Replication

By analyzing value chains, participants can often identify intermediation opportunities that offer increased efficiency, economies of scale, transaction cost reduction, or more value added in the chain. Entrepreneurs and businesses may be the first to identify and act on them, or government and development partners (and their consultants/practitioners) may be the ones to promote such opportunities. The defining characteristic in the context of this tool is that the opportunities offer the possibility of replication within the value chain.

The benefits of identifying and promoting intermediation opportunities go beyond adding value and upgrading the value chain (with the resulting net economic benefit in jobs, wages, and incomes). More than these, use of this tool in countries with a particularly weak private sector and lack of an entrepreneurial culture amounts to investing in the promotion of entrepreneurship. Additionally, as individual entrepreneurs improve on the basic business model, they often generate their own innovations.

Replicable business models can be recognized through a variety of mechanisms and experiences. For example, opportunity can be identified through the simple need to upgrade quality (of both raw materials and processed product) through learning business models that have worked in other regions or countries in related types of value chains. Opportunity may also appear through the application of analytical tools described elsewhere in this Guide, such as identifying needed services, benchmarking and gap analysis, and market analysis. Box 4.6 presents an example of a replicable business model.

The Pakistan Dairy industry also provides a useful illustration (see box 4.7) of a replicable model. Value chain analysis in Pakistan revealed that in several areas near urban centers, 45 percent of milk produced in the country never reached market because, in most areas, only the morning milk (55 percent of potential output) was collected. The rest (evening milk) went to waste. Further, domestic demand was growing at twice the rate of supply. This analysis led to the identification of an intermediation opportunity that could be exploited by entrepreneurs—namely, investments in simple refrigeration centers for the purchase and collection of milk which allowed an increase in the quality and supply of milk, as well as providing farmers an outlet for selling it. This business model is being widely replicated and by April 2008, less than 30 months after efforts began, about 1,000 collection centers were operating.

Once a business model suitable for replication is identified, value chain participants and development practitioners can support and facilitate value chain stakeholders in successfully implementing a pilot enterprise. Once proven, stakeholders can encourage the replication through promotional campaigns, business associations, technical assistance, and other available means. In the Pakistan Dairy example, a public-private institution to promote the dairy sector is facilitating the replication of the collection centers by promoting the business opportunity, soliciting applications for discounted farm cooling tanks (which the institution negotiated with the provider), and identifying commercially appropriate sites for centers.

A STEP-BY-STEP SUMMARY OF TOOL 5: IDENTIFYING BUSINESS MODELS FOR REPLICATION

- Identify intermediation opportunities (business models) to increase efficiency and value added suitable for replication. Many of the tools in this Guide are helpful in this respect.
- Support and facilitate value chain stakeholders to implement a pilot enterprise.
- When an approach is successfully proven, encourage its replication through promotional campaigns, business associations, technical assistance, and other available means.

Box 4.6   Replicable Business Models—Rwandan Coffee Washing Stations

Rwandan coffee was a principal source of foreign exchange for the country until the 1990s. But coffee's contribution to Rwanda's foreign exchange earnings declined through the mid- and late 1990s. Rwandan coffee production never recovered to 1992 production volumes (39,000 mt) because of inefficiencies in the coffee value chain. The country's disparate nature of coffee farming, the poor health of its coffee trees, the lack of wet-milling stations, and low incentives for reinvestment all contributed to inefficiency. Growers were not offered higher prices for better quality beans, so they spent little time grading and separating their bean harvests. Low coffee yields and poor price points influenced farmers to focus on other crops with higher margins, further diminishing coffee's competitiveness in world markets.

Despite the constraints that led to low-quality and low-quantity commodity grade coffee, the government of Rwanda (GoR) and donor partners believed that Rwanda possessed the capacity, environmental conditions, and political will to improve its coffee position in world markets. What Rwanda lacked was technical capacity, market information, and a coherent strategy. Two USAID-funded projects, Partnership to Enhance Agriculture in Rwanda through Linkages (PEARL), and Assistance a la Dynamisation de Agribusiness au Rwanda (ADAR), helped to provide the strategy and technical capacity that assisted in Rwanda's coffee quality and quantity improvements. The projects sought to improve Rwandan coffee by, among other actions, facilitating the opening and equipping of coffee-washing stations in Rwanda's top 50 producing districts. These washing stations filled a crucial gap in Rwanda's production cycle and allowed the coffee's quality to improve.

Source: Carlton Jones, J. E. Austin Associates, Inc.

With an annual budget of almost US$700,000 dedicated to supporting the coffee sector, ADAR worked directly with private investors to open 16 washing stations in 2005. Direct assistance included feasibility studies, business plans, construction planning and supervision, and training in coffee processing. Similarly, PEARL worked with rural cooperatives to assist in cooperative formation, business planning, washing station construction, processing, cupping, marketing, and Fair Trade certification. In both projects, the assistance provided the platform for a replicable business model to be adopted for numerous future washing station openings. In the model, investment opportunities were created via a loan guarantee program that allowed the private investors to construct collection/washing stations and process coffee beans for improved quality. The model was replicated each time a private sector investor sought to open a washing station. The investor took out a loan from the guarantee fund and, along with technical assistance from the projects, began processing coffee for export. By November 2005, 10 of the 11 loans provided by the program, totaling US$1.6 million, went to private sector operators.

As of January 2007, the private sector was continuing to invest in coffee washing stations in Rwanda. The replicable business model provided by the projects has helped to establish 80 functioning stations throughout the country and 120 washing stations by the end of 2008. The washing stations provide an important intermediate role in the coffee value chain and have also proven to be platforms for entrepreneurship and entrepreneurial innovation. Ultimately, Rwanda hopes to have its entire coffee production fully washed by 2010.

Background
An estimated 30–35 million farmers in Pakistan are engaged in raising livestock, which generate 30–40 percent of their income. Ninety-seven percent of fresh milk is either consumed locally or distributed through informal trading routes. The farmers' dairy production has often not reached domestic markets, despite the fact that the market for dairy is growing twice as fast as the supply.

(*Box continues on the following page.*)

Dairy Farmers Want to Invest—But Need to Manage Risk

The dairy value chains in Punjab Province and in the area around Karachi recognized an opportunity to improve the quality and increase the quantity of the milk that they were producing and marketing. The chain participants knew that they had unmet demand because they were able to sell everything they could supply. The industry's strategic working group (SWOG) meetings identified a huge market opportunity that could entice entrepreneurs to invest time and money into meeting this growing need. In fact, the dairy sector was missing out on selling its second (evening) milking, which is 45 percent of the milk produced on the farm.

The most significant issues for the value chain were that 97 percent of the trading was done on an informal basis, and there was no cold chain to handle the storage of a second milking. Of the milk that farmers did sell, 15–19 percent was wasted en route to market, again due to spoilage because of lack of chilling.

Although these facts appeared to present investment opportunity, it can be difficult to create the conditions within the value chain that motivate businesses to invest and that encourage the value chain to upgrade its practices. Buying new equipment and changing their practices means both costs and risks for farmers and intermediaries. These barriers were removed by a facilitated strategic planning process that identified a workable business model. The planning process developed sufficient trust among the participants to create a strong win-win solution and to generate commitment to the model, with risk sharing and up-front financing from Dairy Pakistan, the public-private institution that was designed by the SWOG project.

The Replicable Business Model (Collection Centers/Cooling Stations)

The core of the business model was to encourage entrepreneurs to invest in and to manage collection centers/cooling stations. The entrepreneur puts up 20 percent of the investment and receives a no-interest loan for the remainder, which was subsidized by the government, managed by Dairy Pakistan, and distributed by a consortium of banks. Dairy Pakistan then provided technical training on how to operate the cooling station. The large dairy processors/distributors committed to regular, predictable milk collection.

Communicating the Case for Investment

The SWOG presented the market opportunity to potential entrepreneurs. Dairy Pakistan and the several banks sent out formal invitations for entrepreneurs to submit applications to Dairy Pakistan for investment. The project and Dairy Pakistan supported entrepreneurs with technical assistance in learning to operate the tanks, again reducing the risk of investment. As of mid-2006, the project was facilitating 2,150 collection tanks and had received 3,050 applications. By May 2008, approximately 1,000 additional collection tanks were in place.

Summary and Results

The supply of chilled milk has increased by an estimated 500,000 liters per day. About 7,000 direct jobs have been created in collection and processing. Based on the 2006 results, the entrepreneurs who own and operate the centers will earn an estimated US$63 million (net present value). More than 30,000 farmers now have access to market and are able to sell at higher prices. Additional benefits are the increased profits further down the market chain. The private sector has invested more than $7 million in the program.

Source: Mike Ducker with Marcos Arocha and Martin Webber, J. E. Austin Associates, Inc.

Identifying and Implementing Replicable Business Models—Mozambican Cashews

Carlton Jones and Martin Webber
J. E. Austin Associates, Inc.

INTRODUCTION

Following a tumultuous round of cashew sector reforms in Mozambique, the government of Mozambique and USAID commissioned a cashew subsector analysis[1] seeking innovative means to revitalize the industry while maximizing benefits to small growers. The analysis stressed the importance of replicable business models for value-added processing of cashews.

Rejuvenating the Mozambican cashew sector requires innovative approaches to bring value back to the actors in the value chain. This case demonstrates how small and medium hand-processing plants were identified as replicable businesses supporting that rejuvenation. Mozambique has not yet returned to its former cashew dominance, but those in the sector have learned that, through replicable business models, value chain actions can rebuild the private firms that bolster the sector.

POINTS TO CONSIDER

When reviewing this case consider the following questions:

- What led to the need to identify replicable business models?
- When is it appropriate to consider implementing such a model?
- What role do local entrepreneurs play in implementation?

BACKGROUND

From the 1920s until the mid-1970s, Mozambique was considered the world's leading cashew producer (240,000 mt at its peak in 1973),[2] with considerable domestic capacity in processing quality cashews. By the early 1980s, Mozambique had over a dozen processing factories and was the first African country to process cashews on an industrial scale, rather than through the traditional method of hand-processing by SMEs.

However, by the end of the 1970s, other global producers (India and Brazil) began to threaten Mozambique's cashew dominance.[3] In response, in 1978, the government of Mozambique banned the export of raw nuts. The rationale at the time was to stimulate domestic processing and maintain global processing dominance. But after a variety of events, including a civil war from 1982–1992 and the adoption of policies that fixed raw nut prices, production continued to decline (see figure 4.23) (down to 22,106 mt in 1990; Deloitte Touche [1997]).

In 1992, the government of Mozambique implemented many reforms in the hope of regaining past cashew processing performance. The raw nut export ban was lifted, previously state-owned factories were privatized and sold to local entrepreneurs, and there was a push to invest heavily in new large-scale mechanical processing facilities. However, the government also introduced high taxes on raw nut exports (18–22 percent), again with the goal of pushing the entire industry toward domestic processing. The reforms failed, and the sector essentially collapsed by 1994.

Figure 4.23   Mozambican Cashew Nut Exports since the 1970s

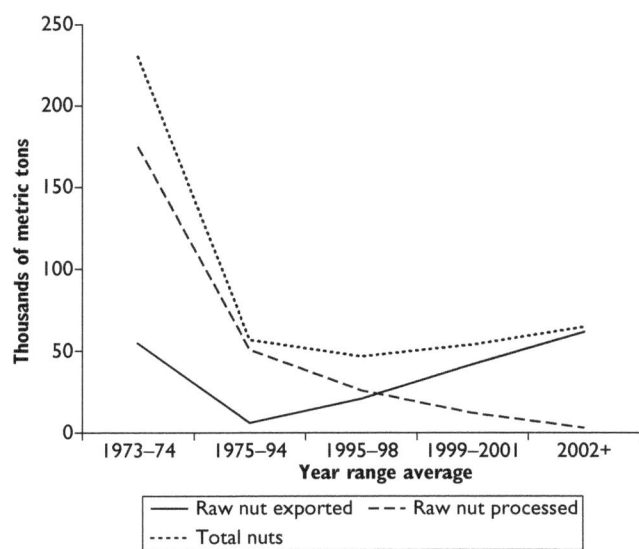

Source: FAOSTAT data.

In 1995, the government of Mozambique liberalized the cashew sector, in part as a condition for World Bank loans. The reduction of export tariffs (from 18–22 percent to 20 percent, then again to 14 percent) slightly increased prices at the farm gates, but, some argue (McMillan, Welch, and Rodrik 2003), also led to the closing of most processing factories. Mozambican processors found it too difficult to compete with traders selling raw nuts to India (where the industry is reportedly subsidized). Additionally, because of low margins, processors did not reinvest or maintain their plants; equipment began to break down, and improper and improperly maintained equipment caused a high level of cashew kernel breakage.

With most processing factories closed, and 7,000 employees out of work, Mozambique's cashew sector suffered another relapse. By the late 1990s, instead of having a vibrant value-added cashew sector, Mozambique exported most of its nuts raw to India for processing and value added. In 2001, local businesses pressured the government to reinstate the export tax on raw nuts.

Concerned about the sector, USAID commissioned a cashew subsector analysis seeking innovative means to revitalize the industry while maximizing benefits to small growers. The study results suggested that small and medium processors could bring value back to Mozambique by processing some of the raw nuts that otherwise would be exported to India (see figure 4.24). Thus, a program was implemented with the goal of establishing a profitable SME processor in the northern province of Nampula that would serve as the pilot. If successful, the processor could serve as the model for other, similar enterprises.

THE LEAD FIRM MODEL

A local businessman, Antonio Miranda, possessed many of the characteristics hoped for in an entrepreneur. He was innovative, thrifty, socially conscious, and had vision. With the support of a technical assistance provider (TechnoServe 2003), a small- to medium-scale hand processor, Miranda Caju, Ltd., was established in 2001 on the grounds of a previously closed facility. The building was reconstructed using local labor, which provided jobs to the surrounding community. Mr. Miranda was able to raise funds for seed and working capital (US$47,000) in the form of a guarantee fund from INCAJU, Mozambique's National Cashew Institute, and he installed new equipment for whole nut production.

In hand processing, each nut is steamed, shelled, dried, and peeled by hand, then pregraded to ensure a higher percentage of whole kernels. After kernels are vacuum packed, they are trucked to exporters in the port of Nacala. The plant had the capacity to employ 460 workers, purchase 12,500 mt of raw cashews from small growers, and process 1,250 mt of cashews that rivaled India and Brazil in quality. When Mr. Miranda announced his intention to hire locally, 1,000 candidates applied to fill the 70 original positions.

Miranda Caju experienced and overcame many challenges. Within months, the processing plant was selling to a major buyer in Holland. Not only was the plant making a profit, but Miranda Caju workers earned, on average, US$300 per year versus the average of US$8 per year in cash income earned by subsistence farmers.

Miranda Caju purchases raw nuts from several sources, including recently formed farmer associations and small growers. Before the plant's entrance into the market, most small growers sold to traders, who then sourced to wholesalers. Miranda Caju was able to locate small growers with the capacity to improve their growing methods to provide better yields and, thus, higher quality raw nuts to the Miranda plant. Miranda Caju's entrance into the market benefited small growers by growing their incomes an average of 20 percent.

REPLICATING THE MODEL

Recognizing the potential for additional small and medium processors to enter the cashew sector, TechnoServe arranged

Figure 4.24 Weaknesses in the Mozambican Cashew Domestic Value Chain

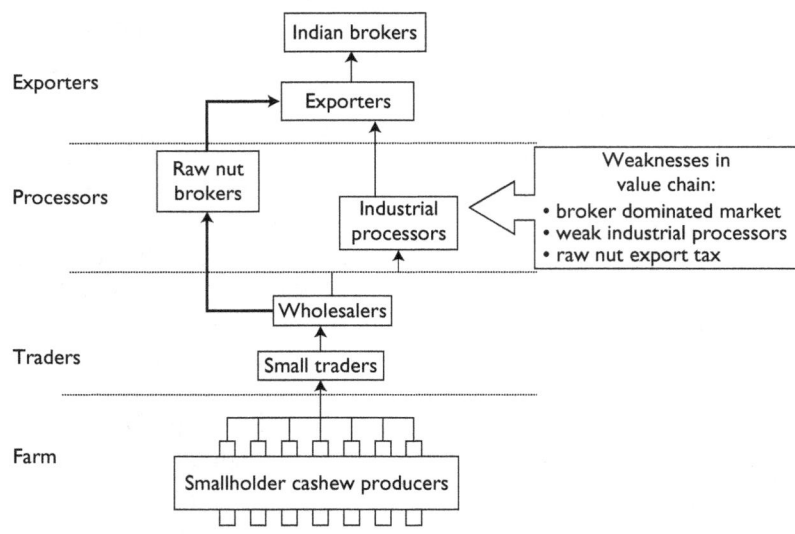

Source: J. E. Austin Associates, Inc. (2007).

Figure 4.25 Mozambican Cashew Domestic Value Chain with Small Processors

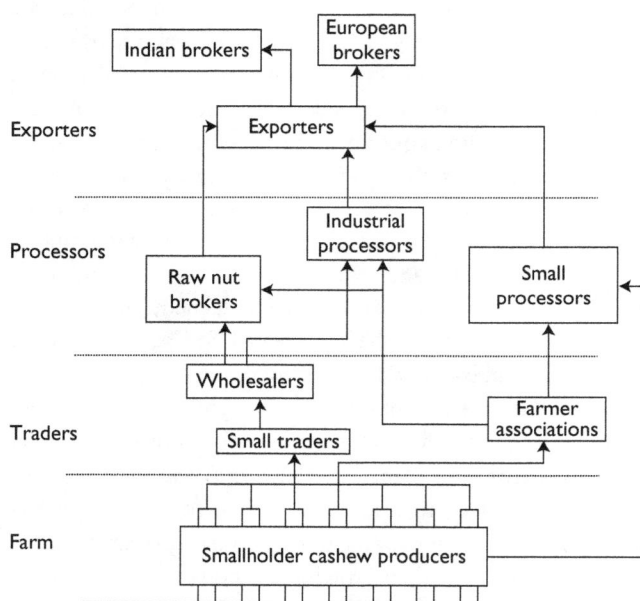

Source: J. E. Austin Associates, Inc. (2007).

for other entrepreneurs to be trained on the Miranda Caju premises to learn first-hand how to run a cashew plant. Mr. Miranda was an instrumental trainer, providing day-to-day experiences and lessons to the entrepreneurs learning the business. His ability to share lessons learned on a variety of topics like operations, cost savings, plant location, financ-

ing, hiring practices, and sourcing raw nuts from growers provided a sound foundation for other entrepreneurs to launch their own processing facilities in 2004. Also in 2004, Miranda Caju opened a second operating plant to meet the growing demand for processed cashews. Miranda Caju served as the model for five additional processing plants to open between 2002 and 2004, with a total processing capacity of 8,750 mt (see table 4.10).

CONCLUSION: REBIRTH OF A SECTOR

Since 2001, 12 processors have now opened under the profitable, replicable business model demonstrated by Miranda Caju (see figure 4.25). They vary in their stages of development and success, with Miranda Caju continuing to lead the small to medium cashew processor market. Of those businesses, Miranda Caju continues to grow and innovate. The firm also hopes to increase the percentage of raw nuts it purchases from farmer associations (currently 40 percent), and it now provides on-farm technical assistance to its small growers in the form of help with seedling replanting, quality control, and improved yields.

The entire value chain has benefited from these interventions, not only in increased volume of quality cashew processing and exports, but also from realizing that profitable manual processing businesses can be created and can improve quality, create jobs, and rebuild the Mozambican cashew brand. Access to investment and working capital has improved, initially through INCAJU's Guarantee Fund, and later by other guarantee funds managed by the Ministry of

Table 4.10	Mozambican Cashew Processing Operations				
Name	**Location**	**Started**	**Processing capacity (mt)**	**Employees**	**Small-grower purchases**
Miranda Caju	Namige, Mogincual	2001–2	1,250	460	12,500
Africaju Lda	Namialo, Meconta	2002–3	1,500	160	10,000
IPCCM	Murrupula Sede	2002–3	1,000	84	10,000
Miranda Caju	Angoche Sede	2003–4	1,500	230	5,000
Alexim Lda	Iuluti, Mogovolas	2003–4	1,000	63	1,200
Moma Caju Lda	Mecone, Moma	2003–4	1,000	63	1,200
Macia Caju	Macia, Macia	2003–4	1,500	70	1,500

Source: Reprinted from TechnoServe (2004).

Industry and Commerce. Since 2001, these processors have had annual sales over US$5.1 million and have employed over 3,000 workers. Smallholders are also benefiting through the increased prices they receive at the farm gate.

Mozambique's cashew industry is examined further as a case accompanying Tool 7, Horizontal Collaboration—Creating and Taking Advantage of Economies of Scale.

NOTES

1. The subsector analysis was conducted by U.S.-based NGO TechnoServe.

2. TechnoServe.

3. In 1978, India was the top world producer, at 165,323 mt. Brazil was second with 77,000 mt, and Mozambique was fourth with 61,000 mt produced (FAOSTAT).

Capturing Value Through Forward and Backward Integration

At the firm level, vertical integration means creating forward and/or backward linkages. A firm becomes more vertically integrated when it takes on more of the activities that take place within its value chain. Vertical integration makes sense if, for example, the business is seeking to ensure supply or otherwise control inputs, capture more value, achieve economies of scale, or ensure access to information. A value chain, by consequence, becomes more integrated through the decisions of firm-level actors.

Vertical integration also takes place at the value chain level when more stages are brought into the country's value chains. This means that a nation's businesses are taking on more of the activities within the global value chain, which adds value, provides more market contact and information, creates employment, and more. Value chain members must decide whether it makes sense for them to integrate—a calculation that includes profit, risk, investor wishes, and other factors. Integration can also mean adding more functions to the value chain and not necessarily incorporating them from other countries. This integration may involve joint commitments or even joint investments.

Companies and enterprises have always made conscious decisions about whether it makes sense to vertically integrate. At the value chain level, one can even think that, before there was international trade, every industry was vertically integrated with a region or nation. This is a tool that examines whether there are gains to taking on more of the value chain's functions.

The value chain understood at the firm level can be very simply illustrated (and, of course, can also be shown with much greater detail). In figure 4.26, each stage represents a link in the value chain. In terms of integration, a firm operating in the production stage can assess its distribution channels and decide that it can transport its own goods more cheaply and efficiently than by using another firm. This firm has then made the decision to integrate forward and take on its value chain's distribution function.

The firm could also make decisions regarding its supply of inputs. At the production stage, a firm might recognize that its suppliers are not producing inputs that are adequate for use at the production stage. Rather than share information and work with one or a group of suppliers, the firm might simply integrate backward and develop its own ability to provide the inputs it needs.

VERTICAL INTEGRATION FROM THE NATIONAL VALUE CHAIN PERSPECTIVE

For most products in most developing countries, relatively simple value chains focus on getting a product (typically a largely undifferentiated commodity) to market (whether that market is domestic or international). From this perspective, the challenges are to achieve low transaction costs, push volumes of product to the market (and sell them), and reduce losses from spoilage, waste, or theft. From the perspective of the in-country value chain participants, such value chains tend to be supply driven and production driven (a situation that poses its own challenges, if the producer's interests are not in line with market requirements). Also, the recipe for business development from this perspective involves reducing production and logistic barriers and removing taxes and levies (or imposing them to protect against cheaper competition or foreign competitors who are willing to buy raw materials at slightly higher prices). A "market information gate" that prevents domestic producers from understanding the export market is often present, thereby presenting both a challenge and an opportunity for forward integration (see figure 4.27).[1]

One typical competitiveness goal is to increase quality and service within the value chain and to offer customers a desirable, higher-value product or service (shown in figure 4.28 as X+Y). This, if achieved, can offer huge increases in productivity and make the value chain and the country as a whole more competitive (see Tool 4, Upgrading and Deepening the Value Chain).

Figure 4.26   Firm Value Chain

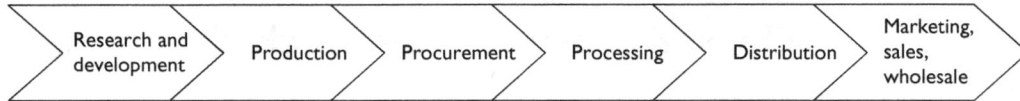

Source: Adapted from Michael Porter.

Figure 4.27   Improving Value Chains (before Value Added)

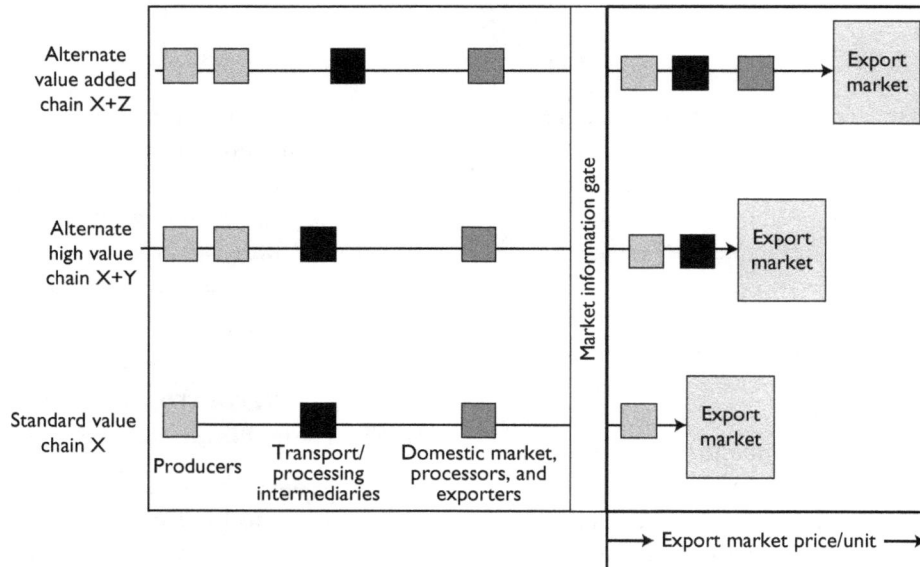

Source: J. E. Austin Associates, Inc.

Figure 4.28   Improving Value Chains (with Value Added)

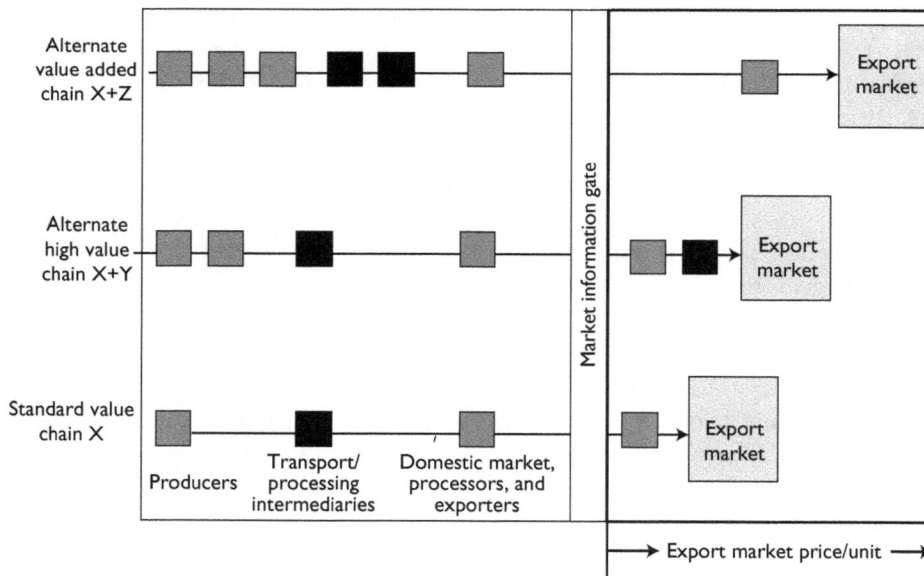

Source: J. E. Austin Associates, Inc.

An even more rewarding goal is to add value along the value chain (shown as X+Z).[2] This can be fairly simple, for example, coffee washing, packaging versus bulk tea, filleted fish, cut and packaged flowers delivered directly to retail outlets, or furniture or furniture components. It is analogous to the Mongolian meat production example described earlier in tool 4, figures 4.20 and 4.21. These value additions contrast with, for example, selling unprocessed logs or lumber or selling unprocessed vegetables for delivery to markets. Value addition can be accomplished by introducing new enterprises into the value chain (thereby deepening it), or by having existing firms take on new activities (vertical integration). Adding value might also mean creating domestic operations that had previously been performed abroad. With cut flowers (as in the Ugandan example), this might include assembling bouquets and packaging for display. In many value chains, it might take the form of producing intermediate or final products rather than raw material (for example, rubber gloves rather than crepe rubber, processed or canned fruits rather than fresh or frozen exports, or filleted and packaged meats or fish rather than frozen products).

CONSIDERATIONS FOR INTEGRATION

There are many reasons to think about integration and several considerations that must be kept in mind when thinking about it. First is strategy: it is important to understand the context in which the firm or value chain operates and whether it can become more competitive through integration. Once a firm understands its position in the value chain, it can determine whether there are profitable opportunities for expansion into adjacent links. A similar calculation must be made when a value chain seeks to vertically integrate through collaborative approaches. There are many strategic questions to ask about integration, and these vary depending on which stage the firm occupies in the value chain. Jim Austin's book, *Agroindustrial Project Analysis* (1992), long a touchstone for investors and practitioners, lists important questions to ask in analyzing agricultural projects. Some are related to vertical integration and are relevant mainly to the production stage of the value chain, including:

- Is there competition in procurement among similar agroindustries?
- How much quality control would be gained if the processor integrated backward to assume the production, storage, transport, and handling functions?

- How do improvements in quality control compare with the cost and with the alternatives for quality control?
- Should the producers integrate backward and undertake transport or production, or both?
- Would backward integration lower the costs of raw materials?
- How much will control of quantity, quality, and timing improve with integration?
- How far back should the producers integrate?
- How much additional fixed investment will be required to integrate?
- How much additional working capital is required?
- How might integration reduce the project's flexibility in obtaining sources of raw materials?
- What are the economic and operational risks of a decrease in this flexibility?
- How will integration affect variable and fixed costs?
- How will integration affect the plant's break-even point?
- Is integration politically feasible or socially desirable?

Second are operational considerations. Vertical integration may be necessary if a firm needs to be able to control its supply of inputs. This need for control is especially relevant if the firm needs highly specialized inputs for its products. Also, by controlling its supply, a vertically integrated firm can more easily ensure availability. Although suppliers can often provide inputs at a lower cost, especially if there is competition within that stage, a vertically integrated firm may actually lower its costs by providing its own supply.

Integration must make basic financial sense: a firm or country must evaluate whether value is being generated in adjacent links and whether it can capture enough of that value to make integration profitable. The firm or country should perform a cost-benefit analysis to identify whether the benefits outweigh the costs. Table 4.11 presents a number of reasons to integrate vertically. Boxes 4.8 and 4.9 present two illustrative examples and the topic is considered more deeply in case study 7.

A STEP-BY-STEP SUMMARY OF TOOL 6: CAPTURING VALUE THROUGH FORWARD AND BACKWARD INTEGRATION

- Analyze the current in-country value chain in the context of the global value chain to identify profitable opportunities for expansion into adjacent links.
- Strategically assess current and future value chain addition activities in the context of the desirable objectives associated with vertical integration. Likely objectives include

Created in the 1980s to Support Diversification into Higher-Value Horticulture Products

In the 1980s, Zambia's three largest horticulture exporters created the Zambian Export Growers Association (ZEGA). Zambian exporters saw an opportunity to use the country's considerable natural advantages to produce and export higher-value horticulture products. ZEGA's founders recognized that they needed critical mass to purchase inputs from South Africa and to negotiate duty-free incentives with the Zambian government. ZEGA was established without any donor support, but, as it evolved, it became an important vehicle for donor support.

Grew in the 1990s by Developing Competence in the Freight Business

Perhaps the main benefit of grower cooperation was to secure airfreight. Zambia's airfreight export tonnage was always less than in competing countries such as Kenya and Zimbabwe, so achieving critical mass to secure competitive rates and capacity was difficult.

In the 1990s, some of Zambia's big horticulture growers started to create linkages with flower markets in Holland and large food retailers in the United Kingdom. With these linkages to sophisticated markets, and with perishable products at stake, the Zambian growers realized that getting reliable, affordable airfreight service to Northern Europe would be key to its long-term competitiveness. During the 1980s, Zambia Airways offered subsidized airfreight rates to Europe for the horticulture exporters, but the airline became insolvent in the late 1980s. ZEGA instead negotiated its first freight contract with British Airways, which nonetheless put Zambia at a cost disadvantage compared to other horticulture exporters such as Kenya and South Africa. However, ZEGA members stood firm; even though they could sometimes get cheaper freight rates on passenger planes, they continued to use ZEGA for freight services so it could amass tonnage. Once producers reached a sufficiently large tonnage of horticulture produce, ZEGA was able to negotiate with African freight carriers to achieve cost competitiveness. Over time, ZEGA developed a competence for managing freight firms, and now has at least one airfreight shipment of horticulture products going out a day. ZEGA even sought to break off the freight business into a separate company, although it continued to grow its expertise and service its clients.

Began Cold Storage at the Lusaka International Airport

Because of EurepGAP standards, the horticulture value chain in Zambia needed to have an integrated cold chain from the farmer to the European importer. The large growers invested in refrigerated trucks while ZEGA handled cold storage and logistics at the airport. This created a full, integrated cold chain for floriculture and horticulture export products.

Backward Integration into Procurement of Inputs

ZEGA supported backward integration by buying farm inputs, such as fertilizer, which has provided the industry with two advantages: bulk purchasing power and thus lower input costs for the sector and important working capital because ZEGA sells on account. Because ZEGA controls the important link to air transport, growers have a powerful incentive to influence other growers to pay their debts.

Results

The vertical integration within Zambia's value chain, led by ZEGA, enabled the sector to increase exports of fresh vegetables and cut flowers from US$6 million in 1994 to over US$33million in 2001 and US$43 million in 2005. This increase in exports was enabled by ZEGA's forward integration into airfreight and backward integration into procurement. ZEGA has filled important gaps within the Zambian value chain and has enabled all value chain participants to benefit from economies of scale. ZEGA has also been a recognized "face" of the industry in dialogues with the Zambian government and the donor community in receiving technical assistance to support Zambia's export growth.

ESA Rose Exports to the European Union

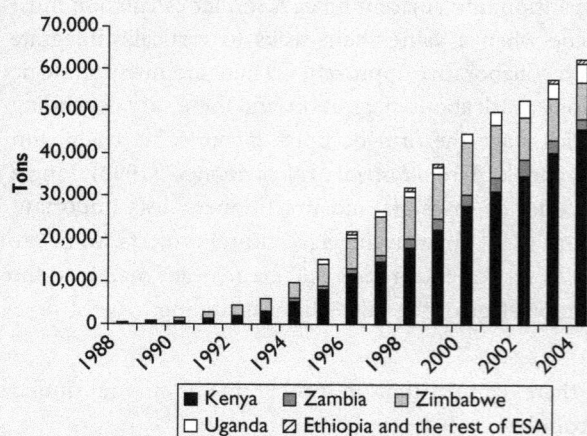

Source: UNCTAD (United Nations Conference on Trade and Development) data, www.unctad.org.

Source: Carlton Jones and Mike Ducker, J. E. Austin Associates, Inc.

Table 4.11 Some Reasons to Consider Vertical Integration

Reasons	Considerations
Control reasons	• Insufficient supply • Inadequate supply • Need for highly specialized inputs • Cost savings
Lack of intermediation	• Ineffective communication and flow of information between members • Nonexistent technical/embedded services
Establishment and expansion	• Solidify position in value chain • Lower costs through economies of scale • Alter competitive landscape
Capture more value	• Opportunities to increase revenues without overstretching resources • Opportunities to undertake more functions without overstretching resources • Opportunities to create value

Source: J. E. Austin Associates, Inc.

Box 4.9 Bulgarian Wine—Integrating Operations to Secure Sourcing of Raw Material

The Bulgarian wine industry is closely linked to Bulgaria's grape production subsector. The traditional value chain (as represented in figure 1) illustrates how winemakers rely on the grape auction and imports for their grape supply. However, a severe frost and low temperatures in 1997–98 significantly restricted grape production at Bulgarian vineyards. More than 50 percent of vineyard production in northern Bulgaria and 20 percent in southern Bulgaria were lost. Wineries in the north were forced to turn to suppliers from southern Bulgaria and Romania.

This increased competition for grapes throughout Bulgaria caused prices to rise quickly. Consequently, Bulgarian winemakers were forced to pay more for their Bulgarian grapes or to import grapes from neighboring countries with little control over the quality and variety of grapes. The poorly controlled imports negatively affected wine production.

The firm Vinzavod-Assenovgrad (VA)[a] is located in a region famous for growing grapes. Prior to 1997–98, VA had never had problems securing grapes from local suppliers for its production cycle.

The grape shortages made the company aware of the need for measures to ensure local supply to maintain quality and varietal differentiation. VA management decided to develop its own vineyards and to create new contract mechanisms to secure grapes from local producers. The company invested in 200 hectares of grape production and has made plans to expand to 350 hectares to secure a reliable and cost-effective supply chain.

Figure 1: Bulgarian Wine Value Chain: Traditional

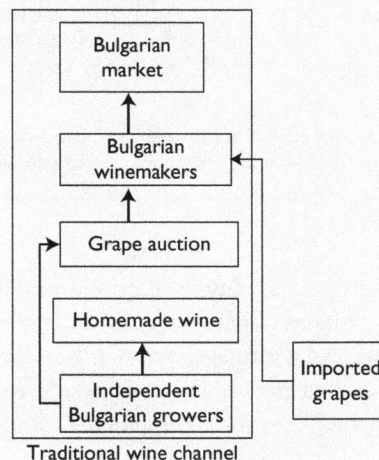

Traditional wine channel

Source: J.E. Austin Associates, Inc.

As shown in figure 2, VA also now secures a portion of its grape supply by offering small vine growers short-term contracts for their grapes and preferential pricing on wine. In the contract's inaugural year, VA sourced 40,000 kg of raw grapes from local smallholders. However, in subsequent years, VA allowed purchases under the new mechanism to decline, once again relying on the grape auction as the primary avenue for domestic purchases. While the new contract mechanism did not radically restructure VA's supply chain, it did institutionalize a new fail-safe for securing local production in years of scarcity.

(Box continues on the following page.)

Figure 2:   Bulgarian Wine Value Chain: Integrated

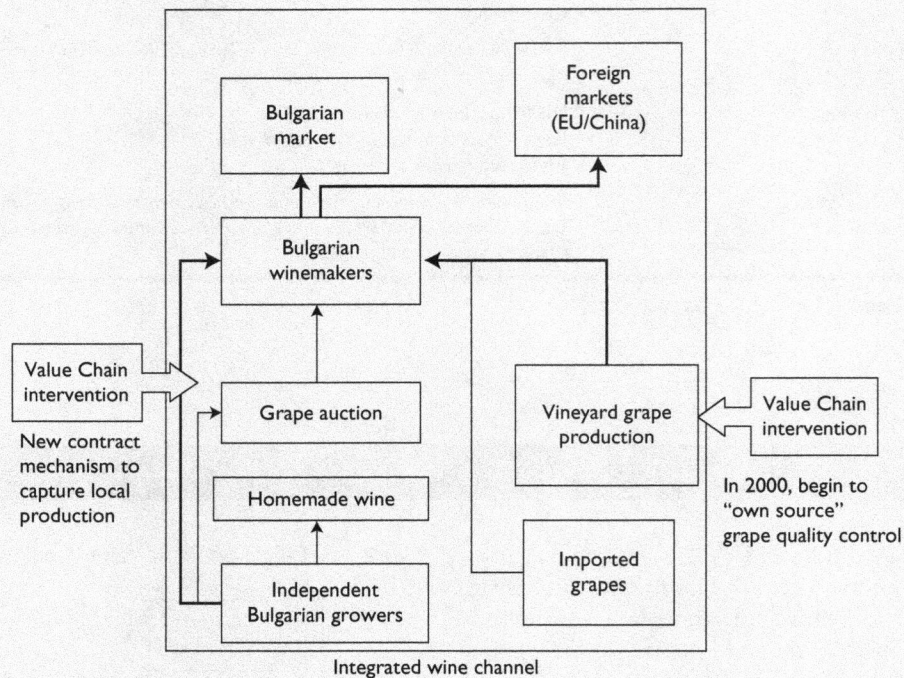

Source: Michael Gorman and Martin Webber, J. E. Austin Associates, Inc.
[a] VA's corporate Web site: http://www.mavrud.com/en/index.htm.

greater control over quantity, quality, and timing of raw materials and reduced transaction costs, among others.

■ Analyze operational advantages and disadvantages associated with vertical integration. This may include lower transaction costs, higher fixed costs, complex logistics, and risk.

NOTES

1. Forward integration by domestic producers often means that they need to access more information about the market to produce products that will sell. There are many ways of doing this. In order to gain a foothold in the export market, the exporter should learn as much about the market as possible and communicate that information to suppliers.

Exporters could also pay the producers (and intermediaries, for example, transporters) a premium at produce at certain quality and delivery standards. From the perspective of producers and intermediaries, who also want to sell more, they should do everything possible to learn about the market's (and the exporters') requirements. This sharing of information will add value and help value chain participants produce the right products in sufficient quantity.

2. In reality, different businesses in competitive, market-driven economies generally participate in a variety of value chains—some simple, some offering higher quality, and some offering considerable value addition. Within an economy, businesses make their own choices according to their business model.

Capturing Value through Integration—The Ghanaian Pineapple Industry and Blue Skies Holdings Ltd.

Michael German and Martin Webber
J. E. Austin Associates, Inc.

INTRODUCTION

Vertical integration generally refers to a firm's ownership or control of vertically related activities. The greater the firm's ownership and control over successive stages of the value chain for its products, the greater its degree of vertical integration. In a value chain context, vertical integration can also be achieved between upstream and downstream firms when there is a high level of integrated systems and information sharing.

One case in point is Blue Skies Holdings Ltd., an example of a successful, vertically integrated exporter of pineapple and other processed fruit from Ghana.

THE GHANAIAN PINEAPPLE INDUSTRY

According to the Food and Agriculture Organization of the United Nations (FAO), there are more than 80 countries producing approximately 17 million tons of pineapples. More than 11 million (65 percent) of the 17 million tons grown are destined for export (FAOSTAT). Pineapples are exported in various forms, and nearly 80 percent of pineapples are found on the market in processed form: 48 percent as juice and 30 percent as canned fruits. Thailand, Brazil, the Philippines, and India are the main producing countries. Thailand, the Philippines, and Indonesia account for 80 percent of the canned pineapple industry. Brazil's production is essentially consumed domestically, as is India's (Imbert 2003).

The fresh pineapple market has traditionally been dominated by Côte d'Ivoire, Costa Rica, and the Philippines (see figure 4.29). Growth in the fresh pineapple industry has averaged 6 percent per year since 2000. Political instability in Côte d'Ivoire has caused its pineapple export growth to fall to 2 percent over the past five years, and it has lost significant market share to Costa Rica and Ghana. In fact, during this same period, Ghanaian exporters have achieved an average growth rate of 45 percent while Cost Rica has nearly doubled its exports to Europe. Costa Rica's success has centered on its usage of the preferred MD2 varietal, as well as the logistical competence and marketing prowess that the multinational Del Monte Foods employs to service the European market.

Ghana's West African location provides an excellent climate for growing fruits and vegetables, as well as advantages for servicing the European market. Ghanaian fresh pineapple exporters face fierce competition from Costa Rica, Côte d'Ivoire, Honduras, Mexico, Ecuador, and others. Costa Rica is the leading exporter of pineapple to the European markets with an annual export of about 300,000 tons, followed by Côte d'Ivoire with exports of 150,000 tons, while Ghana has just reached the third position with 71,000 tons.[1] Ghana's main competitive advantage over Costa Rica is its location, while its political stability and business environment compare favorably with Côte d'Ivoire.

Overall, Ghanaian pineapple exports to European markets have increased in recent years thanks to greater

Figure 4.29   Pineapple Exports

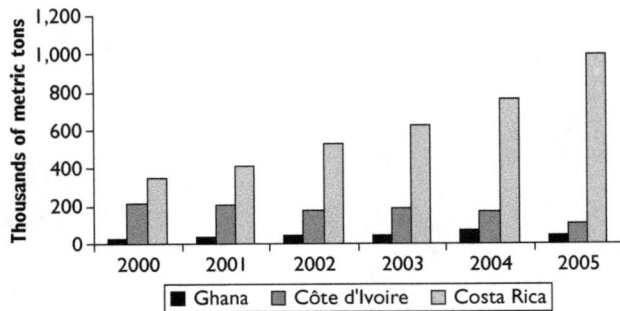

Source: FAOSTAT data.

Figure 4.30   European Pineapple Imports

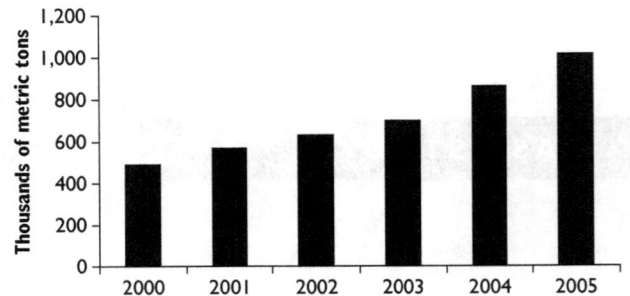

Source: FAOSTAT data.

investment in the fruit export industry from both the private and public sectors. Regulatory reform, tax incentives, market linkages, investments into new varietals, public-private partnerships, and new economies of scale within the value chain have all helped to expand the Ghanaian pineapple industry.

BACKGROUND

The European market

The European market for fresh produce has been expanding with the rising incomes of European consumers. In 2005, the European market imported approximately 1 million metric tons of pineapples (see figure 4.30), of which one-quarter are estimated to be fresh pineapples (Vagneron, Faure, and Loeillet 2005). However, several changing factors are driving the transformation of the produce sector, including supermarket strategies, food safety legislation, supply chain integrity, rationalization of the supply base, and innovation. Consolidation of European supermarkets has, in part, been driving these changes. By the early 2000s, seven of the largest food-retailing chains in Europe accounted for 76 percent of fresh fruit and vegetable sales and 70–90 percent of fresh produce imports from Africa (Hallam et al. 2005). In the United Kingdom, supermarkets are even more concentrated, with just four big chains accounting for 73 percent of sales at supermarkets and convenience stores (*Economist* 2007). Thus, the EU-SSA pineapple export supply chains are characteristic of buyer-driven global commodity chains; the European supermarkets increasingly demand products that are low cost and quality certified (resulting in higher profits via the use of branding), as well as new methods of marketing differentiation.

European populations with higher disposable incomes have increasingly been demanding high-standard, certified fresh fruits and vegetables on a year-round basis. The European market is characterized by several relevant market factors and trends:

- Increases in wealth and demand for high-value products (many of which are imported)
- Exotic produce market growth
- Diversified preferences: national and ethnic
- Revolution in market structure: retail outlet dominance, foodservice, and catering
- New marketing formats: prepackaging and precut vegetables
- Consolidation of sources: direct linkages and faster market response
- Regulatory environment change: lower tariffs but increased safety constraints
- Value chain integration and just-in-time inventory
- Logistics networks: sea freight and airfreight capacity
- Niche markets, biocertification, and fair trade

In Ghana, fresh pineapple is exported by 60 companies, although more than 50 percent of the total export volume is produced by the larger companies, such as Jei River Farm, Farmapines,[2] and Koranco Farms. Exporter association organizations, like the Sea Freight Pineapple Exporters of Ghana (SPEG), the Horticultural Association Ghana (HAG), and the Exotic Fruit Exporters Association of Ghana (EFEG), work to help Ghanaian exporters service the growing European fresh produce market. Processing companies such as Blue Skies, Tonggu Fruits, and First Catering export fresh-cut pineapples to high-quality retailers such as Marks & Spencer and Sainsbury's.

Ghanaian fruit exporters source their products from both commercial farmers (70 percent) and small-scale farmers (30 percent), and the large commercial farming

Figure 4.31   Ghana's Fresh Pineapple Exports to the EU

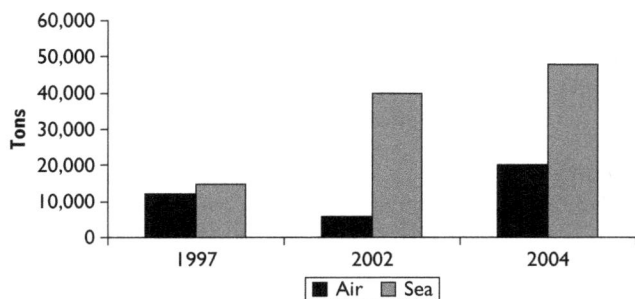

Source: Voisard and Jaeger; Ghana Horticulture Development Study; and SPEG (2004 figures).

enterprises are typically operated as outgrower schemes. While recent market conditions have led export companies to increasingly invest in vertically integrated outgrower operations, nearly all exporters mitigate risk by buying fruit from small-scale farmers to supplement commercial farms' production. By sourcing from small-scale producers throughout the country, exporters ensure a diverse supply chain that is not as susceptible to weather, crop sickness, or other unpredictable risks.

GHANAIAN EXPORTS TO EUROPE

During the late 1980s and early 1990s, Ghana carved a significant niche in the European Union (EU) market as a primary supplier of top-quality, airfreighted pineapples, supplying about 60 percent of the estimated annual 20,000 mt of pineapples airfreighted to Europe.[3] Throughout this period, only a small amount of pineapples were sea-freighted (2,710 tons). Figure 4.31 presents the evolution of total Ghanaian pineapple exports to the EU through 2004. The airfreight market's success was due to Ghana's liberal market regulation, efficient handling services, and the diversity of available and relatively inexpensive flights to all parts of Europe. However, during this period, pineapple export operations remained segmented and spread among many participants, and little integration was accomplished. Ghanaian export volumes were eventually restricted by the limited airfreight capacity of commercial passenger aircraft.

THE BLUE SKIES HOLDINGS LTD. VALUE CHAIN

Established in 1998, the Blue Skies Holdings[4] processes fresh, chilled pineapple, mango, watermelon, passion fruit, and papaya for export (see accompanying operating schedule).

Blue Skies' products are certified to meet the EurepGAP protocols for quality compliance. Fruits processed by Blue Skies are sourced mainly from Ghana's eastern and central regions, with supply gaps being filled by imports. The Blue Skies value chain is highly integrated, having incorporated operations from buying and transporting raw pineapples to delivering certified, cleaned, cut, packaged, and branded pineapple pieces to UK distribution networks. The company has made excellent use of its owner's networks within the EU supermarket industry to achieve market access for its products.

Since 2000, the company has grown tremendously, expanding its value chain by incorporating additional operations into its processing facilities. It has also expanded its local employment. Blue Skies began operations with 38 workers and has since increased its workforce to 1,000, over 60 percent of whom are permanent staff. It has also replicated its business model with similar ventures in South Africa and Egypt. By providing good extension services and farmer training, and by offering higher prices, the company has rapidly increased its production from one to about 35 tons per week. Blue Skies is also known to pay its farmers promptly and at a higher price per kilogram than other pineapple buyers in the Nsawam area of Ghana.

Blue Skies does not provide credit to farmers, nor does it link them to any financial agents; its prompt payment and higher prices are sufficient incentives for farmers to invest in their farms. In addition, the company has assumed technical and financial responsibility for certifying all its suppliers. It also provides inputs and equipment to its producers for purchase. Because of the investments needed to get certification, those suppliers whom Blue Skies has helped obtain EurepGAP accreditation are obliged to sell to the company. Recently, 57 percent (77 of 135) of Blue Skies' small-scale pineapple producers were certified as organic, fair trade producers. Blue Skies operates with individual farmers and not cooperatives.

Several factors contributing to Blue Skies' success reflect concepts discussed throughout this Guide, such as high levels of trust, sharing of information, innovation, value addition, positioning collaboration, and risk mitigation. Blue Skies emphasizes prompt payment to farmers, the provision of training and education on EurepGAP standards, certification of farmers, interest-free loans for dedicated farmers, and willingness to improve local road infrastructure to improve access to farms by company trucks.

CONCLUSION

Blue Skies has been able to take advantage of strong market linkages with the European grocery sector, access to

In less than 48 hours, fresh organic pineapples are harvested in the mountains of Ghana and delivered to UK consumers.

Thursday

9:00 AM:	Pineapples are harvested in Akwapim Mountains (100 km west of Accra)
10:00 AM:	Men cut pineapples and women deliver them to collection point
10:30 AM:	Pineapples are sorted by class at collection point
12:00 PM:	Fruit is loaded onto trucks and heads to Blue Skies factory, 100 km away (2,000 pineapples per truck)
2:00 PM:	Pineapples arrive at factory and are processed
2:45 PM:	Pineapples roll off assembly line and are cleaned; "topped and tailed"; have their skin trimmed; weighed; sealed in Sainsbury-labeled (UK supermarket) tubs; put in holding chillers; and packed into cardboard boxes
7:00 PM:	Refrigerated load of pineapples leaves factory for 100 km journey to Accra

10:00 PM:	Boxes of pineapples are packed onto British Airways flight and take off for the United Kingdom

Friday

5:45 AM:	Pineapples arrive in London and go through customs
8:45 AM:	Pineapples are taken to British Airways perishables-handling center outside of London
9:30 AM:	Pineapples are taken out of cold storage and quality is inspected again
11:00 AM:	Sainsbury truck picks up pineapples and takes them to the supermarket's distribution center 58 km away
12:00 PM:	Fruit is sorted according to Sainsbury store orders

Saturday

4:00 AM:	Delivery to Sainsbury stores made
5:00 AM:	Fruit goes on sale in organic section
7:00 AM:	European shoppers begin to purchase pineapples
9:00 AM:	European consumers eat pineapples for breakfast

Source: Blue Skies corporate Web site, www.bsholdings.com.

---

information on innovative practices, and foreign capital and expertise. It has implemented a highly sophisticated production and quality control model and provided appropriate incentives and support to its suppliers. Blue Skies services a value-added portion of a large, highly competitive commodity market. Starting with the same raw material, the value chain and operating model of Blue Skies are very different from that which the Sea Freight Pineapple Exporters of Ghana has successfully implemented, which we will discuss in tool 7.

NOTES

1. GEPC News, http://www.gepcghana.com/news.php?item=4&n=.

2. Despite its contribution to exports, Farmapines's output has subsequently declined, and it is now a marginal contributor to sub-sector exports

3. Partnerships for Agribusiness Development, Agricultural Trade, and Market Access by TechnoServe for NEPAD, November 2004.

4. http://www.bsholdings.com/.

Horizontal Collaboration—Creating and Taking Advantage of Economies of Scale

Tool 6 focused on approaches to vertical integration within a value chain. Horizontal linkages also offer excellent opportunities for value chain participants to obtain scale advantages through interfirm coordination. By combining resources and sharing information, horizontal cooperation allows participating companies and producers to achieve improved quality, service, and savings through increased access to inputs, more leverage in sales negotiations, and greater ability to design initiatives that emphasize upgrading the value chain.

This tool focuses on the implementation of horizontal collaboration mechanisms and linkages among businesses to overcome problems stemming from small-scale activity by some individual producers or enterprises. This small scale prevents them, for example, from accessing inputs at optimum prices, from reducing the uneconomical unit costs of extension services, or from enjoying enhanced market power stemming from increased volumes of production and nonfragmented marketing.

Typical benefits of collaboration to achieve scale in transactions or operations include reduced costs from activities carried out jointly and increased access to more and better inputs and services, which enables more professional management and marketing due to greater affordability. Looking further, though, horizontal collaboration among enterprises creates a collaboration platform that could later allow the chain to move toward forward or backward integration (discussed in tool 6), or to achieve improved quality (tool 9). Business-to-business collaboration is certainly an approach that enterprises can and should explore independently. There is also potential for development partners and other facilitators to assist the value chain participants in recognizing and creating collaborations.

The first step for enterprises looking to implement horizontal linkages is to identify areas in which they can operate

jointly with increased efficiency and effectiveness. Typically, there will be many opportunities—in marketing, procurement of inputs, management, or logistics.

When enough enterprises have expressed interest in the idea of horizontal cooperation, some type of operational form, such as a simple agreement or a set of actions facilitated by a producers' association, formalizes the arrangement. The benefits of horizontal collaboration can lead to the creation of cooperatives, associations, or new companies, or toward the reorientation of existing organizations to perform the joint activity. For example, joint purchasing of inputs could form a basis for an inputs depot to be run by an association or as a jointly owned commercial venture in which many of the enterprises are represented. The need to obtain quality extension services can similarly be satisfied through a more developed member services association or cooperative. Joint marketing and logistics can lead to the creation of a collection center, which could be responsible for increasing product volume sales and thus obtaining better prices while reducing transportation costs when consolidating shipments. The center could be operated as a company or within a cooperative.

Economies of scale do not necessarily need to be developed through producer associations or cooperatives. Horizontal linkages are in many cases recognized, instigated, and organized by lead firms in the value chain.

A STEP-BY-STEP SUMMARY FOR TOOL 7: HORIZONTAL COLLABORATION—CREATING AND TAKING ADVANTAGE OF ECONOMIES OF SCALE

■ Identify areas in which enterprises performing similar activities in the chain can operate jointly with increased efficiency and effectiveness. Typically, many will be in marketing, procuring inputs, management, and logistics.

- Promote the idea to generate enterprise buy-in.

- Give operational form to the collaboration, such as through simple agreements, cooperative creation, new associations, or companies; reorient existing organizations to perform the joint activity.

Creating and Taking Advantage of Economies of Scale—The Ghana and Côte d'Ivoire Experiences in Fresh Pineapple Exports

Michael Gorman and Martin Webber
J. E. Austin Associates, Inc.

INTRODUCTION

The case accompanying tool 6 described a successful story of vertical integration within the Ghanaian pineapple value chain. This case looks at a story of achieving economies of scale within the same industry. Economies of scale characterize a production process in which an increase in the number of units produced or managed generates a decrease in the average cost per unit. Achieving economies of scale is important when the minimum units required to access desired inputs, services, technologies, or other capacities are quite large. Such minimums are required to dissipate the high usage or acquisition costs of a service or facility over a larger number of inputs in order to increase efficiency.

The term "reaching scale" refers to attaining a level of production that allows the addition of further investment or the incorporation of additional operations and also enables wholesale input procurement. Where individual actors lack such scale, collaborative mechanisms can substitute. In Ghana, pineapple exporters were required to reach substantial volumes (scale) before they were able to access sea-freight transportation. This case describes their success.

CÔTE D'IVOIRE: ORGANISATION CENTRALE DES PRODUCTEURS-EXPORTATEURS D'ANANAS ET DE BANANES

In 1999, Côte d'Ivoire was the largest horticulture exporter in West Africa, exporting US$140 million of fruits and vegetables, primarily bananas and pineapples. A brief look at Côte d'Ivoire in the 1980s and 1990s helps to put Ghana's actions in perspective (Minot and Ngigi 2003).

As a result of increased competition from Thailand, the collapse of state enterprises, and economic reforms that reduced subsidies, Côte d'Ivoire exports of canned pineapple and pineapple juice practically disappeared by the late 1980s. In response, much of Ivorian pineapple production switched over to the export of fresh pineapples to Europe by Sea Freight, using the same refrigerated freighters ("reefers") that are used to transport bananas. This move took advantage of Côte d'Ivoire's proximity to Europe, a factor much more important in the fresh pineapple trade than in the market for canned pineapple given spoilage considerations.

However, by the late 1980s, Côte d'Ivoire began to lose market share to fresh pineapple exporters in Central America and the Caribbean. After supplying close to 90 percent of the European market for fresh pineapple in the mid-1980s, Côte d'Ivoire's market share fell to two-thirds in 1990 (Rougé and N'Goan 1997). But the 1990s also brought several changes favorable to the Ivorian fruit and vegetable export industry.

First, in the 1990s, the Organisation Centrale des Producteurs-Exportateurs d'Ananas et de Bananes (OCAB) was formed to represent the interests of exporters, set quality standards, and facilitate communication. OCAB has reduced the number of "approved" exporters of fruit in an attempt to maintain quality standards. It also organizes the charter of refrigerated ships to transport bananas and pineapples to Europe. Second, in 1993, after much debate, Europe harmonized its banana import policies to make way for the single European market and continued granting former colonies preferred access to its markets. Third, the 50 percent devaluation of the CFA franc in January 1994 helped stimulate the economy, particularly the export sectors.

The net impact of these three factors was that banana exports grew from 95,000 mt in 1990 to 215,000 mt in 1999, while fresh pineapple exports expanded from 135,000 mt to 183,000 mt over the same period (FAOSTAT data 2002). Côte d'Ivoire became the second largest fresh pineapple exporter in the world after Costa Rica (Ti 2000). It is estimated that approximately 35,000 people are employed by the banana and pineapple plantations.

In pineapple production, smallholders continue to dominate. Seventy percent of Ivorian pineapple exports are produced by smallholders on farms of 0.5–10 hectares. The remaining 30 percent is produced by large plantations, including some owned by vertically integrated banana companies such as Compagnie Fruitière and Chiquita. One reason for the greater involvement of smallholders in pineapple production compared with banana production is that the initial investment cost of establishing a plot is estimated to be three to four times greater for bananas (Rougé and Goan 1997).

Several factors lay behind the past success of fruit and vegetable exports from Côte d'Ivoire. First, Côte d'Ivoire had long been known for its political stability. Second, President Houphouet-Boigny had, for the most part, supported agriculture-led growth. Third, Côte d'Ivoire had benefited from its proximity to European markets since it is just 8 to 10 days by sea freighter from Marseilles. Although it also benefits from frequent air connections with Paris, this factor was less important since most Ivorian fruit and vegetable exports have been via Sea Freight. Fourth, the government had relatively limited involvement in production and marketing, particularly in the horticulture sector.

However, with Côte d'Ivoire's current political instability, much of the fresh pineapple exporting industry has shifted to more stable locations such as Ghana.

THE SEA FREIGHT PINEAPPLE EXPORT VALUE CHAIN

The Sea Freight Pineapple Exporters of Ghana was formed in 1995 by Integral Ghana Ltd., Jei River Farms, and John Lawrence Farms[1] to develop sea freight shipments of fresh pineapples from Ghana (see figure 4.32). SPEG chose Union Bananière Africaine (UBA/Dole) of France that same year to

Figure 4.32 Ghana's Pineapple Value Chain

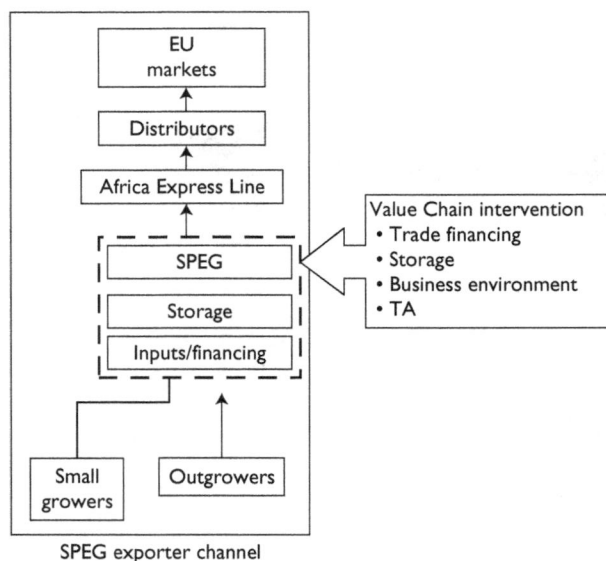

Source: J. E. Austin Associates, Inc.

provide freight services to the Ghanaian industry. The UBA boats are refrigerated vessels transporting bananas from Cameroon, and operators allocate space for Ghana's pineapples based on available free space after the banana loads. Travel times to southern and northern EU destinations are 9 and 13 days, respectively.

Since its formation, and the introduction of sea-freighting, SPEG has become a driving force in the Ghanaian pineapple industry and has been profitable from its inception. As a result, its membership increased from three in 1995 to 22 by mid-2005 (Danielou and Ravry 2005). Pineapple exports from Ghana have increased from 15,764 tons valued at US$5.6 million in 1995 to 57,392 tons valued at US$18.3 million in 2003. The percentage of sea-freighted exports to total pineapple exports increased from 17 percent in 1995 to 68 percent in 2003. At its peak, Ghanaian pineapple exporters had access to two vessels on a regular weekly basis to the European ports of Vado and Vendres in the south and to Port Antwerp in the north. That particular supply chain has subsequently atrophied. Ships now arrive on a less regular basis, with vessels from Cameroon bypassing Ghana.

The availability of regular vessel services since 1995 has benefited all producers. Large-, medium-, and small-scale producers expanded production and generated increases in farm-level incomes and employment. The 10 largest exporters controlled about 71 percent of total exports in 2004 (TechnoServe 2004).

Although initial pineapple exports from Ghana were private sector initiatives, the Ghanaian government is also supporting sea-freighting by dedicating a facility at Port Tema for the consolidation of shipments. Ghana's government and industry players have successfully constructed one handling facility at Port Tema, although the details on who will manage and operate the shed are still being negotiated. The government is also planning a second holding facility at the airport. This facility is planned to be compliant with GlobalGAP rules.

BENEFITS FROM BUSINESS PARTNERSHIPS

The most important partnership developed over the past nine years is the SPEG-Union Bananière Africaine (now Africa Express Line) arrangement for the sea-freighting of pineapples. This strong partnership has ensured the availability of regular vessel services since 1995.

Polycraft, a local carton manufacturer, is also working with SPEG to provide its members with 35 percent of packaging requirements. SPEG also undertakes bulk procurement of agrochemicals from suppliers such as Wienco, Chemico, and Dizengoff for distribution to its members. On average, SPEG budgets about US$50,000 toward the purchase of agrochemicals for its members. The prices that members pay are about 10 percent below market price but include a small margin to cover administrative costs.

SPEG's success in increasing Ghana's primary pineapple exports was at least partially due to the development of sea freight capacity. Another success factor in the industry was Ghana's proximity to the market.

The early airfreighting of Ghana's pineapple exports was attractive because the fruit could arrive at the EU market in six hours. Sea Freight extended shipping periods to between 9 and 13 days to southern and northern EU ports, respectively. Ghana had logistical advantages over Latin American exporters (who have longer shipment periods of 16–20 days to the EU) until recently due to the EU's new preference for the MD2 pineapple, which Ghana was not producing.

In 2005, Ghana lost considerable market share due to its decision not to invest in the MD2 varietal. However, since the

Figure 4.33 Ghana's European Pineapple Exports

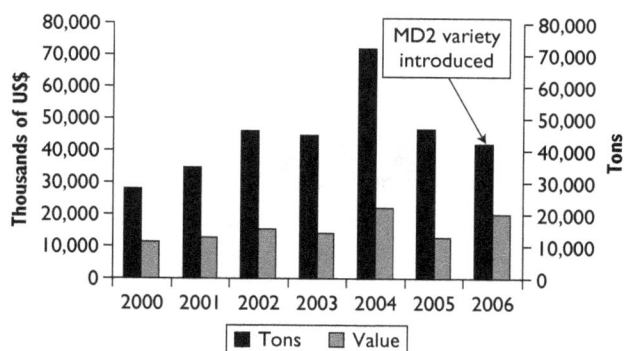

Source: Ghana Exporters Promotion Council.

adoption of MD2, Ghana's pineapple quality and presentation are now up to EU standards and its export revenues have increased in per unit value (see figure 4.33; this topic is further discussed in tool 6).

CONCLUSION

During the period from 1995 through 2006, SPEG was able to increase its share of the expanding European pineapple market by building scale through leveraging its relative logistical competitive advantages over its Latin American counterparts. SPEG is also working with its members to meet EurepGAP standards and implement new traceability, certification schemes and other standards and to provide other services.

NOTE

1. SPEG was formed with support from the Ghanaian government and USAID under the Trade and Investment Program (TIP). The TIP provided technical staff during SPEG's three formative years to oversee the coordination of sea shipments. Ghana's government leased a shed at Port Tema to SPEG solely for the consolidation of fruits before shipment.

Creating and Taking Advantage of Economies of Scale within the Mozambican Cashew Value Chain

Carlton Jones and Martin Webber
J. E. Austin Associates, Inc.

INTRODUCTION

This case demonstrates how firms identified common areas for collaboration and created an association in the Mozambican cashew value chain that enabled the companies to achieve economies of scale in operations. Revisiting the example presented in Tool 5, Identifying Business Models for Replication, this case looks at an analysis commissioned by USAID of value addition opportunities in the Mozambican value chain aimed at revitalizing the country's processing capacity. In the analysis, lead firms were identified to establish new processing centers, and once operational, this model was replicated and implemented by other processors. Those same processors experienced bottlenecks in the value chain and came together to address those constraints through economies of scale. These economies are realized when horizontal linkages occur, and the linkages are most likely to be successful when there is a common platform from which firms can operate. In this instance, Mozambican processors were willing to organize and identified areas in which to jointly operate, creating an association that carried out those shared functions.

POINTS TO CONSIDER

While reading this case, consider the environment and actors that drove the processors to consider organizing, the steps they took, and the benefits they realized once the association was established. There are three principal benefits to horizontal linkages: 1) lower costs, 2) access to services or inputs that are not easily acquired by an individual processor, and 3) pursuit of initiatives that are difficult for processors to accomplish on their own.

Also consider the services offered by the association, as they are good examples of market-driven (demand-side) services that have a stronger likelihood of being sustainable.

BACKGROUND

From the 1920s until the mid-1970s, Mozambique was considered the world's leading cashew producer (240,000 mt at its peak in 1973; TechnoServe 2004) with a considerable domestic capacity for processing quality cashews. In 1978, the government of Mozambique banned the export of raw nuts in an attempt to stimulate domestic processing. Within a few years, Mozambique had over a dozen processing factories and was the first African country to process cashews on an industrial scale. But by 1994, after a variety of events—including a civil war, the adoption of policies that fixed raw nut prices, and the continuation of the raw nut export ban—the cashew sector collapsed (see figure 4.35; FAOSTAT 2003). At the end of the civil war, those policies were abandoned, and the government of Mozambique hoped to reclaim its past reputation of progress by investing heavily in large-scale mechanical processing facilities. Unfortunately, the government also

Figure 4.34   Regions of Mozambique

Source: World Bank.

introduced a high tax on raw nut exports with the goal of pushing the entire industry to domestic processing.

In 1995, the Mozambican government liberalized the cashew sector to meet World Bank conditions for continued loans. (The rationale for this approach was highlighted in the discussion of tool 5.) The reduction of export tariffs did, in fact, increase prices slightly, but it also led to the closure of Mozambican processing factories. With those factories closed, Mozambique's cashew sector entered another decline. By the late 1990s, instead of a vibrant value-added cashew sector, Mozambique exported most of its nuts—raw—to India for processing and value addition.

Seeing an opportunity to assist, USAID commissioned TechnoServe to conduct a cashew subsector analysis, seeking to identify innovative ways to revitalize the industry and maximize benefits to small growers. As discussed in tool 5, a model version of a small hand-processing plant was designed, piloted, and, by 2004, replicated.

The first successful plant, Miranda Caju, provided the replicable business model on which all other plants in Nampula province were based. Afterward, even though processors were established and growing, they still relied heavily on technical assistance. In examining the sector's long-term viability, the processors recognized other extension-service needs that were not being met.

As other small hand-processors entered the market, stakeholders realized that to ensure long-term sustainability of the entire value chain, these extension services needed to be fee-based rather than subsidized. Unfortunately, if the extension services were provided at full price, only Miranda Caju could pay the fees and still operate profitably. This scenario

Figure 4.35   Mozambican Cashew Exports, 1961–2000

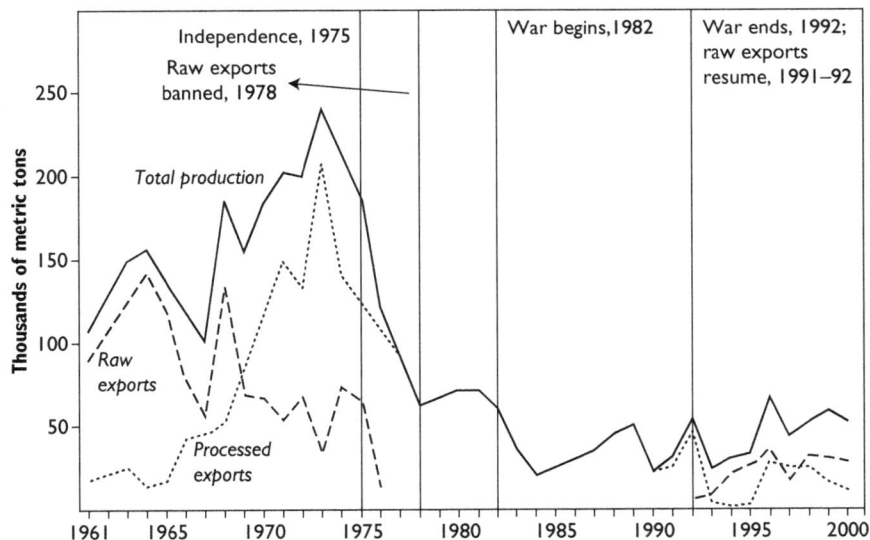

Source: FAOSTAT, Ana Machalela, INCAJU statistician, e-mail communication, July 2001; Raimundo Matule, deputy director of INCAJU, e-mail communications, September 2001 and May 2003. As adopted by McMillan, Welch and Rodrik (2003).

encouraged the processors to link horizontally to distribute the cost of extension services. Better still, this seemed to be a good business opportunity for a firm to provide these services to all processors as the sector continued to expand.

MOZAMBICAN CASHEW PROCESSORS LINK HORIZONTALLY

With the assistance of TechnoServe, Miranda Caju's president and founder, Antonio Miranda, considered by his peers to be an industry leader, brought together Nampula province's other processors to discuss jointly creating a private firm to provide services to everyone in the sector. This lead firm would provide valuable services to processors that would otherwise have a difficult time accessing them. These meetings led to the formation of Agro Industria Associadas (AIA).

SERVICES PROVIDED BY AIA

AIA began in 2004 as a private sector–led services firm comprising seven processor firms in Nampula. Each processor contributed US$500 of seed money to start the firm and was considered an equal owning partner. AIA selected a president, Ali Cherif Deroua, and now provides the services once provided by a consulting firm. Some services are fee based, while others are nonfee based. AIA's fee-based services fall into three main categories: processing, distribution, and marketing. AIA provides the following nonfee services: training, branding, and advocacy.

Its processing services include importing non-nut inputs like packaging and machinery. Distribution services include warehousing and load consolidation at Port Nacala and completing and filing paperwork for export administration. In marketing, AIA provides fee-based services such as selling (order-filling) to global buyers and providing pre-shipment quality control. These quality control measures include ensuring Hazard Analysis and Critical Control Point (HACCP) and EurepGAP compliance by adopting a "three strikes, and you're out" cut rate for suppliers. In this system, suppliers are encouraged to improve their quality measures or risk being excluded from the supply chain if they incur three quality infractions. Adopting this system has reduced instances of poor quality and increased export prices.

AIA provides marketing intelligence to its members through training seminars and advocates on behalf of members by engaging in public-private dialogue. In the past, these discussions have included negotiating with the government of Mozambique for targeted infrastructure investments and improving market regulations. With outside technical assistance, AIA is advocating for a gradual reduction of the export tax on raw nuts, which, at 18 percent, penalizes farmers and hampers competitiveness. In addition to providing these services to existing processor members, AIA also actively recruits and trains new processors.

Branding is one of the most interesting services AIA provides. Again, with outside technical assistance, AIA created the "Zambique" cashew brand. This brand was created to draw international awareness and interest to Mozambican cashews, especially from U.S. buyers.

HOW HORIZONTAL LINKAGES BENEFIT THE MOZAMBICAN CASHEW VALUE CHAIN

With AIA now providing much-needed services to small Mozambican processors (figure 4.36), the following benefits have been realized.

- *Improved quality control.* Through AIA, quality has improved and poor-quality claims have been reduced by over 50 percent. In 2005, 26 containers were cited as having quality problems, while in 2006, only 12 were. It is estimated that this reduction saved producers approximately US$35,000 from 2005 to 2006.
- *Speedier and cheaper access to inputs.* Before AIA, it was nearly impossible to ask for duty exemptions. To qualify for duty exemptions, a processor had to export all imported items within three months. This did not match normal business needs because processing volumes in a year's time were less than a container load, so processors typically could only import their packing needs once a year and not qualify for the exemptions (see table 4.12).

  With AIA, processors were able to combine orders to use temporary import-duty exemptions (IVA – 17 percent + duty 7.5 percent). AIA was also able to reduce shipping freight for its members. Before AIA, the average cost of exports per kilogram (kg) of kernels was US$0.38, while after AIA, this cost dropped to US$0.27, and then again in 2006 to US$0.17 (see table 4.13).
- *Improved market linkages and information sharing.* With AIA, processors now have a timely and credible supplier in the market. AIA carefully selects sea lines and transit shipments, while keeping daily track of all containers. Not only are these shipping records shared among AIA members, AIA also sends reports containing updates on sales, stocks, and receivables to banks on a weekly basis. This has helped banks feel more comfortable about the perceived risks associated with the sector and has made

Figure 4.36   Domestic Value Chain for Mozambican Cashews

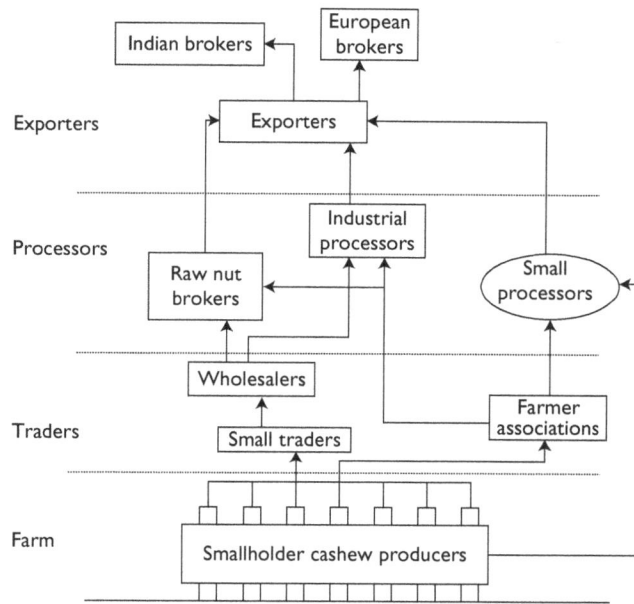

Source: J. E. Austin Associates, Inc.

Table 4.12	Cost of Packing Material before and after AIA	
Item	**Cost before AIA**	**Cost after AIA**
Plastic bags	Bad quality and repacking rate of 12 percent = US$0.72	Good quality and repacking rate of 5.3 percent = US$0.52
Cartons	3-ply (considered too thin) = US$1.10	5-ply with 4 colors and printed Zambique logo = US$0.085

Source: TechnoServe 2007.

Table 4.13	Cost of Shipping before and after AIA	
Item	**Cost before AIA**	**Cost after AIA**
Container to Rotterdam	US$1,850	US$1,450
Port and service costs	US$920	US$750–800

Source: TechnoServe 2007.

credit applications a little easier to file. This improved access to information would not have been possible for individual processors, although information is not the only thing shared among AIA members. Today, the improved communication and collaboration among AIA members has also translated into an atmosphere of cooperation between firms. When one member experiences shortage of an input, other AIA members pitch in to provide those supplies, recognizing that as each firm gets stronger, the entire industry benefits.

■ *Improved industry image through "Zambique" brand.* Time will tell how successful the introduction of a brand will be and how it will impact the Mozambican cashew sector. Early indications suggest that a unified brand has helped buyers recognize that small processors in Mozambique have improved their quality. The brand has certainly improved the solidarity of members within the sector.

LESSONS LEARNED

Horizontal collaboration mechanisms, such as those of AIA members, demonstrate the benefits of joint operation. Increasing producers' market power, enhancing their market linkages, and improving quality are all benefits that other industries can consider when seeking to improve their value chains through horizontal linkage.

Positioning Products and Value Chains for Greater Value and Competitiveness

Building on several of the tools already described, a competitiveness positioning assessment provides strategic direction to many of the actions that the value chain implements to improve its competitiveness. This assessment and collaborative decision making inform the value chain's leadership about the value chain's product offerings, relative to competitors, in key markets. It also forms the foundation for developing a strategic vision and a clear, actionable plan for repositioning the industry in current markets and for penetrating new ones.

POSITIONING THE VALUE CHAIN

In a simple 2 x 2 matrix, the product or service of a company, value chain, or industry can be described in terms of product scope (complexity, value addition) and product differentiation (special qualities, lack of direct competitors). Products and services in the lower left are basic commodities, subject to severe price competition and very restricted profit margins. Products in the upper left have a lot of value added but may still be under severe price competition. Products to the extreme right are highly differentiated and, in that respect, may be able to command higher prices and margins but have little value added. Of course, products and services in the top right are in "competitiveness nirvana," commanding high prices and margins because of their complexity and special qualities in the customer's eye—all assuming, of course, that there is sufficient market demand to interest the value chain participant.

One challenge for value chain participants is to decide where to position the chain's products or services. Where is the product currently positioned in the domestic or global market? Where do we want it to be—and what are the quality, service, and other requirements to be competitive in that positioning? What are the best global performers in any of the positions doing to be competitive? What are the profit margins and likely market demand at each position? Who will our competition be?

In the case of the cashmere industry (see figure 4.37), Mongolia produces the world's best quality raw cashmere (wool from a breed of small goats) in the world. Mongolia produces very few value-added products (and virtually none of quality), so substantial exports are only in the form of raw cashmere or yarn. Mongolia exports most of its cashmere to processors in Italy and Scotland, where the cashmere is processed and transformed into extremely high-value garments and fashions. Figure 4.37 illustrates Mongolia's position in the world cashmere market relative to major competitors and partners, with differentiation represented on the x-axis and product scope represented on the y-axis. (Note that this is an application of benchmarking introduced in tool 3). Each country's market share as measured in revenues is represented by the relative size of the circles. In most cases, higher profit per unit (and certainly higher prices per unit) is implied by a position in the top right corner. However, it is important for this graph to be interpreted in the context of local market conditions and the overall profit and profitability of the activity.[1] While the upper right quadrant is generally associated with high profitability, operations in the lower left may find that high volumes of low value production may generate total profits that outweigh the premium pricing available at other positions.

China was also a major producer of finished cashmere products, but of lower quality than those produced in Scotland and Italy. Seeking new and inexpensive sources of cashmere wool for their high-volume business, Chinese cashmere buyers competed with domestic wholesalers for Mongolian wool stocks. However, Chinese buyers had no incentive to encourage high quality as they planned to feed low value-added industrial garment makers in China. Their advantage in the purchasing marketplace was to offer

In some cases, potential value exists in the value chain and needs only to be unlocked. This can be achieved either by movement toward higher scope or toward product differentiation. Ecuador's cacao industry illustrates this principle.

Ecuador's cacao industry has made advancements in processing and value added that enabled producers to export higher quality cacao and receive premium prices.

The improvements in value enabled a repositioning of the higher quality portion of the Ecuadorian product, and these are being supported by promotional and market channel actions. Historically, Ecuador has received a US$20–US$100 premium over the baseline market price. However, the flavor profile of Ecuadorian cacao is so desirable in today's consumer market that it commands a premium of US$800–US$1,200 per ton.[a]

Premiums for Several Countries' Cacao Products

Country	Premium over market price, May 4, 2007 (per ton, US$)
Venezuela (dried and fermented)	2,000
Java (dried and fermented)	2,000
Ecuador (dried and partially fermented)	800—1,200
Ivory Coast (dried and fermented)	320
Dominican Republic (dried and unfermented)	280
Ghana (dried and fermented)	250

Source: Blommer Chocolate.

Among the companies currently buying cacao from Ecuador is Blommer Chocolate Company, a large manufacturer that purchases raw cacao for grinding and processing into chocolate products. It is the largest buyer in Ecuador and the largest raw cacao processor in the United States. Blommer customers include large, well-known companies and brands such as Mars, Nestlé, and Hershey, among others. Blommer is pleased with the quality of cacao that they are able to purchase from Ecuadorian producers who have been trained through the Farmer Field Schools. Blommer previously used Ecuadorian cacao in a wide variety of dark chocolate products, but because of its premium qualities, Blommer has recently been using Ecuadorian cacao for producing high-end, single-origin dark chocolate.

Single-origin dark chocolate can be a branded, value-added product because buyers are looking for the specific Ecuadorian flavor profile. One indication of the repositioning of the value chain toward greater value and competitiveness is the fact that single-origin chocolate from Ecuador is being sold in international markets at a substantial premium. Additionally, the government of Ecuador (GoE), with support from the Inter-American Development Bank, is promoting Ecuadorian cacao in global, high-end niche markets. Also in line with the repositioning, Ecuadorian farmers and the GoE are encouraging the cultivation and maintenance of Ecuador's heritage cacao trees, which produce the highly desired flavor profile.

Source: Lisa Carse and Martin Webber, J. E. Austin Associates, Inc.
[a] Author interview with Karl Walk, purchaser for Blommer Chocolate, 2007.

immediate cash. With this incentive, Mongolian herdsmen were ready to sell to Chinese buyers. The perceived need to protect breed and wool quality suffered among herdsmen selling to undiscerning Chinese markets.

Mongolia's downstream buyers recognized an opportunity to increase the Mongolian product's quality differentiation by offering price incentives for higher quality and by implementing both a mark (certification) of quality

Leveraging Other Value Chain Initiatives

Box 4.10 illustrated the concept of the hidden potential in value chains. Key to realizing hidden potential in value chains is the pursuit of greater product scope and differentiation. Thailand's Good Agricultural Practices (GAP) cluster is an excellent example of such an attempt.

Thailand's agricultural sector is an important contributor to its economy. Thailand has one of the most developed agricultural product sectors in Southeast Asia and has been a net exporter of agricultural products for decades. It is known in international markets for the quality of its fresh and processed products, and producers from both developed and developing countries view it as a strong competitor.

The Thai GAP cluster carried out a major program to implement EurepGAP standards in western Thailand to gain export certification to service its traditional European supermarket business (discussed in tool 9, box 4.12). The GAP cluster wanted to further leverage its achievement of EurepGAP standards in domestic Thai markets that have similar market requirements. Thailand has many large super- and hypermarkets in its urban areas, including foreign-owned retail outlets like Tesco and Carrefour that desire similar quality products for their customers.

Product Positioning

Although value chain processes produced a quality product that conformed to tough European standards, the Thai GAP cluster wanted to position those same quality products within local super- and hypermarkets in Thai urban areas. This would support a market diversification strategy that reduces the risks of relying on exports linked to its investments in upgrading. The cluster took some of the following initiatives to position itself as a quality vegetable producer:

Source: Mike Ducker, J. E. Austin Associates, Inc.

1. **Branding and certification**: The cluster created the western cluster GAP logo and a grading process for its products, which was approved and certified by the Department of Agriculture. The logo and standards appear on all producers' packaging, and farmers are encouraged to promote the brand. The cluster has also done some local advertising of this brand name.
2. **Unique shelf space**: The cluster was able to work with supermarkets to gain dedicated shelf space for its vegetables. This separated its products from the open-air vegetables. This space was also branded with point-of-purchase (PoP) displays.
3. **Packaging**: The cluster created unique packaging that highlighted product freshness and high quality, and it was also used to promote ready-to-eat vegetables that were in demand by time-conscious urban professionals.

Summary

To leverage the quality improvements made within the value chain, the cluster positioned itself within local markets that had similar requirements as export markets by using branding, certification, unique shelf space, and packaging that promoted quality and freshness. These improvements are estimated to have generated a 50 percent increase in farmers' bottom lines.

Businesses must make these choices with purpose, or they will simply be out-positioned by their competitors or buyers, which makes understanding the competition a critical aspect of repositioning as well. Movements to new positions do not have to happen instantly, and it is often most appropriate to adopt changes incrementally, for example, by adding differentiation through higher quality or better variety, and then adding product scope through processing or improved packaging.

and a Mongolian brand. At the same time, design and manufacture of cashmere products in Mongolia was encouraged, which added value within the Mongolian industry.

The Mongolian cashmere industry understood the actions necessary to change its positioning in the value chain and acted to move to "the right" (greater differentiation) and "upward" (more value added)—a more lucrative positioning with less exposure to competitive pressures.

Once an objective is determined, value chain participants must decide which actions are necessary to achieve the desired positioning. Boxes 4.10 and 4.11 provide brief examples; case study 10 examines a case more deeply.

Figure 4.37 Product Positioning—Mongolian Cashmere Industry

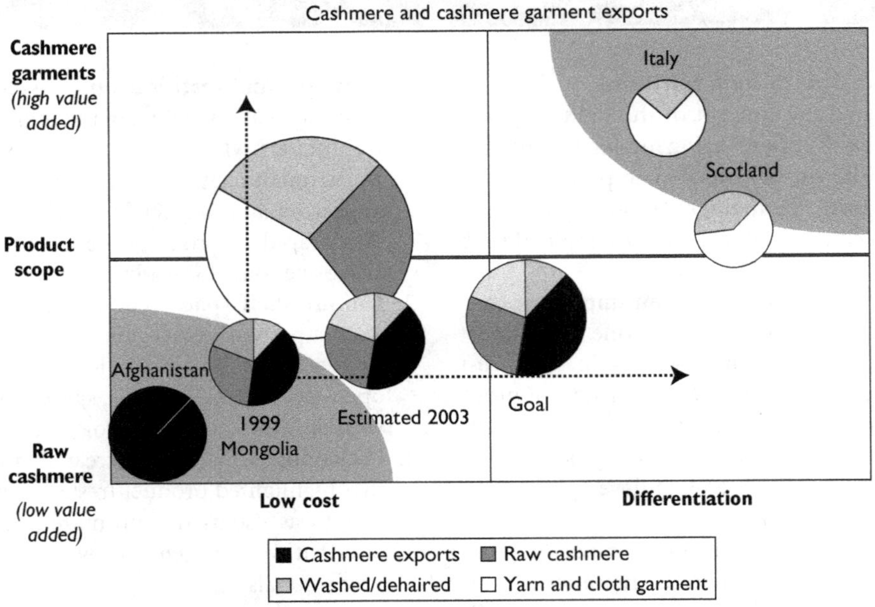

Cashmere and cashmere garment exports

Source: Nathan Associates Inc. and J. E. Austin Associates, Inc. for USAID.

A STEP-BY-STEP SUMMARY OF TOOL 8: POSITIONING PRODUCTS AND VALUE CHAINS FOR GREATER VALUE AND COMPETITIVENESS

- Assess and benchmark size and share of market. Collect net sales for each product segment and each competitor in each product segment.
- Assess and benchmark product scope (or product "offer"). Collect industry value added for each product and competitors' products. If industry value added is not available at the product level, the number and type of value-added activities taking place in-country can be substituted.
- Assess and benchmark product differentiation. Product differentiation should be measured by a combination of both the average price point at a given level of value addition, as well as specific product attributes and customer perceptions of the sources of product value. Product attributes and customer perceptions are qualitative measurements but can be assessed quantitatively through market research tools, such as consumer surveys.
- Understand the possibilities and requirements for repositioning the product, and develop a repositioning strategy. Repositioning a product in a more competitive space requires a combination of activities that both enhance

product differentiation and increase in-country, value-added activities.

NOTE

1. Once completed, the graph is strategically revealing; however, compiling the information for the analysis is not straightforward, apart from the size and segmentation of the circles. Once basic sales data are compiled for the value chain's key product segments, the circles must then be positioned on the graph. If available, the most accurate data to measure product scope is industry value added. In some cases, reliable data on value added for a specific industry may not be available. In this case, product scope can be gauged by assessing the numbers and types of value-added activities that occur in-country. Product differentiation can be measured in a number of different ways. Market price can be a reflection of the differentiation of a product in a given market, but this is not always the case. Also, at the aggregated level, average price across a number of markets can be diluted and mask differentiation. As a result, differentiation should be measured by a combination of both the average price point at a given level of value addition as well as specific product attributes and customer perception of the sources of product value. Product attributes and customer perception are qualitative measurements but can still be measured through market research tools such as customer surveys.

Value Chain Strategies for Market Repositioning—Rwandan Coffee

Carlton Jones and Martin Webber
J. E. Austin Associates, Inc.

INTRODUCTION

In the 1990s, export revenues from coffee, an important source of hard currency for Rwanda, declined. This case discusses a government-led initiative to improve the competitive position of Rwandan coffee. Before 2001, Rwanda was an unknown in the specialty/high-value coffee sector. Today, it is a sought-after supplier of specialty coffees to Europe and the United States. This case touches upon the successes of the government of Rwanda's initiative and also speculates about the likely outcomes if the government had more closely followed its own strategy.

FACTORS TO CONSIDER

When reviewing this case, it is important to keep these questions in mind:

- Where is Rwandan coffee positioned currently, and what factors influence that position?
- Where does the industry want to go, and what are the quality, service, and other requirements to make it competitive in that positioning?
- Who are the best global performers, and what puts them in this position?
- What price points and profit margins exist in the various quadrants?

BACKGROUND (1904–2001)

Coffee was introduced in Rwanda in 1904 and was first exported in 1917; it was quickly seen as a major source of income for the country. In 1933, the cultivation of coffee was made compulsory, and, in 1963, the government of Rwanda passed laws making it illegal to uproot coffee trees.

Because of coffee's historical role as a principal source of foreign exchange for the country (averaging 56.7 percent of all exports in the 1990s) and its broad political support, the state was heavily involved in all stages of production, including marketing and dry milling. Nearly all production of coffee ceased, however, during the genocide of 1994. Regionally, Rwanda competed with its southern neighbor Burundi, yet Burundi's coffee was considered to be slightly better in quality than that of Rwanda. Neither country produced coffee that was considered specialty grade, as in Ethiopia and Kenya. Despite the fact that some of the coffee grown in Rwanda, such as the Bourbon varietal, had specialty grade potential, all of Rwanda's coffee was considered below commodity grade, and, when exported, was only used by roasters in blends of low-end, mass-produced coffee destined for Europe and the United States (table 4.14; figure 4.38).

Within the value chain, the GoR supported the coffee industry by establishing OCIR-CAFÉ (Rwanda Coffee Development Authority) and through it, distributed seedlings, fertilizer, phytosanitary products, and other inputs to growers for free or at dramatically reduced prices.

Figure 4.38   Rwanda's Coffee Product Position, 1990–2000

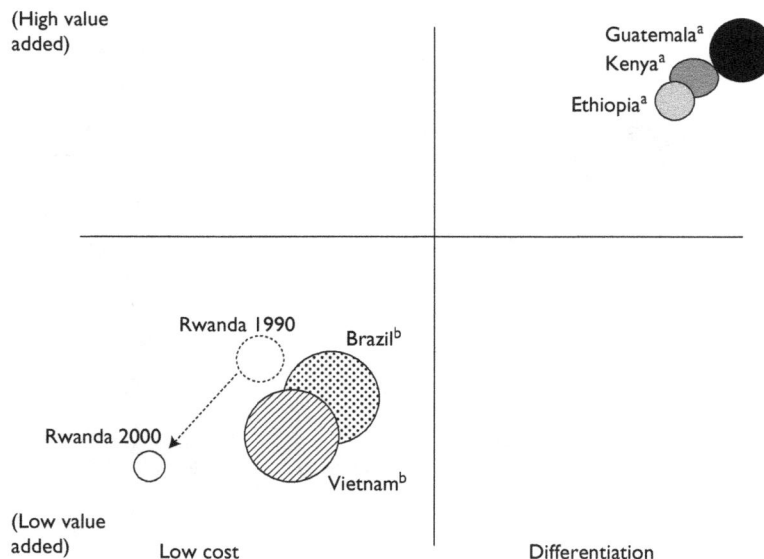

(High value added)

Guatemala[a]
Kenya[a]
Ethiopia[a]

Rwanda 1990
Brazil[b]

Rwanda 2000
Vietnam[b]

(Low value added)

Low cost   Differentiation

Source: J. E. Austin Associates, Inc.
[a] Represents specialty coffee/not drawn to scale.
[b] Represents commodity coffee/not drawn to scale.

Table 4.14   Rwandan Coffee Production

	1986	1987	1988	1989	1990	1992	1993	1995	1996
Production (metric tons)	35,424	43,026	43,026	39,091	39,575	38,970	28,495	21,829	15,239
Standard coffee (percentage)	48.18	30.8	19.4	2	7	0.32	4.25	2.4	0.25
Ordinary coffee[a] (percentage)	38.59	60.2	75.7	94.7	86.9	93	88.7	92.7	82.9

Source: OCIR-CAFÉ 2006.
[a] Ordinary coffee is nonexport grade, while standard coffee is exportable, commodity grade coffee. Neither is considered specialty grade.

Growers would apply the inputs to their crops and harvest, and sell semiwashed beans to RWANDEX, the monopoly responsible for dry milling and exporting coffee. The GoR was a majority owner of RWANDEX and set the prices that growers received from their coffee sales. In fact, the GoR continued to set prices for coffee up until 1998. Though coffee producer associations existed in Rwanda, they were agents of the state that distributed inputs and did little else.

GLOBAL COMPETITION DRIVES DOWN PRICES AND PRODUCTION

Coffee's contribution to Rwanda's foreign exchange declined in the 1990s. Production declined both before and after the 1994 genocide, even as world prices reached near record highs. During the same period, Vietnam and Brazil responded to high prices by increasing output of commodity grade coffee. Beginning in 1997, this growth of supply dropped worldwide prices to historic lows. By 2001, average global coffee prices were US$0.52/lb. Rwanda received US$0.40/kg (US$0.18/lb.), which, on average, was below the price of production. With prices this low, each actor in the Rwandan coffee value chain lost money: small growers, processors, exporters, and even the banks that provided lending.[1]

RWANDA'S IN-COUNTRY CONSTRAINTS

World coffee prices were not the only determining factor for the decline in Rwanda's coffee industry; the country's coffee

production never recovered to 1992 production volumes (table 4.14) because its existing production process was inefficient. This resulted from Rwanda's disparate methods of coffee farming, the poor health of its coffee trees, the lack of wet-milling stations, and the absence of incentives for reinvestment. Growers were not offered higher prices for better-quality beans, so they had little reason to invest in more sophisticated processes of production, harvesting, cleaning, or separation of their bean harvests. Low coffee yields coupled with poor price points influenced farmers to focus on other, higher-margin crops, further diminishing Rwandan coffee's competitiveness in world markets.

Despite the constraints that led Rwanda to produce low-quality, low-quantity, commodity grade coffee, the GoR and donor partners believed that Rwanda possessed the capacity, environmental conditions (elevation, climate, soil quality, Bourbon trees, and others), and political will to improve its coffee position in world markets. What Rwanda lacked was technical capacity, market information, and a coherent strategy.

REPOSITIONING THE OFFER FOR RWANDAN COFFEE

In response to the steady declines in production, quality, and export revenue, the GoR and its donor partners began strategy sessions aimed at improving Rwandan coffee's positioning in world markets. These sessions resulted in coffee-sector liberalization strategies that, when implemented, began the task of improving Rwandan coffee. Armed with market information, the private sector learned that higher-value coffee was very attractive to global markets, that cupping/taste results indicated Rwanda had significant potential to produce specialty coffee, and that Rwanda could compete with higher-end producers such as Ethiopia, Guatemala, and Kenya. The Rwandan repositioning strategy is illustrated in figure 4.39.

Contributing to Rwandan coffee repositioning

For Rwanda to move from being considered a commodity grade to a specialty grade coffee producer, its coffee-producing sector needed to address three key areas:

- **Increase production, since production levels were insufficient to attract global demand.** Activities included distributing improved inputs, supporting growing associations, replanting coffee trees, and constructing wet-mill stations in Rwanda's top 50 coffee-producing districts.
- **Improve quality.** Activities included educating producers on quality and cupping, establishing quality-control mechanisms, investing and technical assistance in wet-mill techniques and operational and financial management,

Figure 4.39 Rwanda's Coffee Positioning Goals for 2010

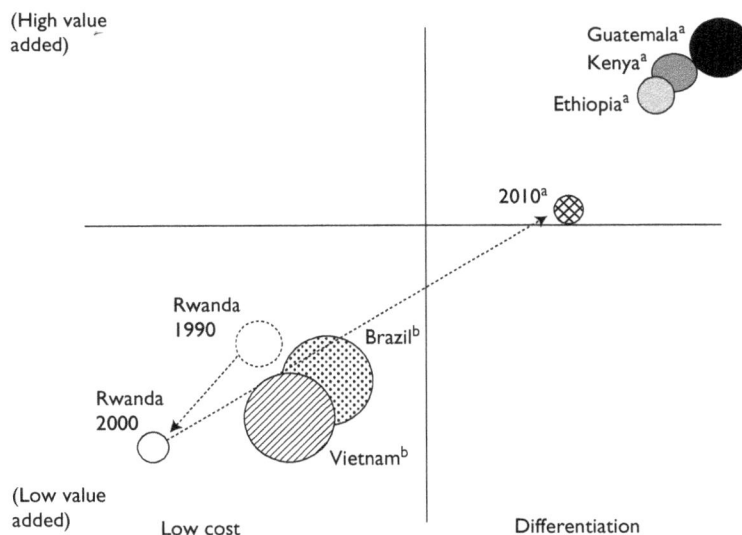

Source: J. E. Austin Associates, Inc.
[a] Represents specialty coffee/not drawn to scale.
[b] Represents commodity coffee/not drawn to scale.

Figure 4.40   Generic Coffee Value Chain

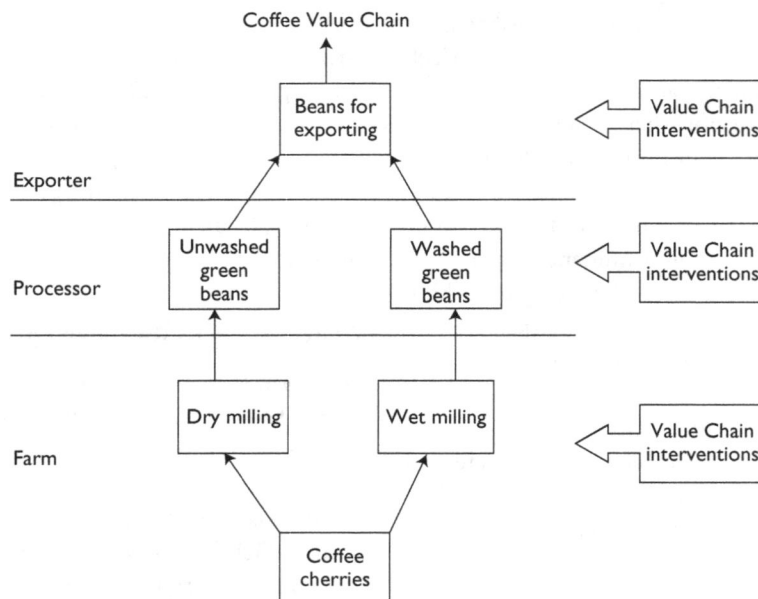

Source: J. E. Austin Associates, Inc.

improving infrastructure, strengthening cooperative and association management, strengthening existing institutions (like OCIR-CAFÉ), and providing financial mechanisms throughout the coffee value chain.

■ **Promote the Rwandan brand.** Activities included establishing and improving market linkages through trade-show visits, sharing information about the local and global coffee markets with the private sector, and instituting other innovative promotional activities.

These activities were carried out through a variety of implementing partners and sponsored by various donor partners (see figure 4.40).

IMPLEMENTATION AND OUTCOMES

Through these interventions, Rwanda was effectively able to reposition its coffee and compete in higher-grade, higher-priced markets (see figure 4.41; tables 4.15 and 4.16). July 2002 saw the country's first sales of commercial volumes of specialty coffee, including a sale of 33 mt to Community Coffee in the United States. By March of the following year, privately financed and operated wet-mill facilities produced fully washed coffee. Production and quality continued to increase, and after visits to and from trade show buyers, Rwandan specialty coffee made its first sale to Starbucks Cof-

fee Corporation in June 2004. In November 2005, Starbucks selected two privately owned wet-milling facilities for an exclusive distribution program, which provided coffee to 5,000 Starbucks retail outlets.

In 1990, Rwanda's commodity grade coffee fetched US$1.18/kg (0.54/lb.), but by 2001 its price had decreased to US$0.40/kg (US$0.18/lb.). However, through the above interventions, which were implemented with support from the Partnership to Enhance Agriculture in Rwanda through Linkages and Agribusiness Development Activity in Rwanda projects funded by USAID, specialty coffee production and its subsequent price both increased. Without the wet-milling interventions, Rwanda's ability to improve the quality of its beans from ordinary to standard and specialty would have been impossible. Also, if Rwanda had only tried to maximize profits and decrease costs within its value chain without attempting a repositioning strategy, it would have been more difficult to obtain the same results.

RWANDAN COFFEE TODAY AND INTO THE FUTURE

In addition to the increased production and price/kg that Rwandan specialty coffee has realized, the new wet-milling stations created 4,000 new jobs, and 5,000 rural households saw their incomes more than double (Chemonics 2005).

Figure 4.41   Results of Rwandan Coffee's Positioning Efforts, 2005

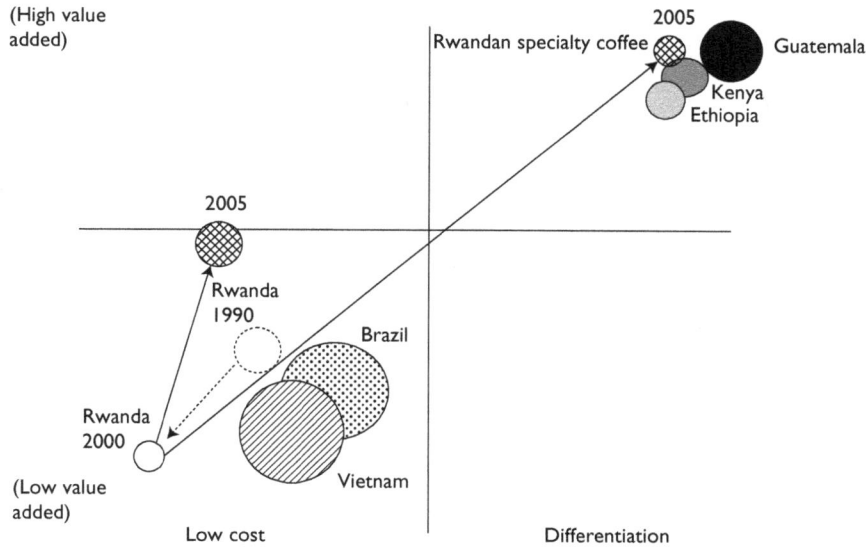

Source: J. E. Austin Associates, Inc.

Table 4.15   Rwandan Coffee Production and Prices, 2003–05

Year	Metric tons produced	Price/kg (US$)
2003	162	1.56
2004	747	2.40
2005	1,190	3.10

Source: OCIR-CAFÉ 2006.

Initial success from these interventions has sparked further donor interest in supporting Rwanda's value-added coffee sector. Partnerships with the GoR have spawned plans to continue increasing production through the construction of an additional 164 wet-milling facilities. Continued investment in the existing wet-mill facilities is required to make better use of water sources and to equip them with water recycling pumps. These, and other interventions, will allow Rwanda to continue to support its growing specialty coffee industry.

As Rwanda gets closer to 2010, continued product positioning will be required to help chart new strategies for the Rwandan coffee market (see figure 4.42). OCIR-CAFÉ has developed a plan to move away from standard coffee altogether and focus only on specialty varieties. Rwandans could also choose to diversify their product offerings by seeking broader markets for standard coffee while simultaneously maintaining focus on higher prices for specialty coffee. This would leverage the Rwandan coffee sector's increased capacity and maturing coffee acumen and could enable Rwanda to broaden its coffee production to more diverse markets.

In fact, this latter situation is ongoing, and Rwanda is more than midway into its positioning strategy. However, it will most likely have future opportunities to revisit its strategy and take advantage of future market opportunities.

Has Rwanda been successful in repositioning its coffee industry? In many aspects, yes. By understanding its position in world coffee markets and then implementing a strategy to reposition itself, Rwanda's coffee industry has revitalized itself and has improved the earning potential of many small growers.

Table 4.16 Standard and Ordinary Coffee Percentages, 1998–2005							
Year	1998	2000	2001	2002	2003	2004	2005
Production (tons)	14,268	16,098	18,267	19,796	14,175	29,000	17,000
Standard coffee (percentage)	7.40	19.5	18.5	29.28	32.4	40.0	45.0
Ordinary coffee (percentage)	80.5	72.4	75.0	58.57	55.0	50.0	45.0

Source: OCIR-CAFÉ 2006.

Figure 4.42   Rwanda's Coffee Positioning, 2010 and Beyond

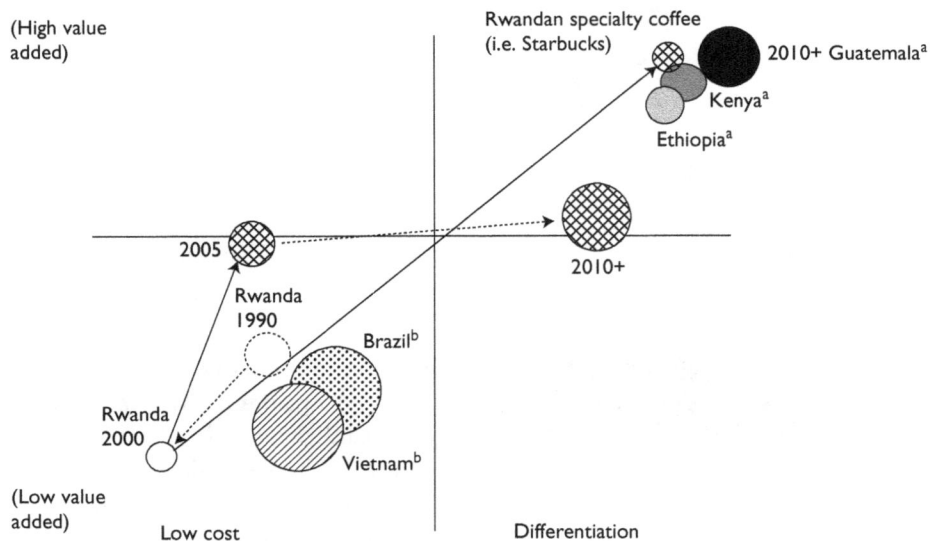

Source: J. E. Austin Associates, Inc.
[a] Represents specialty coffee/not drawn to scale.
[b] Represents commodity coffee/not drawn to scale.

NOTE

1. Rob Henning, OTF Group.

Applying Standards and Certifications to Achieve Greater Quality

Meeting a variety of quality and performance standards is integral to the success of agricultural value chains. However, the importance of specific qualities, standard measurements, and informational or other characteristics may not be readily apparent to all the actors in a value chain if they are not familiar with the target market. Aside from normal ethical, consumer health, and safety requirements, the market side of the value chain pays increasing attention to standards and certifications. National and regional markets are imposing increasingly strict requirements for basic market entry (for example, HACCP and EurepGAP). Powerful buyers and retailers, especially supermarkets, impose additional requirements on their supply chains.

As a result, the value chain must meet increasingly stringent requirements relating to product health and safety, intrinsic product qualities (shape, color, taste, texture, and others), packaging and labeling, and accompanying information.

Value chains are also beginning to understand that meeting recognized standards is not just a condition for market access but a powerful way to compete for market share and higher unit values. Value chains can obtain price premiums if they meet these standards, especially if they achieve valued product and production certifications. These certifications can go well beyond market entry requirements and appeal to special customer segments that are willing to pay premium prices (see figure 4.43). Thus, value chains are increasingly recognizing the opportunities inherent in providing certified, organic, fair trade, bird-friendly, and other high-standard products, as well as the value of marketing and quality-control initiatives that are promoted through seals of quality.

Because a product is affected by many factors—from farm to market—achieving quality standards and certifica-

Figure 4.43 Standards Plotted against Product Value

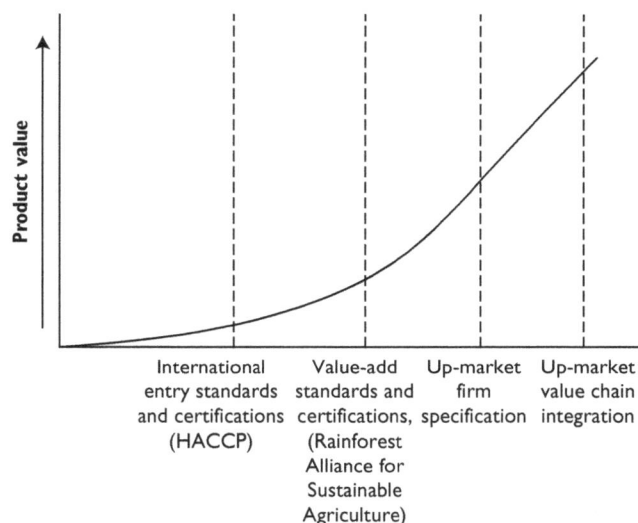

Source: J.E. Austin Associates, Inc.

tions is a value chain issue, and the strategies must be value chain–wide strategies.

VOCABULARY

- **International trade standards**: Standards applicable to trade, imposed by trade agreement or market-governance fiat.
- **Value-added standards**: Geared to the specific requirements of niche or segmented markets; make a product more specialized or unique.
- **Quality standards**: Additional, specific buyer standards such as appearance, size, and packaging.

INCREASING PRODUCT VALUE THROUGH STANDARDS

Choosing and targeting standards should be part of a strategic market exercise. Many export markets have standards and/or certifications that are needed for entry. By achieving international certification or standards, local value chains have the opportunity to export to other countries and select the market positioning of their products. However, implementing standards does not automatically mean that the value chain can sell in those export markets; the chains must still market and sell to customers in those countries.

Value-added standards allow for entry into certain niche markets; for example, Rainforest Alliance standards for coffee products appeal to many coffeehouses and specialty marketers in the United States (see figure 4.44). Many individual importers and retailers have their own quality standards that appeal to their particular customer base.

Implementing the processes and systems to meet standards does take resources, so it is important that the value chain's leaders and firms choose the most strategically appropriate target market segments. Comparing implementation costs and the local value chain's capacity to incorporate standards against the benefits of selling up-market is a strategic choice that must be considered before incorporating standards.

Elements of standards

Implementing standards within a value chain means discussing three elements:

- Certification bodies
- Information channels
- Management oversight and governance structures

CERTIFICATION BODIES

Many standards and certificates have international bodies that certify that products meet certain standards. Several have the ability to certify products and services in developing countries, but cost and timing can be a major issue in bringing these international bodies into developing countries. Therefore—and especially if large numbers of producers or exporters will receive certification—it is often better to set up institutions in the local country. Although it is beyond the scope of this Guide to discuss

Figure 4.44   International and Value-Added Standards

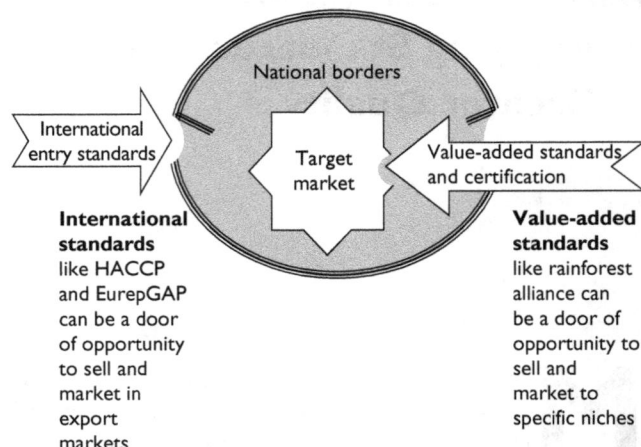

Source: J.E. Austin Associates, Inc.

how to set up a certification body, it is worth noting that several options are available:

- Private companies
- Industry associations
- Nongovernmental organizations (NGOs)
- Government agencies

Governments are typically geared to certify products and services to protect their citizens' health and welfare, but are typically not best suited to certify based on other criteria. NGOs, associations, and private firms around the world have successfully set up certification agencies based on international standards.

INFORMATION CHANNELS

Entrepreneurs—businesses and producers, in general—must be motivated to change the way they produce goods and services to meet standards, and they need information and economic incentives in order to do this. These incentives must include shared knowledge of the requirements (and ideally, the logic behind them), as well as price points that reflect the additional costs and work involved in meeting requirements. There must also be trust within the value chain that the process is stable.

One aspect of creating trust is ensuring that proper information channels are available and being used; these will give small and medium enterprises and producers confidence that they will obtain fair rewards for the costs of implementing new processes to meet standards. This means that the value chain must communicate formally and informally. Formal communication can occur through meetings, cluster activities, integrated supply chain systems, industry associations, conferences, and exchanging price information. Informal channels can be created by having a transparent culture within the value chain, especially within the SMEs' supply base. For example, if a farmer sees another farmer in the village benefit from an investment to meet standards or gain a certificate, the second farmer is more likely to upgrade processes based on the observed model.

MANAGEMENT OVERSIGHT AND GOVERNANCE

A value chain that is upgrading its standards requires some institution to take responsibility for managing the supply base to meet standards and specifications. Because the value chain is comprised of independent firms and actors that often have different motivations, this can be a difficult task. Credible governance, clearly able to link value chain performance to market rewards, is always needed if the supply response of the value chain is to be coordinated and targeted to market needs.

Typically, there are three types of institutions for management of the value chain:

- Supply chain management instituted by an exporter, processor, or other lead firm
- Associations and cooperatives
- Government agencies

The success of these various forms of oversight and governance rests with their ability to understand market requirements and translate them into in-chain procurement standards, communicate information effectively, and motivate suppliers to respond with needed investments and operations.

LEAD FIRMS

Many lead firms have made a "mindset" change that allows them to view the effective management of their supply chain as an opportunity for growth creation and larger profits, rather than simply as an additional imposed cost. This mindset shift is based on the fact that if the participants in a value chain work together, the value chain can more easily meet changing market needs and reduce transaction costs. Therefore, the lead firm should take responsibility for managing its supply base, which includes ensuring that that base is certified or is meeting market standards. In fragmented industries, lead firms are sometimes unable to manage the supply chain to meet market standards, and so the industry would then have to leverage other institutions. The need for a coordinated response within a fragmented production environment is a key motivator for integration and consolidation within value chains.

ASSOCIATIONS AND COOPERATIVES

In fragmented value chains, associations and cooperatives can help manage value chain elements to meet market standards. These institutions are often important when first implementing standards in a value chain; institutions that are producer owned, visible, and well known can build trust in the standardization process. Properly resourced, they can be very effective in training and outreach activities. In some cases, involving a credible third-party institution (as in the example of Kaesetsart University and the Thai GAP cluster, box 4.12) can help overcome initial mistrust between producers and processors/exporters and can help focus all parties on a coordinated approach to meeting standards.

GOVERNMENT AGENCIES

In many countries, and often in keeping with traditional, historical/colonial, or even philosophical backgrounds, government has played the role of industry governance, including standard setting, inspection, extension, and communication. Marketing boards or authorities are one prominent set of examples. However, while some state-run agencies are effective in their governance and oversight role—and, in some cases, even step in to redress serious sectoral problems—there are also problems with such models. Government agencies are often slow to understand and respond to market trends, limited in their strategic focus, inflexible in promoting varying standards and price points, subject to public sector inefficiencies and political and budget pressures, and liable to communicate poorly with the value chain.

SUMMARY

It is a strategic decision to instill standards or certifications into the value chain based on target market requirements. The choice of standards and certifications needs to be an informed one. To implement these, effective elements of certification bodies, information channels, and management oversight must be established.

In the early 2000s, the GAP cluster in western Thailand was able to reorient its production to meet the specific certifications needed to enter European and U.S. markets. This cluster was also able to develop and market certifications that add value to its products. These results were achieved through close collaboration among value chain participants.

Importance of Implementing EurepGAP through the Value Chain

Thailand has long been able to successfully export high-value horticulture products to Europe. Once EurepGAP certification and traceability requirements were put in place, however, Thai vegetable exports dropped by 20 percent. The drop in exports was felt throughout the value chain—by exporters, packers, and growers. The exporters and government made several attempts to implement EurepGAP within the value chain, though without success. This was largely attributable to mistrust among the exporters, government, and growers.

A cluster approach was used to provide training and certification services by incorporating a local university, Kaesetsart University. The exporters collaborated closely in identifying market requirements, and the university trained 2,000 growers on EurepGAP compliance, sending them to train other farmers. Growers were more willing to accept the new processes when presented by a respected third party (the university) with information support from the exporters. This allowed the exporters to gain market share and increase their exports. The growers benefited by receiving a 50 percent increase in their prices for certified products.

Use of Certification and Branding for Local Markets

To further leverage the output of growers who participated in the EurepGAP training and processes, the cluster developed a western Thailand GAP logo. The cluster worked on sophisticated packaging, branding, and smaller packages that were geared toward the large supermarkets in Thai cities. It is expected that each party in the value chain will gain greater value by leveraging this certification and brand.

Source: Mike Ducker, J. E. Austin Associates, Inc.

Figure 1: Thai Vegetable Export Value Chains

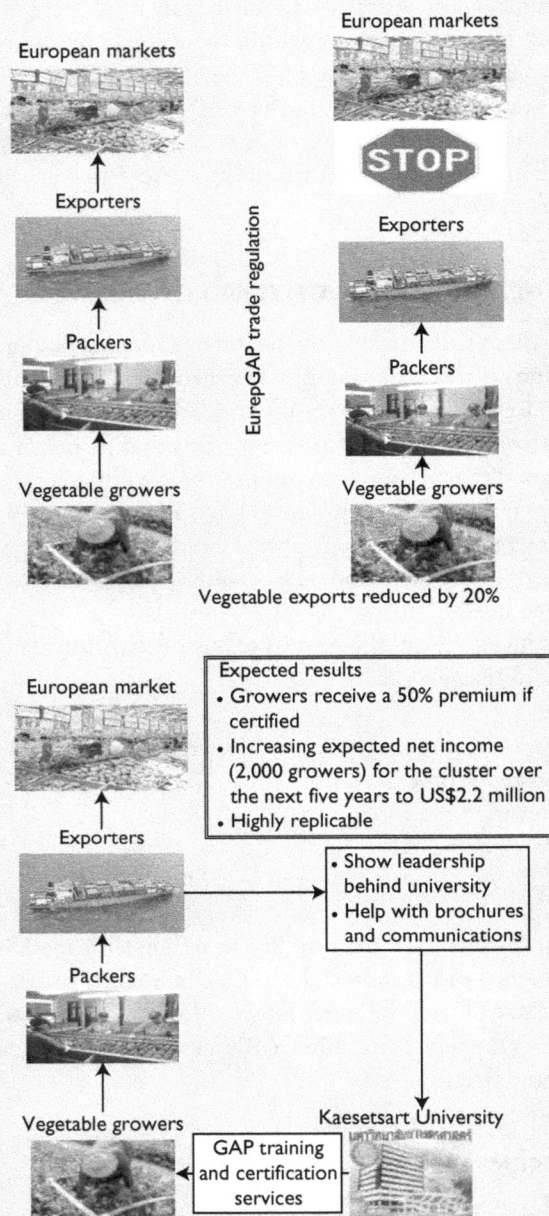

European markets — Exporters — Packers — Vegetable growers

EurepGAP trade regulation

European markets — STOP — Exporters — Packers — Vegetable growers

Vegetable exports reduced by 20%

European market — Exporters — Packers — Vegetable growers

Expected results
- Growers receive a 50% premium if certified
- Increasing expected net income (2,000 growers) for the cluster over the next five years to US$2.2 million
- Highly replicable

- Show leadership behind university
- Help with brochures and communications

Kaesetsart University

GAP training and certification services

Source: J. E. Austin Associates, Inc.

In 2003, the government of Ecuador (GoE) launched an alternative development project focused on the border region between Ecuador and Colombia, which is a locus for cultivation of illicit crops. An assessment of the income and employment potential of other current crops grown in the area pointed to five potential crops, including cacao.

There are two main types of cacao: forastero and criollo. Forastero cacao accounts for approximately 95 percent, most of the remaining 5 percent is criollo.[a] Criollo cacao has traditionally been produced in Latin America, while forastero cacao has been grown in Africa and Asia. Cacao is graded based on several criteria, including mold content, level of fermentation, and percentage of cocoa butter, all of which affect the flavor profile of the chocolate produced. Criollo cacao is generally more flavorful, but it does not necessarily always command a premium. Cacao buyers and processors pay more attention to the local characteristics that create the particular flavor profile of the product, rather than to the type of cacao grown.[b]

Ecuador mainly grows criollo cacao, and its flavor profile is particularly well suited to producing fine dark chocolate, a market segment that has grown exponentially during recent years.[b] However, quality control problems and poor handling practices destroyed the conductivity of fine flavor and aroma in about 50 percent of the harvest in Ecuador. This meant that even though Ecuador was growing the criollo variety, 50 percent of the crop could not be sold at a higher price or was unfit for export.

Cacao buyers typically do not buy directly from producers (see figure 1), preferring to work through collection centers. This is due to the fact that cacao is not a plantation crop, and there is largely an absence of associations that can sell cacao in sufficient quantity.

A value chain analysis revealed several constraints in the cacao sector, including poor production technology, mixing different types of beans without quality differentiation, and selling wet and unfermented cacao.[c] Fermentation changes cacao's flavor profile—sometimes positively and sometimes not. Ecuador's criollo cacao naturally possesses a desirable flavor profile for higher-end dark chocolate products, so producers sought to address quality problems as well as reduce postharvest losses.

Figure 1: Ecuadorian Cacao Value Chain

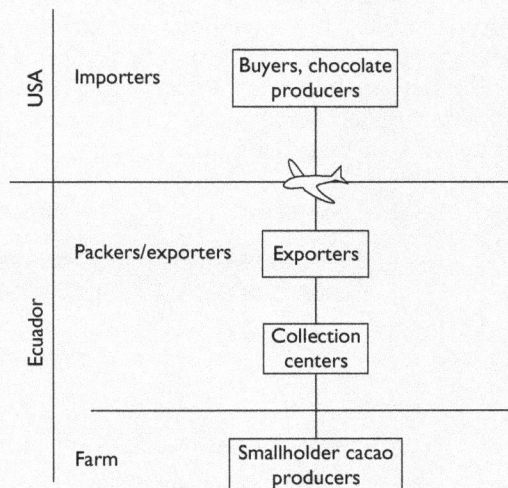

Source: J. E. Austin Associates, Inc.

Prices and Production of Cacao Farmer Field Schools, supported by USAID, helped educate farmers to better cultivate and protect their trees, add value to their product by differentiating between types of beans, and to ferment and dry the beans. Farmers who provide value-added services receive a higher price for their beans; those who sell beans after fermenting and drying them can receive US$60 per quintal, versus US$28–30

Figure b: Prices and Production of Cacao, 1971–72 to 2004–05

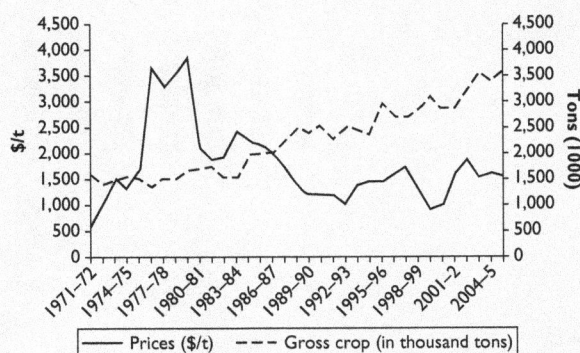

Source: UNCTAD, based on the data from the International Cocoa Organization, quarterly bulletin of cocoa statistics.

(Box continues on the following page.)

per quintal if unprocessed.[d] Cacao beans are sold on the New York and London exchanges, where a baseline market price is offered; then, premiums or discounts are applied depending on the country of origin, the quality of the shipments, and other factors. Between 50 percent and 75 percent of Ecuadorian production is currently of sufficient quality to be sold at a higher price.

As described in box 4.10, Ecuador has historically received a US$20–US$100 premium over the baseline market price. However, because of its desirable flavor profile, Ecuadorian cacao currently commands a premium of US$800–US$1,200 per ton.[b] Through the Farmer Field Schools, farmers learned how to add more value to their product by maintaining bean quality, fermenting, and drying the beans before taking them to the collection centers. These actions have led to the production of higher quality cacao and, in turn, to the farmers who receive a higher price for their cacao.

Prices of Various Countries' Cacao Products

Country	Premium over market price, May 4, 2007 (per ton, US$)
Venezuela (fermented)	2,000
Java (fermented)	2,000
Ecuador (partially fermented)	800–1,200
Ivory Coast (fermented)	320
Dominican Republic (unfermented)	280
Ghana (fermented)	250

Note: This is the same table that appears in box 4.10.

Figure 3: World Production of Cacao Beans

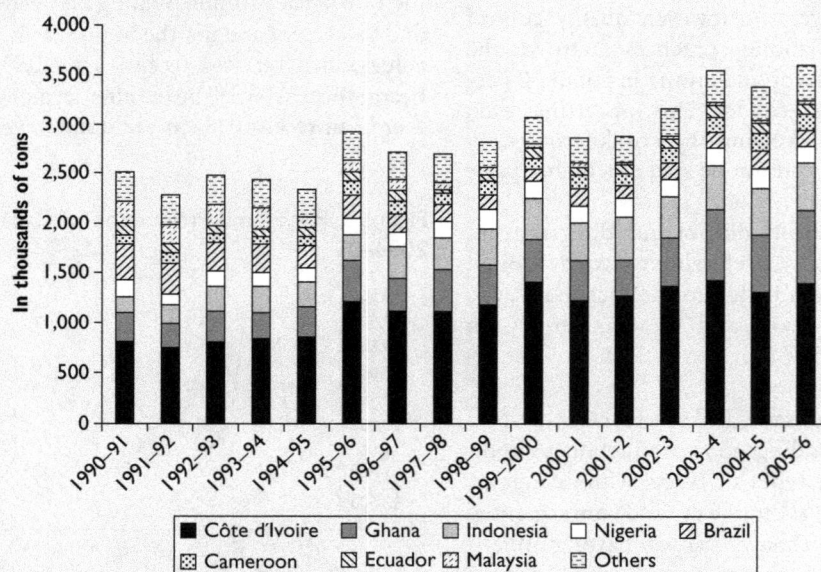

Source: Lisa Carse, J. E. Austin Associates, Inc.; UNCTAD, based on the data from the International Cocoa Organization, quarterly bulletin of cocoa statistics.

[a] http://www.unctad.org/infocomm/anglais/cocoa/quality.htm.

[b] Author interview with Karl Walk, purchaser for Blommer Chocolate, 2007.

[c] The process of drying cacao reduces the likelihood of developing mold; currently, the U.S. Department of Agriculture rejects shipments of cacao that exceed 4 percent mold content.

[d] Technical Evaluation of the Ecuador Northern Border Income and Employment Project Implemented by ARD, Inc.

A STEP-BY-STEP SUMMARY OF TOOL 9: APPLYING STANDARDS AND CERTIFICATIONS TO ACHIEVE GREATER QUALITY

- Analyze market data for price premiums associated with individual standards and quality certifications. In addition to quantifying opportunities within existing markets, look at the potential for certifications to open up new niche markets. Identify the market risks of not meeting standards or certifications.

- Contact other businesses that have obtained certification, particularly lead firms, to discuss the economics of value added relative to traditional production.

- Identify and understand the technical requirements to meet standards or certification, and evaluate the actions and costs that will be necessary. Contact certification bodies to discuss the time and resources necessary to obtain certification.

- Identify the process, pricing, training, and other requirements to meet standards or certifications.

- Assess the firm level and value chain capacity for quality control. Also assess the quality and consistency of services provided by other value chain actors needed to obtain and maintain certification. Assess value chain linkages and relationships to identify key elements that need coordination, and the actors that will ensure coordination.

- Investigate public sector support and services for producers and enterprises seeking certification or value-added production.

Ugandan Nile Perch Quality Management and Certification

Michael Ducker and Martin Webber
J. E. Austin Associates, Inc.

POINTS TO CONSIDER

This case study looks at certification processes that help ensure safety and quality for the final consumers of Nile perch. The case considers the Nile perch export value chain in Uganda, which extends from Lake Victoria fishermen to dinner tables in Europe and around the world, and how quality and safety issues impact the value chain. The Ugandan value chain successfully improved its quality management when faced with potentially losing its sizable European market. This case also highlights the value that different certifications have within the value chain.

BACKGROUND

Opportunistic growth in the 1990s led to an undisciplined value chain (figure 4.45) that caused sector quality issues.

In the early 1990s, Kenya, and then Uganda, started exporting Nile perch to Europe. Fish became a major Ugandan export during the mid-1990s. Despite the profitability of these initial years, the Ugandan fish industry failed to invest in quality control measures central to the value chain's long term strength.

From 1997 to 2000, several health incidents in the European Union and in Uganda caused the EU to place numerous bans and restrictions on Nile perch imports (and other fish) from Uganda, as well as on other countries that export fish from Lake Victoria. (See box on the Nile Perch Certification Timeline for details.) Problems first surfaced

when Spanish and Italian authorities found contamination in Nile perch and issued bilateral bans. These steps forced the European Commission to send several missions to Uganda to test the product and the processes within the value chain. Some of the problems that were identified from these missions included:

- Fish-processing plants failed to meet conditions laid out in EU regulations
- The Uganda National Bureau of Standards (UNBS) issued health certificates incorrectly
- Lack of microbiological tests to support government health certificates
- Lack of routine government monitoring for presence of chemicals in fish and water
- Lack of sanitary infrastructure and fencing at landing sites
- Fish handling was not hygienic throughout the chain

In response to the missions' findings, two Ugandan processing plants were prohibited from exporting Nile perch to the EU.

In 1999, the Ugandan press reported instances of fish poisoning in Lake Victoria. The UNBS notified the EU that it could not guarantee the safety of fish exports, and the EU then banned all fish imports from Lake Victoria. The EU import bans had wide-ranging effects in Uganda; in addition to lower fish exports and export revenue, fishing communities suffered tremendous damage, as did fish processors and

February 1997: Spain and Italy claim that their authorities have detected high levels of bacterial contamination, and impose bilateral ban on fishery product imports.

March 1997: EU inspection confirms "serious microbiological contamination."

April 1997: EU requires mandatory tests on imports of Nile perch from three East African countries.

December 1997–June 1998: Following an outbreak of cholera in East Africa, the EU bans fresh fish imports and imposes mandatory tests on frozen fish from East Africa.

November–December 1998: EC sends a Food and Veterinary Office mission to Uganda to assess compliance in production conditions; two processing plants are found not compliant. The two noncompliant plants are removed from the list of approved establishments. In the same month, the Ugandan press reports instances of fish poisoning in Lake Victoria.

March 1999: Based on press reports, a number of district authorities ban fish sales. UNBS notifies the EU that it cannot guarantee the safety of fish exports.

Source: DISS 2005.

April 1999: EU meets in Brussels with representatives of authorities from Kenya, Tanzania, and Uganda to discuss test results; the EU announces a ban on fresh and frozen fish from the three countries.

August 1999: EU mission assesses resources and capabilities of competent authority in Uganda in relation to control of pesticide residues; mission provides 10 recommendations; UNBS responds to EU report but does not provide all requested documentation or details. A private laboratory is established in Kampala, accredited to perform pesticide-monitoring tests; industry adopts the "voluntary code of practice" for quality control; Department of Fisheries (DFR) revises inspection manual. Transfer of competent authority from UNBS to DFR.

July 2000: Ban lifted when the EU accepts guarantees that Uganda has put in required procedures for safety of exports; country qualifies for temporary certification in List II (see About EU Fish Import Lists box).

May 2001: Uganda goes back to List I (see About EU Fish Import Lists box).

---

related service industries (packaging, transport, and others). As a result of the bans, three plants closed down completely. The remaining plants worked at 20 percent capacity, while 60–70 percent of employees were laid off.

INTERVENTION

The EU bans shut off the supply of a product that was much in demand in the EU marketplace, and the market had few substitutes. Pressures on both the demand and supply sides of the market therefore provided major incentives for actors throughout the value chain to face the problem. The members of the Uganda Fish Processors and Exporters Association (UFPEA), European fish importers, the government of Uganda (GoU), and the EU worked together and took action to deal with the issues. The GoU and UFPEA had several working group meetings to design an action plan. Their major initiative was to restructure the government agencies responsible for

managing Uganda's certification process. Since Europe was the fish's major destination, the government and industry wanted its certification process to match the EurepGAP process.

CREATING A EUREPGAP CERTIFICATION PROCESS IN UGANDA

The GoU streamlined its fish regulatory and inspection systems, with the Department of Fisheries (DFR) formally becoming the sole competent authority for fish safety issues. DFR would be responsible for certifying fish exports as EurepGAP compliant, and it needed to achieve HACCP accreditation to regulate the value chain to EurepGAP standards.

The DFR completely revised its guidelines as well as its monitoring and inspection systems. A manual of standard operating procedures was established to guide inspections, and training programs were carried out for inspectors.

Figure 4.45 Ugandan Nile Perch Value Chain

European markets

Fish processors/exporters

Landing sites

Fishermen

Source: J. E. Austin Associates, Inc.

In 1998, the EU started segregating fish-exporting countries into three lists. List I countries could export fishery products to the EU from any establishment approved by the competent authority. List II countries were authorized to export on the basis of a specific list of approved establishments. List III countries were deemed unable to provide guarantees of appropriate inspection and monitoring. In order to export from these countries, additional documentation and checks were needed and only individual establishments approved by the EU could export.

In 2008, DFR's central offices were staffed with 17 inspectors who monitor the overall system and operations at processing plants. Another 20 or so inspectors operate at the 14 landing sites that are approved as sources of fish for export. These inspectors issue local fish-health inspection certificates that are required to move fish from a landing site to a processing factory. These certificates contain information on both the supplier and buyer of fish at the landing site and on the fish's origin. However, DFR did not have the capacity to handle quality control with the fishermen or at many of the landing sites away from major urban centers. There are 600 total landing sites in Uganda, but only 14 are approved for export. As a result, different monitoring procedures were put in place at the local level, including the formation of committees at landing sites and Beach Management Units (BMUs) that started registering boats and gear. This approach follows what, in fisheries, is known as comanagement—power-sharing between state and local communities and a shift of responsibilities from the former to the latter. In this framework, BMUs are supposed to coordinate with local governments via the formation of Lake Management Organizations (Ponte 2005). As of 2004, BMU-managed landing sites were not authorized to export to Europe, so many processors, agents, and traders transfer fish at one of the 14 approved landing sites.

THE IMPORTANT ROLE OF PESTICIDE LABORATORIES IN THE CERTIFICATION PROCESS

The EurepGAP certification process requires biochemical tests to check for pesticide residue. No laboratory in Uganda could perform the pesticide residue test, so samples were being shipped to Belgium, where a Belgian firm, Chemipher (U) Ltd., did the tests. Chemipher recognized that there was sustained business for them in Uganda, so they opened a laboratory there. Having a local lab helped streamline the certification process and reduce costs.

ISO 9001 CERTIFICATION

Many of the fish processors and exporters wanted to add another layer of quality standards to their production, mostly to demonstrate (and to help the market perceive) that they were serious about quality. With the assistance of a USAID-financed project[1] that trained the fish processors in ISO 9001 (a subset of ISO 9000, see figure 4.46) processes, the processors were then certified by an outside consulting firm.

INDUSTRY-LEVEL CERTIFICATIONS

The association of fish processors, UFPEA, has adopted a voluntary code of Good Manufacturing Practices (GMPs). The fish processors implemented HACCP and good quality management systems (see figure 4.47) with support from EU funding, and 11 processors were upgraded to handle fish for export (see figure 4.48). The voluntary GMPs were monitored by UFPEA and proved helpful in improving processors' practices.

THE RESULTS: A MORE COMPETITIVE INDUSTRY THAN ITS NEIGHBORS—AND ONE THAT HAS GAINED A REPUTATION FOR GOOD QUALITY

In short, compliance with EU standards (including HACCP procedures) by the Ugandan fish industry in reaction to the import bans resulted in:

- Streamlined regulation under a single, strong, and competent authority (DFR)

- Formulation of a new fisheries policy
- Improved monitoring and inspection systems supported by inspection manuals, standard operating procedures, and the training of inspectors
- Regional efforts for the harmonization of handling procedures in the three countries sharing Lake Victoria
- Upgrading of a (small) number of landing sites and plans for upgrading a substantial number of others
- Upgrading of processing plants' procedures and layouts
- Opening up of the U.S. market, which also requires HACCP compliance
- Installation of two local laboratories (Chemipher and UNBS) and general improvement of service provision to the industry
- Increased number of processing plants and improved export performance (see figure 4.49)

LESSONS LEARNED

- There was and still is a strong incentive for the value chain and government to work together to ensure a quality product. The potential total losses of poor quality management were apparent to all parties.
- Paradoxically, banning the supply of all Nile perch from the Lake Victoria region created incentives for European fish importers and the EU itself to support Uganda because there were few replacement sources.

Figure 4.46   ISO 9000 Certification Process

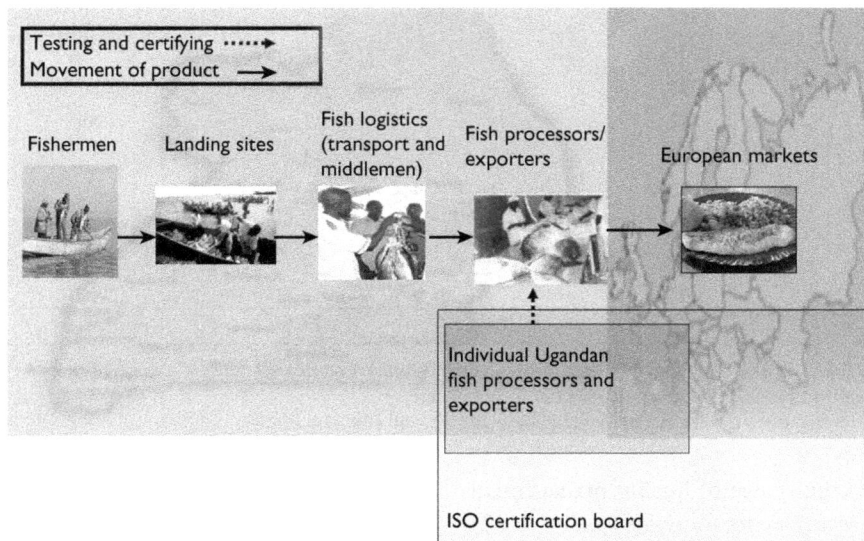

Source: J. E. Austin Associates, Inc., 2007.

Figure 4.47 Good Manufacturing Practice and HACCP

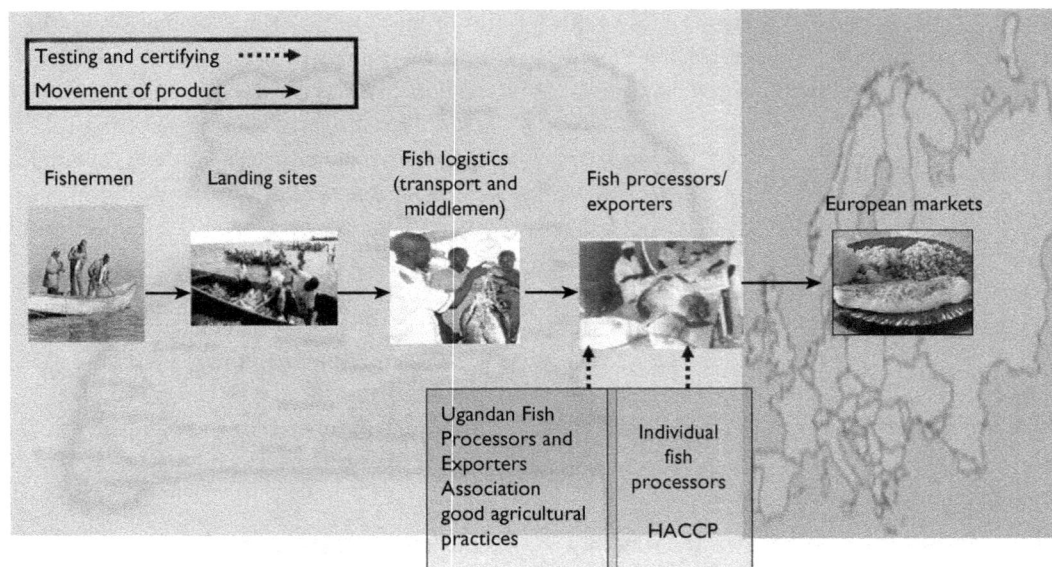

Source: Stefano Ponte, "Bans, Tests, and Alchemy: Food Safety Standards and the Ugandan Fish Export Industry." Danish Institute for International Studies 2005.

Figure 4.48 HACCP Implementation

Company code	HAACP complaint begins	HAACP compliance begins	Number of plants upgraded[a]	Length of process of achieving compliance (months)	Total estimated cumulative expenditure to reach HACCP compliance, capital cost (thousands of US$)	Extra recurrent costs (US$/year)[b]
A	Y	1998	2	12		39,600
B	Y	2001	1	12		
C	Y	1997	1	48	1,927	65,800
D	Y	1997	1	12	1,000	
E	Y	2000	1	24		45,000
F	Y	1995	1	36		72,000
G	Y	1998	2	36	1,000	70,000
H	Y	1997	1	12	1,500	80,000
I	Y	2000	1	12	200	43,000
Average			11	23	1,125	59,343

Source: Stefano Ponte, "Bans, Tests, and Alchemy: Food Safety Standards and the Ugandan Fish Export Industry." Danish Institute for International Studies 2005.
[a] Plants built after 2001 (already to HACCP specifications) are not included here.
[b] Estimate includes product testing, extra quality management labor, materials, and annual training.

■ Recognition of the importance of quality management, and of building a secure reputation for quality, led to actions beyond the minimum needed, such as implementing ISO 9001 and GMPs.

■ The fish processors and exporters were natural actors to take the lead in determining and disseminating information about the standards required within the value chain. They were responsible for a large part of the value-added

Figure 4.49   Uganda's Nile Perch Exports

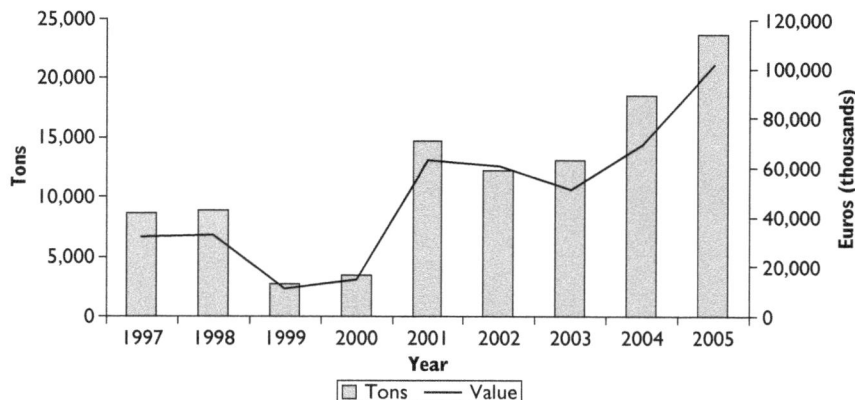

Source : EUROSTAT data, calculations by J. E. Austin Associates, Inc.

process and were the portion of the value chain most knowledgeable about export markets' requirements. They could serve as the "control point" for the rest of the value chain. The government had reason to listen to them because they employed a large number of people and recognizably controlled the market linkage that tens of thousands of people working within the value chain helped to supply.

- There is multilayer monitoring at the fish processing and export stages, but monitoring is much weaker at the landing sites and with the fishermen. Currently, local governments do not have the capacity to do much monitoring, so the exporters and processors have most of the responsibility to ensure that they receive fish that meets the EU market's quality requirements.

- Fishermen and fish traders also understand and remember that markets can be "turned off" and, consequently, have incentives to supply fish that meets quality requirements.

NOTE

1. Under the SPEED project, this and other assistance to the fish industry was provided by J. E. Austin Associates, Inc., and the prime contractor, Chemonics Inc.

Identifying Needed Support Services for the Value Chain

Profitable value chains are supported by services that allow the chain to grow, be more efficient, and enhance its competitiveness. The overall objective is to improve the depth and breadth of services currently being provided to the value chain, enabling them to be commercially sustainable, and to help those services emerge where they are not being provided. The availability of new and better services should enhance the profitability of the whole value chain. Commercially sustainable services will typically involve specialization on the part of the service deliverer; thus, there are important linkages with the deepening of the value chain, as discussed in Tool 4, Upgrading and Deepening the Value Chain.

The range of services that can add value and strength to a value chain is vast. Examples include input supply, market information and product development support, business management and consulting, transportation and logistics, quality assurance (including certifications), skills, extensions and training, veterinary services, and credit and other financial services. Box 4.14 describes an example of an enterprise-linked extension services model. Box 4.15 describes the actors of a sector organization.

It is absolutely in the interest of businesses, entrepreneurs, and associations to ensure provision and access to services that would enhance their value chain's profitability. In many cases, demand for services can also offer opportunities for small and medium enterprises to enter the value chain market as suppliers.

In the specific case of financial services, relationships between value chain actors can also enable financial flows by

---

Box 4.14   Ugandan Cotton—Enterprise-Linked Extension Services Model

Uganda's cotton production dramatically decreased during the 1970s, and the sector has not yet fully recovered. Supported by USAID,[a] the government of Uganda (GoU) sought to increase Uganda's cotton production and revenue by encouraging small farmers to grow more and higher quality cotton. Greater production would enable ginneries to operate closer to full capacity. By involving private business in serving the needs of the farmers at the input and financing stages, the ginneries were able to encourage farmers to increase the supply of cotton available to the ginneries. This was accomplished through a model that has been successfully replicated through eight lead ginners representing the interests of supporting ginners in eight designated cotton production zones; the model has also been extended to other sectors.

The Enterprise-Linked Extension Model for the cotton industry begins with a ginnery that is performing at undercapacity, where there is nevertheless market demand for cotton. For example, the Nykatonzi ginnery has a productive capacity of 20,000 bales per year, yet in the early 2000s, it was only processing about 10,000 bales annually.[b]

The farmers already had supplier relationships with the ginneries; however, the industry and the GoU recognized that these farmers needed extension services if they were going to produce cotton in sufficient quantities for the ginneries to operate efficiently.

Inputs and service needs were identified by analyzing the underperformance of the sector compared with historic levels, including value chain and GAP assessments. Farmers did not have access to needed inputs,

(Box continues on the following page.)

and they lacked the technical knowledge to increase their yields. The identified needs included:

- Training and extension
- Technical advice
- Access to inputs
- Financing of inputs
- A guaranteed buyer

Since output could be boosted through the use of these inputs, the ginneries worked with stockists to provide these inputs to the farmers. The purchase agreements between the ginnery and the farmer provided a risk-mitigation mechanism for the stockists' investment. The farmers' need to purchase these inputs led to the development of financial services programs for the farmers. The ginneries worked with financial service providers to give the farmers access to the financial resources they needed. All of these steps were able to take place because the farmers had guaranteed buyers in the ginneries through purchase agreements.

For extension services, ginneries were encouraged to communicate their needs and engage directly with farmers. The ginners, with support from the USAID/ Agricultural Productivity Enhancement Program (APEP), set up demonstration plots and trained farmers in cotton production techniques, including the use of fertilizers and pesticides; farmers were trained by lead farmers, collaborating farmers, and site coordinators. An employee of the ginnery, called a site coordinator, oversees the plots, coordinates field trips, provides information to farmers, and supervises lead farmers who act as extension agents. Lead farmers pass on cotton-production technologies to collaborating farmers for adoption through trainings, field days, and hands-on exercises. Technical advice is provided by the ginneries and USAID/APEP.

The benefits to the ginneries included increased and more reliable cotton supply, greater operational efficiency, and greater loyalty among farmers to the ginnery. The benefits to the farmer included increased production, productivity, and profits; greater knowledge of the market; sophisticated production techniques; and a guaranteed buyer for their supply. The model has successfully increased cotton production and revenues in Uganda. More ginneries are in operation, and farmers have been able to increase their yields threefold to around 600 kg/hectare. As a best practices benchmark, Australian yields in 2005 were 2,080 kg/hectare.

Results

The model successfully increased cotton production and revenues in Uganda. It has now also been replicated in several sectors, including maize and sunflowers. In the maize sector, corporate linkages have been strengthened, farmers have been economically empowered, and support services have been created. Production and sales volume of maize remain high, and quality has improved. In the sunflower sector, an additional US$6 million dollars in farm income has been generated in three years, with 35,000 farmers joining a dedicated production system.[c]

Sources: Lisa Carse and Martin Webber, J. E. Austin Associates, Inc.; Uganda Bureau of Statistics.
[a] Initially the SPEED (Support for Private Enterprise Expansion and Development) Project, and subsequently APEP. Both projects were implemented by Chemonics, Inc.
[b] Ralph Chaffee, April 2, 2002, Enterprise-Linked Extension Services in Uganda; SPEED Project.
[c] Mark Wood, USAID/APEP Project, 27 March, 2007.

making the potential client more attractive to traditional financial institutions. The benefits of these buyer-supplier value chain relationships—specifically, a more secure market and improved skills—make potential borrowers (suppliers) more creditworthy to financial institutions.

Services can be delivered through many appropriate mechanisms. Services along the value chain can be provided by both public and private entities; commercially sustainable approaches are certainly preferable. Additionally, services may be delivered as part of another commercial transaction, such as in the case of embedded services. For example, a processor extends credit in the form of "virtual" working capital to a small farmer when the processor provides seeds, fertilizer, or pesticides as part of an outgrower scheme.[1] In this context, for example, formal financial institutions can enter the equation and make credit flows available, perhaps

Box 4.15   Sri Lankan Cinnamon

World trade in spices, their related products, and herbal health care products are estimated to be US$200 billion per year with an annual growth rate of over 5 percent. In Sri Lanka, growing and processing spices provides cash income to over 400,000 smallholders and many processors. Sri Lanka commands over 80 percent of the world's true cinnamon production and exports close to 13,000 mt per year in the form of quills in different grades, mainly in bulk form, at a value of US$50 million.

Cinnamon zeylanicum, the source of the spice, is a small, unassuming evergreen that is native to Sri Lanka's west and southwest. Cinnamon has been popular for ages, imported to Egypt as early as 2000 BC. Demand for cinnamon helped drive the European "age of discovery" beginning with Vasco da Gama's first trip to Asia in 1497. There is "true" Ceylon cinnamon, and there are other spices which are incorrectly referred to as cinnamon, such as Cassia (*C. aromaticum*), Indonesian cinnamon (*C. burmannii*), and others (e.g. *C. loureirii*). The price differential between true cinnamon and Cassia is 4:1. While European and Latin American markets distinguish the varieties, the U.S. market does not. Thus, in the U.S., low-quality cassia sells for a fraction of the price of the Sri Lankan product.

Members of the spice industry cluster formed the Sri Lankan Spice Council (TSC) in 2001 to establish Sri Lanka as one of the top five branded, value-added spices and allied products marketers in the world. TSC has worked hard to differentiate its Ceylon cinnamon from lower-quality substitutes. One problem that TSC addressed was that Ceylon cinnamon and Cassia are classified under the same Harmonized System (HS) code of the World Customs Organization (WCO). In collaboration with the U.S. Department of Commerce and Sri Lanka Customs, and after deliberations with the WCO, TSC succeeded in obtaining a separate subheading for "Ceylon cinnamon" in the HS code.

TSC has carried out several actions to improve product quality and market access. TSC carried out a market analysis to locate the best sales prospects for whole spices and to identify the kind of bottling and packaging that is required for optimal value creation in the United States. TSC has also worked with local spice smallholders and suppliers to improve postharvest handling and management of spices in order to increase the quality of spices that are delivered to Sri Lankan exporters.

Figure 1: Value of Sri Lankan Cinnamon Exports

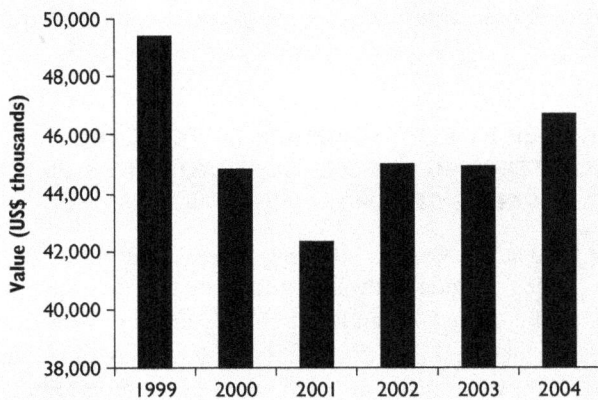

Source: Michael Gorman, J. E. Austin Associates, Inc., and FAOSTAT data.

Figure 2: Cinnamon Exports' Value Chain

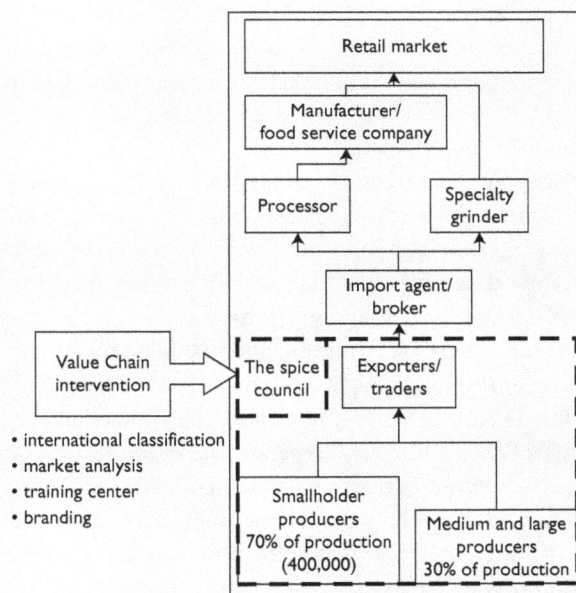

Source: J. E. Austin Associates, Inc.

Figure 4.50   Mapping Actual and Potential Business and Financial Services

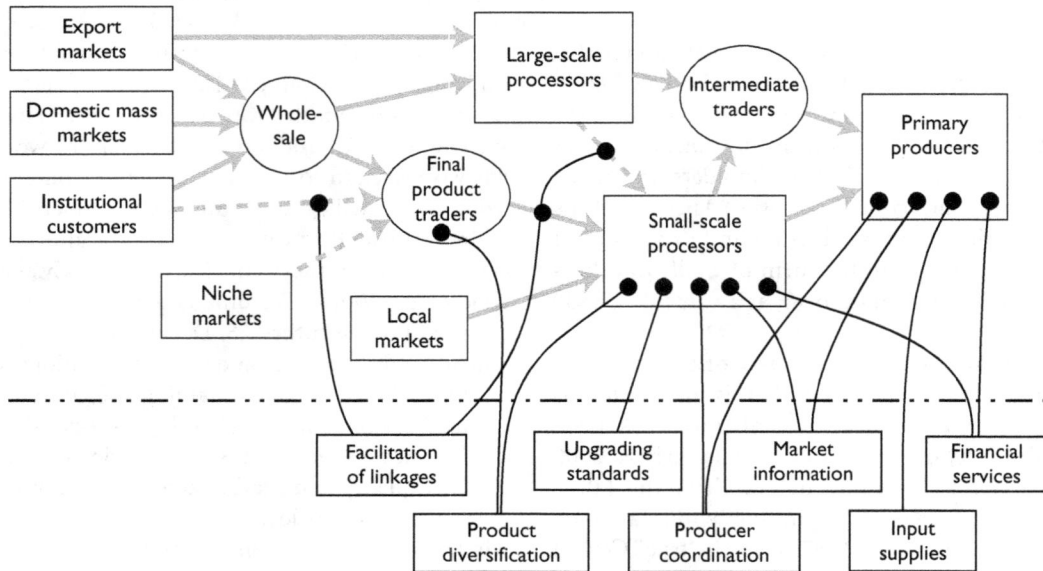

Source: Albu and Griffith (2005), "Mapping the Market: A Framework for Rural Enterprise Development Policy and Practice," at *www.practicalaction. org/?id=mapping_the_market.*

even extending the offer to other financial services (savings, transfers, and longer-term loans). This would extend the depth, breadth, and sustainability of the services that were previously provided (mainly short-term working capital).

To implement this tool, it is useful to map the particular services that are currently being provided (their sustainability, quality, and location within the chain), as well as those services that are potentially viable that can improve the chain's performance. Figure 4.50 provides an example of what the resulting map could look like.

The mapping is, of course, related to Tool 2, Designing Informed Strategies across the Value Chain, as well as to Tool 3, Conducting Benchmarking and Gap Assessments of Value Chains. Indeed, sound value chain analysis involves mapping the actors and, by benchmarking against competitors, identifying needed services that could enhance the value chain. The focus here, though, is in implementing the results of analytical methods and, given its importance and potential, this implementation is treated as a separate tool in this section.

Once the map of current and potential services is complete, interventions can be developed to introduce a service for which there is potential demand within the chain, as well as to improve the quantity, quality, and sustainability of those currently being offered.

Entrepreneurs, businesses, and practitioners will need to carry out feasibility analyses and develop business plans.

Within development projects, the approach will often involve one or more pilot initiatives carried out in close collaboration with value chain participants, providing adequate support to encourage emergence of the market for service. In most cases, services that are provided on a market basis will be more sustainable, as well as those provided by specialized institutions. As many of the services are from sound, replicable businesses, they can be good examples of the replicable business models discussed in tool 5.

A STEP-BY-STEP SUMMARY OF TOOL 10: IDENTIFYING NEEDED SUPPORT SERVICES FOR THE VALUE CHAIN

- Along the value chain, map services that are currently being provided as well as those services that are potentially viable and can lead to improvements in the chain's performance. Benchmarking and analyzing gaps against other value chains are particularly useful tools for identifying potential services not being provided.

- Include in the map indications of the services' sustainability, quality, and location within the chain.

- Conduct feasibility studies and develop business plans to introduce services for which there is potential demand within the chain and to improve the quantity, quality, and sustainability of those currently being offered. In most cases, services that are provided on a market basis will be more sustainable, as well as those provided by specialized institutions.

NOTE

1. The term "outgrower scheme" is often reserved for schemes where agribusiness has considerable control over the smallholder production process, providing a large number of services, such as input credits, tillage, spraying, and harvesting. The smallholder provides land and labor in return for this comprehensive extension/input package. The high-value horticulture export sector is currently the focus of considerable development of outgrower schemes (for example, Hortico in Zimbabwe and Homegrown in Kenya).

Identifying Needed Support Services for the Value Chain— Zambian Cotton

Carlton Jones and Martin Webber
J. E. Austin Associates, Inc.

INTRODUCTION

Commercially viable extension services can be vital to a value chain's health. In the case of Zambia's cotton industry, support services were provided in a variable market that featured too many independent cotton traders and service providers, ultimately resulting in significant loan defaults, decreases in production, and the failure of many service providers. This case examines how a large private firm identified and altered the way it provided extension services to small growers, helping to stabilize and reinvigorate Zambia's cotton value chain.

POINTS TO CONSIDER

When reviewing this case, consider the following questions:

- What led to the need to provide support services?
- When is it appropriate to consider implementing different models?
- What role does the private sector play in implementation?

BACKGROUND

From the late 1970s until 1994, Zambia's cotton purchasing, processing, and marketing was controlled by the state-owned Lint Company of Zambia (LINTCO). During that period, LINTCO purchased seed cotton from an estimated 140,000 small farmers at a fixed price and extended services such as the provision of certified seeds, pesticides, sprayers, bags, and advice on growing techniques. LINTCO was the principle buyer of seed cotton, the sole provider of extension services, and the sole distributor of inputs on credit. Production fluctuated during this period but generally trended downward (figure 4.51). By the early 1990s, LINTCO was operating at a loss, having accumulated substantial unpaid debts.

These trends began to change in 1994. Zambia's president, Frederick Chiluba, implemented a wide-ranging restructuring of Zambia's economy, including privatizing the cotton industry through the Zambia Privatization Agency (ZPA). ZPA facilitated the sale of LINTCO to Lonrho Cotton and Clark Cotton, two private ginners and exporters. The two firms operated in different regions of the country, and both worked through direct outgrower schemes that offered inputs and extension services on credit to farmers. When farmers sold their cotton to ginners, the cost of the inputs and services they received before harvest was deducted from their selling price. Because both ginners operated in otherwise underserved markets, their practice of providing seed, other inputs, and services on credit involved minimal risk. Repayment rates averaged 86 percent.

The expansion of cotton production attracted four new ginners and delinters to the market.[1] National cotton production increased through 1997.

To serve the increased demand for cotton, some ginners contracted with independent outgrower agents to recruit more farmers to produce and source cotton to them. These outgrower agents received inputs from the ginners, distributed

Figure 4.51   Zambian Cotton Exports, 1990–94

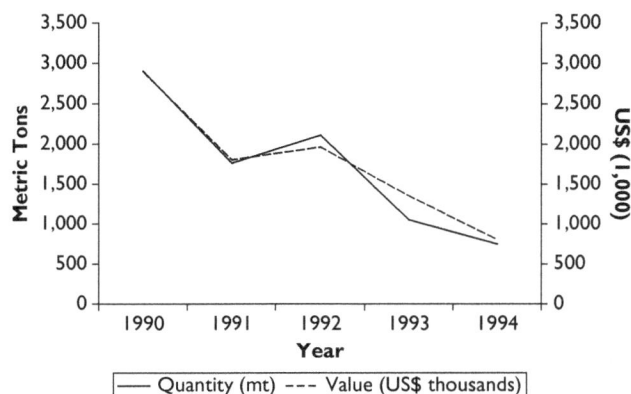

Source: FAOSTAT data.

Figure 4.52   Zambia's Cotton Value Chain

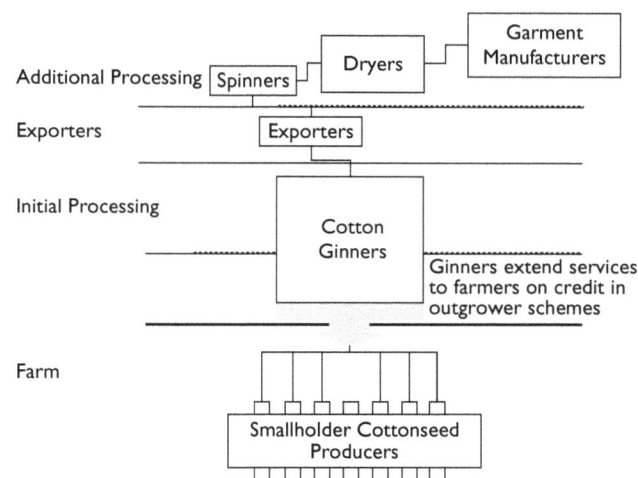

Source: J. E. Austin Associates, Inc.

them to their farm networks on credit, and when harvest time came, sold the cotton gathered from the farmers back to their respective ginners. In the same way that the increased cotton production attracted new ginners, the apparent success of the outgrower agents attracted additional independent agents to the market. These agents purchased inputs from other sources and offered them to any farmer on credit. In return, that farmer would sell cotton back to the independent agent, who would sell to any ginner willing to pay.

This unchecked proliferation of ginners and independent agents led to many problems. By 1998, ginning capacity exceeded production by 50,000 tons per year (Tschirley, Zulu, and Shaffer 2004). With too many agents competing for a limited number of farmers, sourcing was chaotic. This competition led to growing distrust and a lack of transparency in price setting, with agents and ginners vying to outbid each other for cotton. Some farmers, despite having agreed to outgrower contracts with specific ginners, sold their cotton to any agent willing to pay more than the contract price. Some agents purposefully sought to outbid outgrower contracts to acquire cotton. The entire value chain became volatile as ginners and outgrowers experienced increased incidences of defaulted loans. Some agents compensated for large portfolios of defaulted loans by marking up the inputs they sold to the remaining farmers who had remained loyal. This made it even more difficult for those remaining farmers to make a profit and resulted in even higher rates of loan defaults.

By 1999, the entire Zambian cotton value chain was in a crisis (figures 4.52 and 4.53). At this time, Lonrho, while negotiating its own sale to Dunavant, began laying the groundwork for a new service and extension model. At the time of its sale, Lonrho was projected to post a US$2 million

per year shortfall. To lower the likelihood of their own default, the remaining ginners stopped making embedded service contracts with growers. In 2000, with no other means to finance production, farmer output decreased to 50,000 mt, with just 2,500 mt exported (both less than half of 1998 levels). Many of the outgrower agents that contributed to the repayment crisis closed down, and the entire value chain had an average credit default rate of 53 percent. Amaka Holdings, a ginning company, went out of business, leaving the remaining ginners to retool in an effort to survive the market crash.

DUNAVANT'S DISTRIBUTOR MODEL

After taking over Lonrho's operations, Dunavant, a privately held U.S.-based cotton company, further implemented and perfected Lonrho's service and extension model. The new approach impacted Zambia's cotton industry in two ways. First, the service-extension model showed that outgrower schemes could work with little risk of loan defaults if the schemes were properly designed and managed. Second, Dunavant used its distributor model to significantly expand its production network (see figure 4.54).

Dunavant's distributor model was very different from previous schemes. In the past, Lonrho relied on a large number of direct company employees, including almost 800 extension agents, to carry out the required activities. Overhead in the previous model was significant, and this burden was greatly exacerbated when borrowers defaulted. In the new distributor model, Dunavant used almost no direct-hire employees to

Figure 4.53   Zambian Competition for Cottonseed

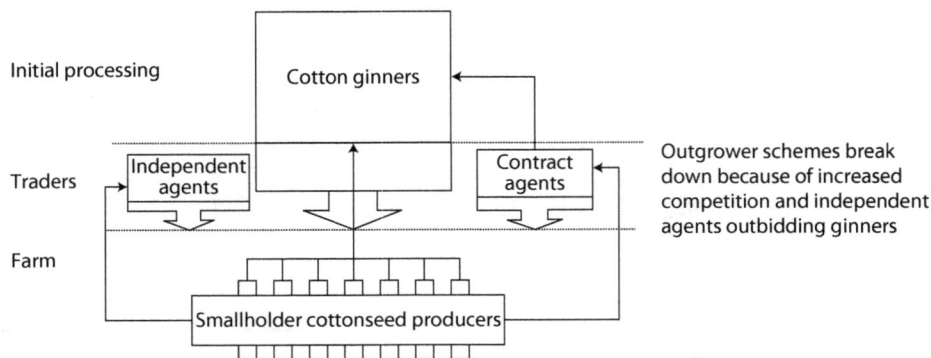

Source: J. E. Austin Associates, Inc.

Figure 4.54   The Dunavant Distributor Model

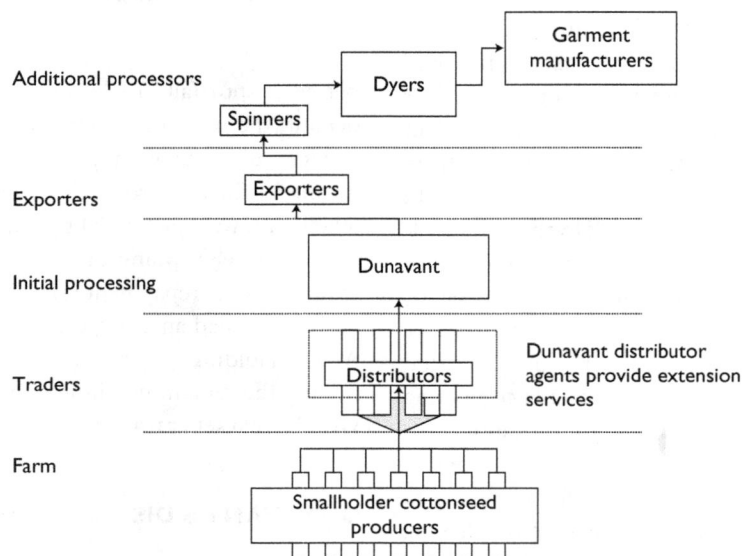

Source: J. E. Austin Associates, Inc.

deliver services. Instead, "distributors" were mobilized via formal written contracts to identify farmers. The distributors would acquire the inputs from Dunavant on credit, deliver them along with technical advice to the farmers, and ensure that farmers sold their cotton back to Dunavant in order to recover the input credit. In this scheme, the distributor's compensation was directly tied to the amount of credit recovered. Paid on a graduating scale, the more credit a distributor recovered, the more the distributor earned.

Table 4.17 illustrates the distributor compensation plan. Distributors could earn up to 21.5 percent ($0.65 \times 0.05 +$ $0.85 \times 0.075 + 1.0 \times 0.125 = 0.0215)^2$ in commissions based on their efforts. To maintain performance, Dunavant dropped any distributor who could not bring in a minimum of 50 percent of their credit portfolio. By 2003, the company raised this minimum credit recovery rate to 60 percent. In some of the better-performing regions, the cut-off rate went to levels as high as 80 percent.

Another unique aspect of Dunavant's distributor model was the "work-in, live-in" principle. Distributors were required to farm cotton themselves and live in the same area as their farmer network.

Table 4.17   Dunavant Compensation Plan

Recovery percentage	Compensation rate
65–84	5 percent of the total credit
85–99	Additional 7.5 percent of the total credit
100	Additional 12.5 percent of the total credit

Source: Dunavant, 2006.

Dunavant showed its commitment to the success of the program by offering two types of training: credit management and cotton production and harvesting best practices. These courses laid a strong foundation of sound business operations and management for the distributors, allowing them to assess farmers' creditworthiness while rapidly growing their portfolios.

As Dunavant's distributor network grew, its outgrower network followed suit with the average distributor handling 65 growers each. In step with this growth was Dunavant's realized increase in credit repayments. In the year prior to the scheme's implementation, Dunavant's reported recovery rate was 67 percent. After one year in the system, the rate grew to 80 percent—in the second year, to 88 percent and, after three years, to 93 percent.

CONCLUSIONS: GROWTH OF A SECTOR

Dunavant's successful rollout of its distributor model of providing services to farmers encouraged other ginners to follow with similar arrangements. Not all ginners replicated the model exactly, and most did not place as rigorous an emphasis on training and distributor selection as Dunavant. Still others, such as Zambia's other large ginner, Clark Cotton (Clark's southern African holdings were purchased by Cargill in 1996), maintained the old model and continued to extend services to farmers via its own employees.

In all, the entire Zambian cotton value chain has experienced rapid growth since the sharp drop of the early 2000s (figure 4.55). This rapid recovery was led entirely by the private sector, in large part because of Dunavant's ability to identify, design, and deliver innovative ways to extend services to small farmers. As of the 2005–06 season, Dunavant was outperforming other Zambian ginners in terms of volume and produced an estimated 115,000 mt of cotton lint. Clark/Cargill is second in the Zambian market with 60,000 mt.

Figure 4.55   Zambia's Cotton Lint Exports, 1995–2004

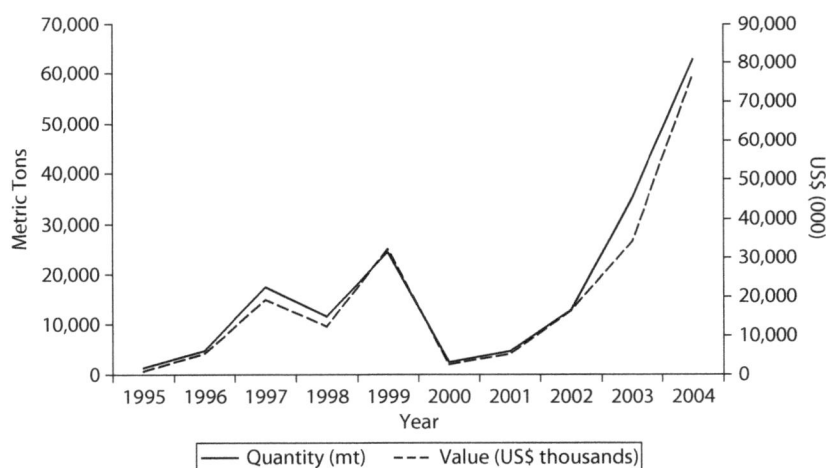

Source: FAOSTAT data.

NOTES

1. Amaka Holdings opened in 1997, but is now closed, having gone into receivership. Continental Ginnery opened in 1997, Mulungushi Textiles (now Zambia China Mulungushi Textiles) opened in 1999. Northern Growers began service in 1986, and expanded in 1997.

2. Tschirley (2004).

Improving the Operating Environment by Promoting Public-Private Dialogue

ENABLING ENVIRONMENT

The enabling environment for business is critical to the development and growth of a vibrant private sector and its firms. Constraints in the enabling environment can limit business growth, such as through:

- Increasing costs
- Decreasing competitiveness
- Decreasing product and service quality
- Increasing business and investment risk
- Decreasing foreign and domestic investment
- Constraining businesses' willingness to pursue long-term strategies

The value chain's ability and willingness to upgrade and make strategic choices often depends on the development of a long-term strategy. However, a burdensome regulatory, legal, and policy environment can severely hinder the growth of industries, and diminish competitiveness and success in global markets. A poor business environment not only limits local firms' capital investments, it also obstructs foreign investment. Reforming policies so that they are favorable to businesses can encourage dynamism and efficiency.

Value chains' integrated nature makes them susceptible to constraints in the enabling environment at any level. Constraints affect their costs and ability to act, from the most basic supplier of raw materials to the broker who arranges for a large international shipment of finished goods.

Government is often the principal actor in changing regulatory issues and is responsible for improvements and reforms. Often the private sector's interactions with government (and those of development partners as well) tend to be on the national level. However, to a value chain, the capacities and wisdom of local government can be even more important due to their impact on strategic portions of the supply or value chain. Lacking incentives and experience, local governments tend to be less sophisticated in their understanding of the constraints faced by value chain members in the enabling environment. Businesses within the value chain often have more personal relationships with local officials, which can be both a benefit and a barrier to enacting pro-growth change. Often, and especially in lower-income countries, the private sector feels powerless to effect change or believes that promoting change is not their responsibility. However, the private sector must often serve as the impetus for reform and sometimes even lead the search for solutions by providing government officials with irrefutable data and a plan for change through an open dialogue process.

PUBLIC-PRIVATE DIALOGUE

Through both official and ad hoc forums and vehicles for dialogue between the public and private sectors, the value chain can communicate its opportunities and challenges within the enabling environment. Through the value chain's sharing of industry strategies developed through analytical tools such as positioning and benchmarking, the public sector can understand the impacts of its own actions, decisions, and capacities and more effectively prioritize issues and actions to align with private sector needs.

Public-private dialogue (PPD) implementation can take several forms but generally follows the format described below (see also table 4.18). This applies to national, subnational, or sector-specific dialogues.[1]

- **Establish a mandate.** This can include memorandums of understanding, formal government mandates, or temporary initiatives.
- **Align with an institution.** Possible choices would be investment promotion agencies, government ministries,

Table 4.18 Sample Checklist of Issues to Address at Various Stages of the PPD Process

	Range of issues to identify and tackle while designing or maintaining partnerships
1- Ignition	Government willingness Cross-spectrum support Business priorities Linkages with existing organizations Sense of urgency Establishing credibility
2- Participation	Selection mechanisms Terms of membership Choosing key individuals Striking a balance in representation Including SMEs Civil society participation
3- Structure	Permanent secretariat Individual leadership Working groups Government structure Transparency and rules of engagement Institutional flexibility
4- Goals and outputs	Mission statements Managing expectations Quantifiable outcomes Reform type and importance Monitoring and accountability Clarity and credibility
5- Role of donors	Type and level of support Public image Quality control Avoiding favoritism Sponsorship versus direction Ownership transfer
6- Outreach	Branding and marketing Using the media Engaging the grassroots Enlisting the public Targeting decision makers Sharing experience

Source: www.publicprivatedialogue.org.

donor agencies, or a newly created and independent institution. Institutional alignment also includes the location of meetings and where the initiative's secretariat will be housed.

■ **Clearly defined structure and rules for participation.** The PPD process should have a secretariat and working groups for specific issues. The secretariat will serve as the coordinating body, and working group members will come from the private sector, governments, associations, academia, and possibly donors. Participants should be decision makers and influential members of the private sector who want to facilitate change. As broad and representative a group as possible should be chosen and should include small businesses, minorities, and women to the extent possible.

■ **Identify and support a champion and a facilitator.** A strong but not overly powerful champion should be chosen from the constituency to represent and drive the process. Also, dialogue facilitators should serve as brokers and help participants negotiate and set timetables and priorities.

■ **Set clear goals and reach them.** Determine the types of outputs the PPD process will generate. These can take the form of roadmaps, a policy white paper, or reform proposals in addition to softer outputs such as cooperation, which emerges through dialogue. Quantifiable results early on can help build momentum and credibility for the process.

■ **Public outreach and communication.** This step is vital for disseminating broader-scale changes in the enabling environment and generating larger-scale buy-in for reforms. It can include branding of the PPD initiative, media education and awareness campaigns, and social marketing.

■ **Monitor and evaluate outcomes.** Documentation of clear successes and obstacles is important to building trust and generating traction for change.

It is important to have channels of communication open with national and local municipal governments, because they each have a different influence on limiting or facilitating investment and growth. For example, businesses cannot take advantage of an excellent customs system with low tariffs if the roads leading to the port are impassable. The value chain must know which levels of government determine the policies that most affect their operating environments and work to engage them. The value chain may also be able to join with local public sector leaders to advocate at the national level. In order to effectively communicate as a unit, value chain participants (or industries they represent) must first develop a clear consensus strategy that outlines and prioritizes the policy changes needed.

PPD can be a tool for encouraging policy changes that enhance the competitive position of the firms within the value chain and link the value chain's strategy to the dialogue process. PPD's success rests on several factors that affect the quality of the dialogue and its strength as a forum for advocacy. First, the private sector must clearly

Tanzania has the climate and altitude to produce high-quality coffee, but several constraints prohibited it from competing seriously in the global specialty coffee market—the only growing segment of the market and the one offering attractive prices. These included an aging population of coffee trees, a scarcity of well-operated wet-milling stations, and a restrictive enabling environment that forced all coffee to be sold through a blind national auction system. These constraints limited the industry and resulted in low prices to growers, providing them little incentive to produce high-quality coffee or reinvest in their plantations. The coffee sector actors wanted change but were unaware of their options. Likewise, the government of Tanzania (GoT) knew that something needed to be done to improve the enabling environment but didn't know where to begin.

In 2001, TechnoServe helped coffee growers form the Association of Kilimanjaro Specialty Coffee Growers (now called KILICAFE). The organization is a farmer-owned association that provides services to its members. These services include coffee marketing, provision of inputs, quality coffee production, lobbying for regulatory change, and cupping services for quality identification.

Recognizing that changes in the enabling environment would be important to the sector, TechnoServe brought the coffee sector's various stakeholders together for roundtable discussions. These discussions included the Tanzanian Coffee Board, KILICAFE members, and private buyers. Participants noted that they were the first discussions that actually involved all actors in the coffee sector. As a result, in partnership with stakeholders, TechnoServe undertook the Coffee Taxation and Benchmarking Initiative (CTBI) to investigate Tanzania's taxation policies and regulations governing the sector.

The study involved benchmarking comparisons with five "peer" coffee-producing nations: Costa Rica, Ethiopia, Guatemala, Kenya, and Uganda. In addition, TechnoServe facilitated a tour for Tanzania's Minister of Agriculture to Costa Rica to meet his counterpart, as well as other coffee stakeholders in the country. Findings from the study showed that, compared to the

other countries, Tanzania had the highest taxes on coffee producers (up to 21 percent) and the lowest rate of reinvestment. In some instances, countries levied significantly lower taxes, and these lower taxes helped alleviate the effect of major price drops and improve competition.

TechnoServe and the other stakeholders discussed the CTBI study and reached out to the GoT, making the following recommendations:

- Harmonize taxes
- Reduce steps and fees for licensing
- Allow smallholder growers of specialty coffee to bypass the national auction system (Moshi Coffee Auction) and negotiate/sell directly to specialty buyers (direct export)

In June 2003, Tanzanian Minister of Finance, Basil Mramba, announced sweeping reforms that included the CTBI study's recommendations. The tax and marketing law reforms took effect in October 2003. In March 2004, KILICAFE, able to bypass the Moshi Coffee Auction and negotiate directly with specialty buyers, sold over 23,000 pounds of fully washed Arabica coffee directly to Peet's Coffee and Tea, a U.S.-based specialty coffee roaster. This sale involved five small-grower groups, which represented 645 small growers. The small growers received a 150 percent price premium on the coffee sold to Peet's compared to other growers. This was the first direct grower-to-roaster transaction in Tanzania's history. Later that year, Peet's and KILICAFE created the "Tanzania Kilimanjaro Limited Edition" coffee brand, which was sold exclusively by Peet's coffee stores and distributors.

Today, taxes in the Tanzanian coffee sector have decreased from 21 percent to a range of 14–16 percent. The steps and fees associated with licensing are also fewer, and lower, respectively. However, the reform that has helped spark revitalization in the industry was the ability to directly export specialty coffee. Since the Peet's sale in 2005, KILICAFE has continued to negotiate and sell high-grade coffee to Peet's, Starbucks, Illycafe, and a range of other global specialty buyers.

Source: Carlton Jones, J. E. Austin Associates, Inc.

understand the public sector's role in the value chain. The public sector may often be blamed for, or looked to for solutions to, problems that are or should be more in private producers' control. It is also helpful to understand that the policy and regulatory environment have both legal and enforcement components and that these may differ substantially. The infrastructure environment and political power dynamics between various stakeholders will make up the climate of dialogue.

A benchmarking activity of specific business environment elements can be a starting point for generating a forum for constructive dialogue among stakeholders along the value chain, as it will generate credible information for decision making. Sound prioritization and decision making are difficult if parties are seen as advocating biased or unfounded positions or asking for special favors.

Once parties have agreed to discuss their common interests, a PPD must establish certain parameters for effective discussion. Some general, overarching principles must be in place for the forum to be effective in reducing barriers to value chain efficiency. A PPD must include the "right" people from both the public and private sectors. This means that key decision makers and knowledgeable, credible opinion leaders must be present, rather than just the highest-ranking member of an organization. Participants must also be encouraged to commit to the process and leave egos and political infighting at the door.

They should all be operating from the same base of information and have access to the same data. This may be the benchmarking data gathered through a previous exercise. The use of benchmarking data can be especially helpful if it is obtained through public-private collaboration.

The dialogue should have clear goals, collaboratively agreed upon. It is important that all of the stakeholders involved agree on the discussion's topics and goals to avoid sessions that get off track or that degenerate into blame and fault-finding. Every PPD mechanism should have a method for providing feedback and input into policy formation.

The private sector must make a credible case for change through the strength of its strategy and by clearly communicating its goals. By using sound data, credible and objective outside experts to provide analysis, and well-facilitated discussion, the private sector can create a nonthreatening and constructive dialogue environment.

It is helpful for the private sector to explain the tax and revenue impacts for the public sector if changes are put in place. The private sector should be able to link changes to meeting government goals, job creation, and revenue increases.

PPD can encourage action that benefits the value chain by educating and informing the public sector. The private sector should be able to communicate those points at which the greatest value is added (or subtracted) from the value chain and ways to make it easy for the public sector to decide on actions that will contribute to the value chain's strength.

Associations and institutions for collaboration, as Michael Porter has called them, are either formal or informal organizations that facilitate the exchange of information among members and can help foster cooperation. They can take the form of regional, social, or professional networks or they can be industry or professional associations that cut across various industry sectors and value chains. These institutions play a significant role in strengthening and promoting the value chain or industry agenda. There are types of institutions called business membership organizations (BMOs) that serve a variety of specialized functions (see table 4.19).

BMOs can improve the business environment by building and supporting trust among its members; establishing a forum for dialogue, collective strategy, and planning; increasing the ability to communicate with one voice through advocacy activities; and assisting with other actions (see tables 4.19 and 4.20).

The International Finance Corporation and the World Bank have an excellent resource detailing best-practice implementations of PPD initiatives. These cases, along with guides and comprehensive information on PPD, can be found on the online forum, www.publicprivatedialogue.org.

A STEP-BY-STEP SUMMARY OF TOOL 11: IMPROVING THE OPERATING ENVIRONMENT BY PROMOTING PUBLIC-PRIVATE DIALOGUE

- Identify burdensome regulations, laws, and policies negatively impacting the growth and competitiveness of the value chain.
- Qualify and quantify the impact of the current business environment on growth and competitiveness using empirical metrics, such as benchmarking activity. This will provide basic data as a platform for public-private dialogue.
- Establish a clear mandate for the public-private forum. This can include memoranda of understanding, government reforms, or temporary initiatives.
- Identify institutions whose support will showcase official commitment to the public-private dialogue and resulting decisions and actions.

Table 4.19 Types of Business Membership Organizations and Their Functions

BMO type	Defining factor	Typical functions and services
Trade/industry associations	Occupation/industry	Arbitration, quota allocation, industry standards setting, lobbying. quality upgrading
SME associations	Size of firm	Entrepreneurship training and consulting, finance schemes, group services
Women's associations	Gender	Entrepreneurship training, microfinance, gender-specific advocacy
Employers' associations	Labor relations	Interest representation vis-à-vis unions, professional information, and training
Confederations	Apex bodies	High-level advocacy, general business information, research, coordination of member associations
Binational associations	Transnationality	Trade promotion, trade fairs, matchmaking
Chambers	Geographic region	Delegated government functions, arbitration courts, basic information services, matchmaking, local economic development

Source: World Bank (2005), "Building the Capacity of Business Membership Organizations: Guiding Principles for Project Managers," Second Edition.

Table 4.20 Pursuing Effective Dialogue

Ineffective	Effective
■ Individual company	■ Value chain stakeholders
■ Ad hoc complaints	■ Comprehensive vision
■ Operational level	■ Strategy
■ Laundry lists	■ Priorities
■ Anecdotal evidence	■ Data and analysis
■ Concessions	■ Co-responsibility
■ Opposite sides	■ Same side of table

Source: J. E. Austin Associates, Inc.

■ Clearly define the structure and rules of the public-private dialogue.

■ Encourage individual firms and organizations, which are capable of facilitating and following through with PPD, to be leaders in the forum.

■ Identify measurable outcomes for the dialogue.

■ Monitor and publicize the progress of the dialogue and its outcomes.

NOTE

1. Source: PPD Handbook, World Bank.

Improving the Operating Environment through Public-Private Dialogue—Botswana Cattle Producers Association

Carlton Jones
J. E. Austin Associates, Inc.

INTRODUCTION

Understanding the role the private sector plays in facilitating change at the local, regional, and national government levels is important when considering changes to the enabling environment for value chains. If the private sector does not speak with an informed, unified voice, does not have a common agenda, and does not understand how to engage the government, change is unlikely.

In this case, Botswana's parastatal meat monopoly addressed a startling sector contraction through public-private dialogue, organizing the Botswana Cattle Producers Association and soliciting its help in designing a sector revitalization strategy. The dialogue is ongoing and is still catalyzing change within the sector. It demonstrates how change is occurring after private sector participants in Botswana's red meat value chain organized to effectively engage the government for mutually beneficial changes in the red meat sector.

POINTS TO CONSIDER

Look for some of the steps outlined in the tool:

- Was a mandate established?
- What institutions did the private sector align with as it organized?
- Who was identified as a champion or facilitator for the group?
- What were some of the goals, were they clear, and how were they achieved?
- What vehicles were used to engage the government?
- Are there any measurable outcomes?

BACKGROUND

In Botswana, the red meat industry (figure 4.56) is one of three main economic pillars (behind only diamond mining and tourism) that support the economy. But with declining exports and losses experienced by cattle farmers and the state-run Botswana Meat Commission (BMC), something had to be done to turn the situation around. From contributing around 30 percent of GDP at independence in 1966, the sector shrank to 3 percent or less of GDP in 2004. Likewise, over the same period, the contribution of beef to national export revenues fell from 70 percent to 1.7 percent (Jefferis 2005). In 1998, beef export value was US$92.57 million. By 2004, it was US$46.38 million (FAOSTAT). Over the same period, export quantity fell from 25,000 tons to 8,600 tons (figure 4.57).

Established in 1966, the BMC is the country's sole exporter and domestic wholesaler of beef. This status, in addition to other privileges, is conferred by the BMC Act. Botswana's main beef export market is the European Union. Protected as a monopoly, the BMC acts as the country's single industrial processor and export channel and sets the prices it pays to cattle producers. The BMC operates abattoirs in Lobatse,

Figure 4.56 Botswana's Red Meat Value Chain

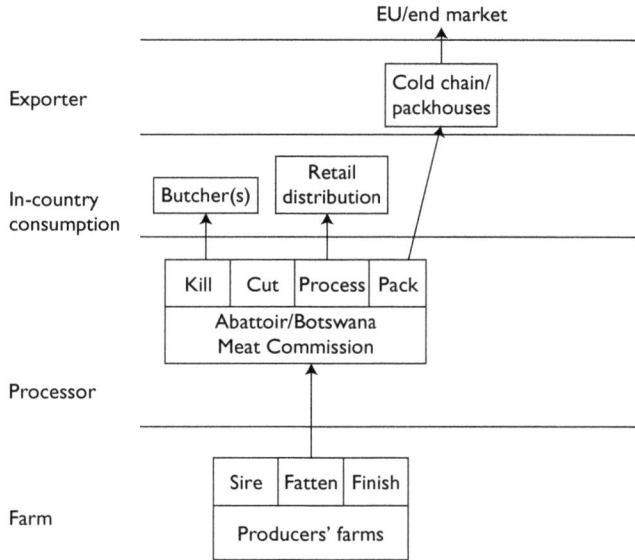

Source: J. E. Austin Associates, Inc.

Figure 4.58 Locations of Botswana's Abattoirs

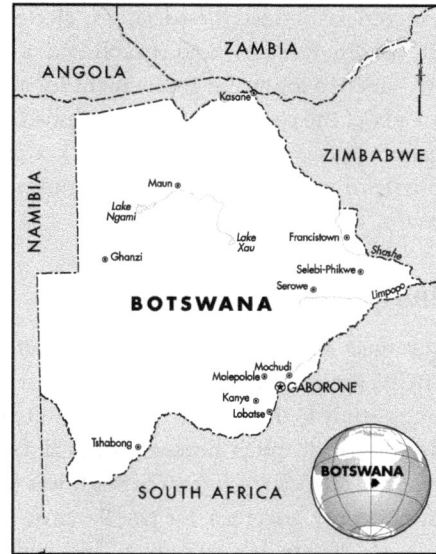

Source: World Bank.

Figure 4.57 Exports of Botswana's Beef, 1990–2004

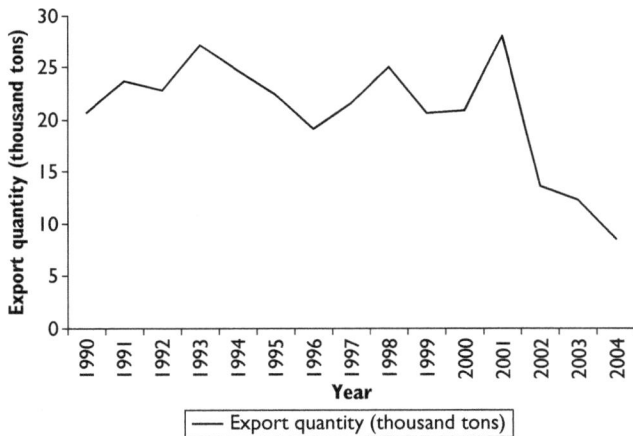

Source: FAOSTAT data.

Francistown, and Maun (figure 4.58) that were designed to handle an output of 8,000 cattle and 500 small stock per day (Lobatse), 400 cattle and 140 small stock per day (Francistown), and 100 cattle per day (Maun)—but each operated at levels well below their capacity. The Maun abattoir was permanently closed in 1996 after an outbreak of cattle lung disease necessitated the culling of all cattle in Ngamiland (Botswana Meat Association 2006). Despite the closing of one of the three abattoirs, the remaining two abattoirs were still underutilized. This underutilization drove up unit costs, and the BMC began losing money. Around the same time, EU beef prices leveled, followed by the revenues from cattle sales in Botswana. Cattle producers were severely impacted as well, and were being paid well below export parity (the price neighboring cattle producers received in Namibia and South Africa).

Botswana's cattle farmers often complained among themselves and recognized that it was becoming increasingly difficult to operate, but never organized to generate change in their institutional and enabling environment. However, when losses continued and export revenue continued to decline, cattle producers could use neither their land nor their cattle as collateral against loans. Led by Philip Fischer (a producer himself), cattle producers approached a USAID-funded project, the Southern Africa Global Competitiveness Hub (SAGCH), for assistance in forming a national association. Its goal was to have existing regional cattle-producing associations speak with one voice to create a common agenda and to lobby that agenda for policy change.

BIRTH OF THE BOTSWANA CATTLE PRODUCERS ASSOCIATION

SAGCH was able to provide the technical assistance that led to the formation of the Botswana Cattle Producers Association

(BCPA), an organization that represents the country's 60,000 cattle producers. The BCPA organized, drafted by-laws, registered as an official industry association, elected its first chairperson (Philip Fischer), and established a common agenda from which to lobby the government for action. Initial components of the common agenda included the desire to receive export price parity for their livestock, an improved production system, and the liberalization of Botswana's entire red meat sector.

UNCOVERING THE PROBLEMS

Energized by their ability to organize and hopeful for the future, the BCPA again approached the SAGCH for assistance in conducting a study to uncover all the constraints in the red meat market to provide much-needed statistical data to support their planned advocacy efforts. The study was conducted by the former deputy governor for the Bank of Botswana, Keith Jefferis. Mr. Jefferis is currently an independent consultant and is highly respected within the country. His study produced several key findings.

Declining national herd

Though the data was poor, Mr. Jefferis's study suggested that the national herd population in Botswana was decreasing from its peak of approximately 3 million animals in the early 1980s to about 2.5 million. Rising costs, drought, and cattle producer cash flow problems were all cited as contributing to the herd population decline.

Additionally, he noted that the existing production system, which produced mature cows and oxen, would not provide enough "offtake" to keep up with rising demand. The combination of a declining herd size, stagnating offtake, and rising domestic demand for beef were all contributing to reduced cattle sales to the BMC, and hence reduced throughput and capacity utilization.[1]

High costs throughout the value chain

With high fixed-unit input costs, and abattoirs operating at around 50 percent capacity, the BMC operated at levels severely below built capacity. This inefficiency caused the cost per unit of output to rise. Compared with neighboring countries, Botswana was operating at less than half the volume levels that were expected for a competitive, commercially run operation to survive (Jefferis 2005). Jefferis concluded that this excess capacity was, in part, the result of the 1990 opening of the Francistown abattoir.

Declining revenues

As the BCPA suspected, the study also revealed that the declining prices paid by EU markets resulted in revenue declines and subsequent lower prices paid to cattle producers (in real terms, after adjusting for inflation). Coupled with the government of Botswana's (GoB's) desire to make the consumption of beef affordable for all the people of Botswana, prices remained artificially low. Export cattle producers, without competitive alternative markets for their beef, were limited to selling to only one buyer, the BMC monopoly. This limited their ability to increase profits.

The sector conducted a benchmarking exercise that compared Botswana's cattle market to those in Namibia and South Africa. Comparing these markets, the study also determined that Namibian abattoirs paid 40 percent more than the BMC paid its cattle producers, while South Africa paid twice as much to its producers.

Operating under monopolistic conditions

The study also highlighted a glaring problem: The BMC was operating as a money-losing monopoly whose inefficient operation was leading to the unsustainability of the entire red meat market in Botswana. BCPA producers of export-quality beef were forced to sell at below-market prices to the BMC for exporting. Live cattle exports were banned, as were beef imports. This artificial market structure meant that, without interventions, the national herd would continue to decline, and cattle producers would continue to lose money and possibly be forced to close their operations or move to other countries to survive.

BCPA PUBLISHES FINDINGS AND ENGAGES GOVERNMENT OF BOTSWANA

Shortly after the research was concluded, the above findings were published in a policy paper, "How Trade Liberalization Can Contribute to Solving the Crisis in the Cattle and Beef Sector." This paper, also prepared by Mr. Jefferis, highlighted some of the industry's challenges and made policy recommendations meant for consideration by the government of Botswana and BMC. In May 2005, the BCPA assembled industry stakeholders with the assistance of the SAGCH, and formally presented its findings and Mr. Jefferis's recommendations, several of which are outlined in the following sections (see also figure 4.59).

Figure 4.59   Recommendations for Botswana's Red Meat Value Chain

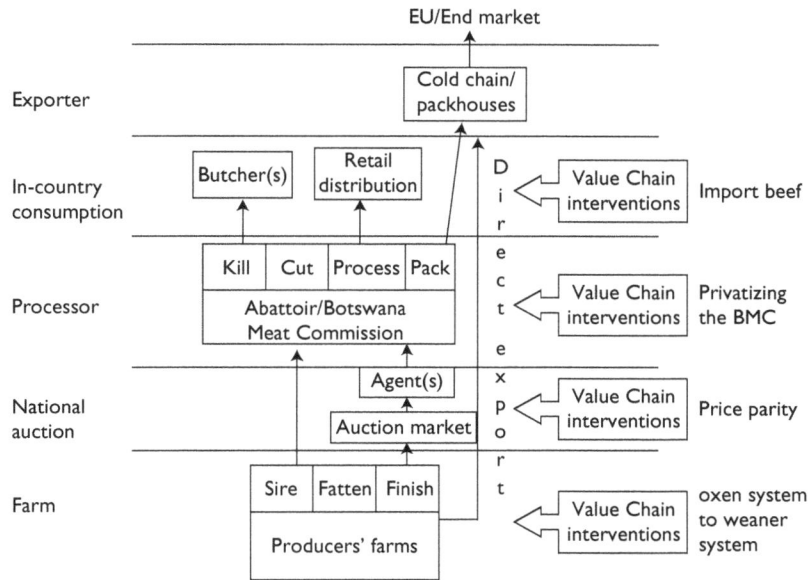

Source: J. E. Austin Associates, Inc.

Changing the cattle production system

Shifting to modern production techniques in Botswana would increase offtake rates and keep up with anticipated demand. As mentioned earlier as a finding from the research, Botswana's production system (the oxen system) was based on selling mature male and female cattle to abattoirs. The modern "weaner" system is the recognized, preferred method of cattle production in the world. In this method, male calves are sold to feedlots as soon as they are weaned. While in feedlots, these weaned male calves are intensively fed and fattened for three to four months, then sold directly to abattoirs. At the farm, remaining herds are then comprised predominately of cows and calves.

In production, the benefits of the weaner system are that farms have higher proportions of (productive) cows, rather than (unproductive) oxen. Farms adopting weaner-system production methods are able to provide younger, better-quality meat because weaners (aged less than a year) are sent to abattoirs instead of mature cattle (whose average age is three years). Additionally, environmental impacts are reduced since animals graze for shorter periods and are younger, reducing the amount of land needed for them to graze.

Weaner-produced cattle are also less impacted by drought, as they make fewer demands on the land for grazing.

This change from an oxen system to a weaner system is a more efficient means of production and could potentially increase offtake from the existing 270,000 to 700,000 per year. More importantly, this production increase does not rely on increasing the national herd size.

Unfortunately, shifting to a weaner system is not possible until prices for cattle are more aligned with costs. That means that BCPA members need to be paid export-parity prices, which did not occur under the existing legislation.

Revising the BMC Act

In Botswana, the BMC Act of 1966 reserves the exportation of live animals or their edible products for the abattoir unless the Minister of Agriculture permits otherwise in writing. In addition, such a permit should be issued with the BMC's consent according to section 21, which addresses controls on the export of cattle and the licensing of export slaughterhouses.

Jefferis's policy recommendation was to revise the BMC Act to remove the prohibition on non-BMC export slaughterhouses and beef exports, and to lift the ban on live-cattle beef imports. Jefferis also included the introduction of a national auction system as the primary method of cattle sales and price determination, accompanied by widely available beef-pricing publications. This would allow the entire beef and cattle industry to be regulated by competition and free-market principles, instead of the existing structure where prices are set solely by the BMC. With BCPA members able to get export-parity prices, they would then be able to afford the switch to weaner production systems.

Based on estimates, if the BMC Act were revised to allow for competition, prices would approximate those found in South Africa, allowing the entire cattle market in Botswana to recover.

Privatizing the BMC

Operating as a monopoly, the BMC hindered growth in the sector. Selling off noncore assets, closing unproductive abattoirs, and restructuring BMC functions toward governance and health enforcement and compliance would allow the industry to move away from its existing protectionist position to being competitive.

To disseminate its research and findings, the BCPA invited key stakeholders and the national press to hear about the challenges faced by Botswana's cattle producers. The event sparked a national debate about how to address the challenges of BCPA members. Just as important, the BCPA was able to produce credible data from which to make its case and, for the first time, BCPA members felt empowered to continue to press for change in their sector.

OUTCOMES

As with several of the cases illustrated in this Guide, this case is still evolving. There have been reforms (see figure 4.60), but more liberalization is necessary to enable BCPA members to export to preferred markets. One immediate success for the BCPA was its ability to garner support, which influenced the GoB to strongly consider its recommendations. Their organization is now a recognized partner of the GoB and is actively engaged in policy discussions that affect the red meat industry. The policy paper which sparked the public-private dialogue that revitalized the industry was later translated into Setswana for the House of Chiefs and other stakeholders in Botswana. The report is seen as one of the single most important outputs that allowed the BCPA to influence the GoB.

In December 2005, the BMC increased the prices that it pays to producers by an average of 40 percent, so they are now in line with neighboring Namibia. It is expected that this price increase will offset some of the losses experienced by BCPA members and will allow them to increase the off-take sent to abattoirs. In March 2006, a further 40 percent price increase for top-grade (prime) beef also went into effect. By July 2006, the GoB and the BMC publicly adopted the BCPA's two primary objectives—to pay export-parity prices and to support conversion to a weaner and feedlot production system (see figure 4.61). Both price increases still affect BMC profitability, but as profits for cattle producers

Figure 4.60   Initial Implementation of Recommendations—Red Meat

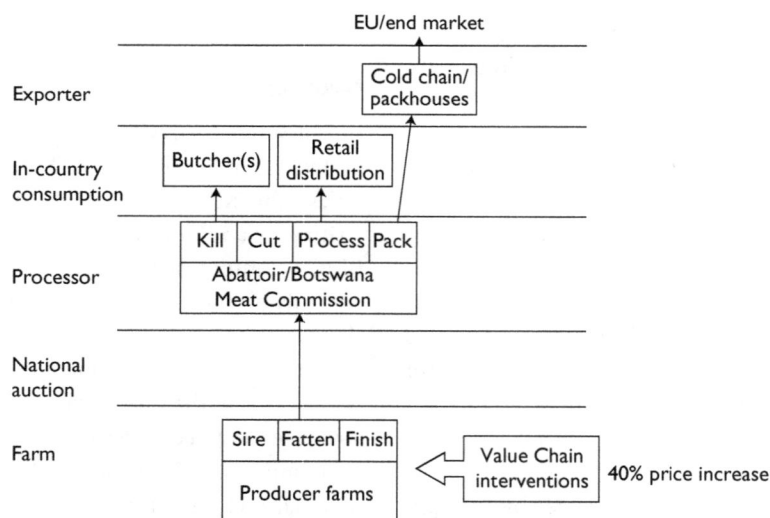

Source: J. E. Austin Associates, Inc.

Figure 4.61   Next Steps for Botswana's Red Meat Value Chain

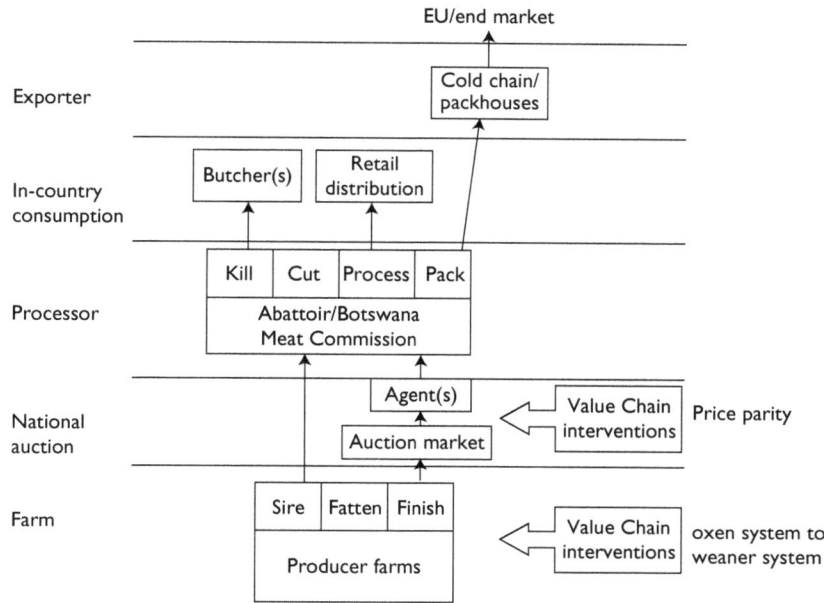

Source: J. E. Austin Associates, Inc.

increase, they will be able to invest in increasing their off-take, which will also positively affect abattoir operations.

CONCLUSIONS: PPD EFFECTS ON THE RED MEAT VALUE CHAIN

Producers are still not being paid full export-price parity. Yet, the latest price increases and the GoB's commitment to adopt weaner production and export-price parity signify to the BCPA that their long-awaited reforms are closer to becoming reality. The BCPA is now working to assist the GoB in implementing the reforms. As the weaner system is adopted, new service providers (feedlot operators) will be necessary to support the industry. Some cattle producers are now looking to expand their businesses into feedlot operations in anticipation of the changes.

Going forward, there are several levels of the value chain that could be affected based on the BCPA's policy recommendations. The most notable are the adoption of a national auction system and the possibility of exporting directly to other markets (bypassing the BMC altogether). The BCPA continues to press for change in its industry and recognizes that continued research and reliable economic data are its best ammunition. As one observer said, "Having a unified voice was important, but more important than that was the sound economic data we presented to the government. Without that data, a unified voice would have been discounted."

NOTE

1. Jefferis Interview 2007.

Achieving Synergies through Clustering

BACKGROUND ON CLUSTERS

Cluster strengthening and cluster-development initiatives began to gain popularity as economic development tools in the 1980s. Since the late 1990s, cluster development and promotion programs have been applied with success in developing and emerging economies, and are starting to take hold in Africa. The cluster approach emphasizes collaboration among cluster members to achieve objectives that are beyond the capabilities of individual firms or even value chains.

"Clusters are geographic concentrations of interconnected companies, specialized suppliers, service providers, and associated institutions in a particular field that are present in a nation or region."[1] Associated institutions can include trade organizations, funding organizations, universities, research organizations, and labor unions, among others. Thus, for our purposes, the cluster is not linear as with a supply or value chain; it is an associated, highly communicating collection of participants, coordinated to focus on achieving objectives that are important to the value chain, or more often, to multiple value chains.

Clusters, which have a geographic focus, arise naturally or can be encouraged to grow around existing assets, firms, or value chains. However, the process of clustering, approaches that encourage cluster-style communication and interaction, and associated cluster initiatives, can play a large role in strengthening firms, value chains, and the economic regions in which they operate.

As a collection of related firms, the cluster benefits from proximity and can increase those firms' competitiveness in the marketplace by exploiting synergies and linkages such as:

- Improved market access
- Firm specialization
- Access to information and market intelligence
- Bargaining power

- Policy change
- Collaboration
- Implementation of standards
- Producer-marketer collaboration
- Supply chain management
- Branding and image
- Shared investment in workforce development, certification and skills, technology, and services

Cluster-based approaches help firms and value chains reduce transaction and information barriers, and, therefore, costs and inefficiencies, as they identify common interests and develop common strategies. This, in turn, can lead to a more formal public-private dialogue process, build collaboration, and exploit synergies among the cluster's organizations. Cooperation that arises from clustering cannot only increase productivity but can also align firms to solve common problems. The strengthening of existing clusters and the fostering of cluster development can begin with a mapping exercise that helps identify potential synergies that could lead to the benefits described above.

THE RELATIONSHIP BETWEEN VALUE CHAINS AND CLUSTERS

At their core, clusters are centered on elements of one or many value chains. Because clusters emphasize locational factors or other commonalities, they can incorporate many value chains or portions of them that operate across clusters. Clusters can form across many links in the value chain or deepen a specific link. From a development perspective, assistance to the value chain is part of the cluster approach. Clustering is a tool to strengthen firm relationships through development of a private sector–led strategy, building of foundations for dialogue, and creation of opportunities for upgrading of skills and technology.

CLUSTER INITIATIVES

An initiative to develop clustering approaches or to strengthen clusters will reinforce the value chain's interests. In developing countries, the most successful cluster initiatives are typically a facilitated but private sector–led process.

When a cluster is promoted by an industry or value chain, its proponents, of course, tend to select a value chain focus. When implemented with government or development partner assistance, clusters need to be selected for participation in the cluster initiative. Thus, it is important to first identify several potential core industries or value chains and then help them to self-select based on their resources, industry willingness to participate, and growth potential. Since the cluster initiative is a facilitated but private sector–led process, the second step is for the facilitator(s) who will be engaging with the industry to gather as much information as possible on broader economic and industry data, principal firms within the industry, and interests for the firms and associated stakeholders.

A clustering initiative (CI) typically takes place in five phases:

1. Initial research and engagement leading to the formation of a cluster initiative (usually through a memorandum of understanding)
   - Develop and present the rationale for cluster cooperation based on data gathered with identified leadership.
   - Generate strong interest in cooperation leading to mutual commitments within the cluster. Can be facilitated through a specific association or organization.
2. Industry diagnostics leading to strategy development
   - Cluster coordinators, industry consultants, and facilitators work with cluster members to evaluate and analyze the current state of the industry and identify potential solutions.
   - A private sector–led industry strategy (including objectives, strategy, and an action plan) is designed and agreed upon.
3. Initial implementation of strategic initiatives
   - Issues outlined in the strategy are prioritized and action plans designed with coordination of those involved.
   - "Quick win" projects, lobbying for policy changes, or initial coordination with academic or associative bodies may be implemented with little funding.
4. Identification of projects and sources of financing
   - Larger-scale projects may need funding from within the industry, government, banks or other sources of investment.

5. Building sustainability
   - Continuity of cluster efforts after the CI depends on creating a strong sense of ownership and on finding leaders who champion continuing improvements.

A cluster map is a valuable planning tool for analyzing the current state of the cluster and can identify where various value chains link into it. Using the map for benchmarking and gap analysis can also identify weaknesses in cross-cutting areas such as skills availability, transport, support, and infrastructure. Figure 4.62 offers an example of a cluster map for cut flowers in Kenya.

Strategic objectives of the cluster should be clearly outlined, and cluster members should be strongly committed to those goals. Implementation often includes dialogue with government and advocacy for changes in regulations and procedures. This process is easier if the cluster has a champion in government who can create traction for the implementation plan and who acts as a facilitator with the government. Intractable government policies, such as promotion of strong state-owned enterprises, could limit the growth achieved through clusters.

A successful cluster-strengthening process can help attract foreign direct investment and the participation of multinational corporations. If a cluster can develop and implement a successful strategy, it can generate internal firm investment, government investment, and external and co-investment opportunities. In addition, clustering projects can be used in conjunction with national initiatives such as special economic zones or export processing zones.

Business associations, trade associations, industry groups, and similar institutions can play an important role in cluster development and sustainability. They have convening power, can provide services in line with the industry strategy, and can advocate on behalf of the industry cluster. The cluster itself can be institutionalized for these same reasons; however, it is important that this does not happen until processes are firmly in place.

CLUSTER EVALUATION

Clusters and cluster initiatives can be evaluated in several ways. The most important indicator of success is whether firms and cluster members are reaping the benefits of the strategies they have implemented. Such successes could include new sales and exports, reduced costs, and increased access to necessary machinery and markets, as well as to appropriate labor and technology. One framework for evaluating successes is the PAID approach

Figure 4.62   Kenya's Cut Flower Cluster

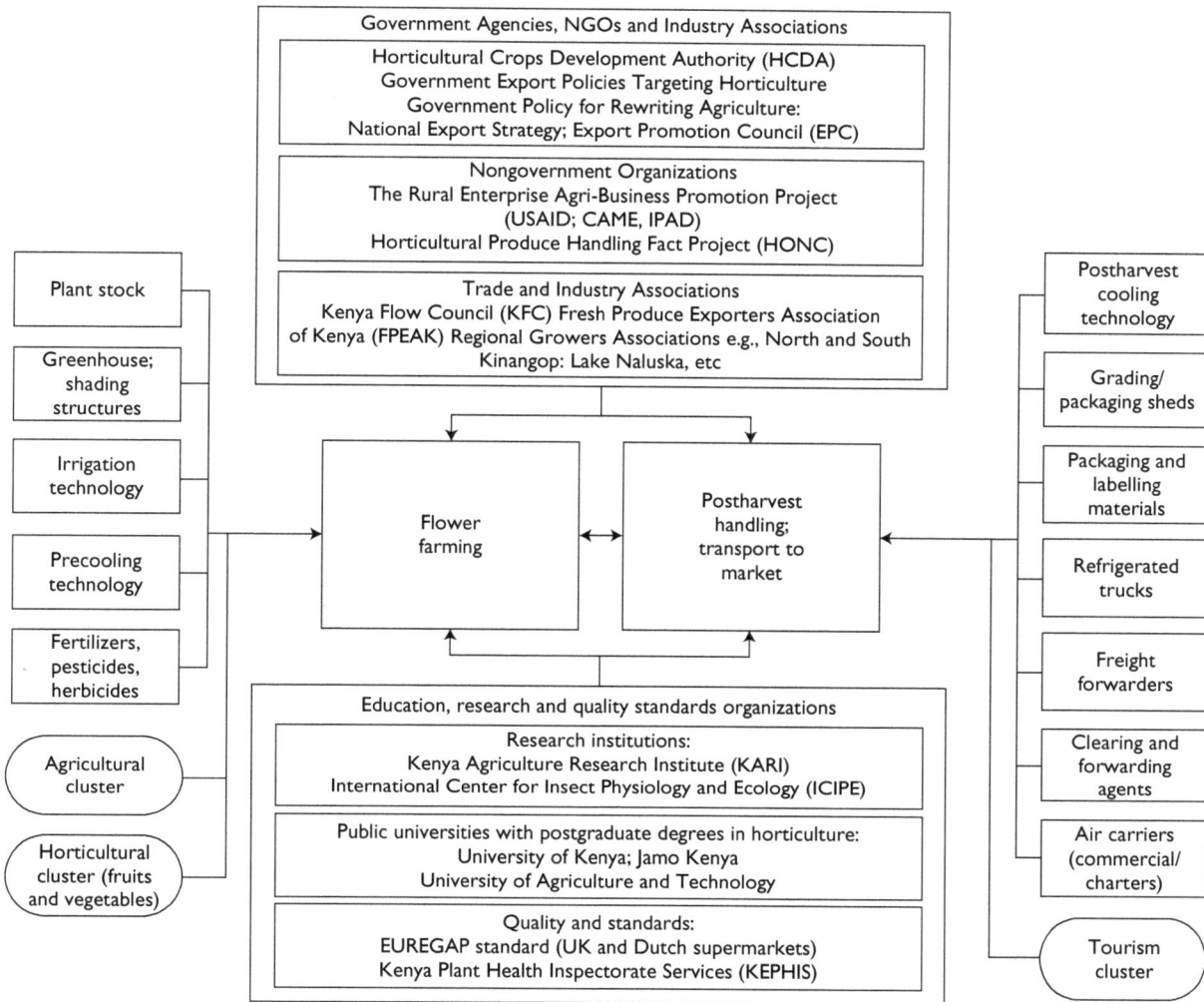

Source: Hornberger, Ndiritu, and Ponce-Brito et al. (2007); Microecomics of Competitiveness, Harvard Business School (2007).

developed by J. E. Austin Associates. This approach, described in more detail in the discussion of tool 13, looks at improvements in four areas:

1. Process indicators
2. Action indicators
3. Investment indicators
4. Delivered results

A STEP-BY-STEP SUMMARY OF TOOL 12: ACHIEVING SYNERGIES THROUGH CLUSTERING

- Cluster coordinators, industry consultants, and facilitators work with cluster members to evaluate and

analyze the current state of the industry and identify potential opportunities for cluster-based initiatives. Potential cluster relationships should be centered on geographically proximate elements of several related value chains.

- Generate strong interest in cooperation leading to mutual commitments within the cluster.
- Assist the private sector in developing a cluster strategy (including objectives, strategy, and an action plan). Present these for discussion within the cluster.
- Prioritize interventions toward achieving the cluster strategy. Focus initially on initiatives that will demonstrate short-term success and that require modest funding.

- Identify financing for larger-scale initiatives from within the value chains, government, banks, or other sources of investment.
- Encourage leadership among cluster participants so that members create norms of cooperation and champion continuing improvements even after the initiative has ended.

- Monitor and publicize clustering results.

NOTE

1. Institute for Strategy and Competitiveness, Harvard Business School.

Achieving Synergies through Clustering—Kenyan Avocados

Carlton Jones and Martin Webber
J. E. Austin Associates, Inc.

INTRODUCTION

The term "cluster" is often used loosely and commonly incorporates a variety of value chain elements. In most instances, it is meant to involve a geographic concentration of similar businesses within the same or related value chains. Generally speaking, this Guide has accepted the definition of "cluster" as a geographic concentration of interconnected companies, specialized suppliers, service providers, and associated institutions in a particular field that are present in a nation or region.[1] These clusters can incorporate or work across value chains, and, thus, are not linear. This case examines how a Kenyan market-linkage strategy, along with a cluster initiative, strengthened firms and the overall value chain in the fresh avocado sector. The case first introduces the Kenyan avocado value chain, then describes initiatives to create and then to strengthen the value chain's market linkages. The case describes the broader avocado cluster map and the role of cluster actors.

POINTS TO CONSIDER

When reviewing this case, consider the following;

- Clustering is a tool to strengthen firm relationships through the development of a private sector–led strategy, build a foundation for dialogue, and create the opportunity for upgrading skills and technology.
- What were the steps taken to facilitate clustering?
- What were some of the benefits realized from establishing the avocado cluster?

BACKGROUND

Mexico and the United States have dominated the global avocado export market for the last three decades. During that time, Kenya has consistently ranked as a top 20 producer. Its best ranking was eleventh, in 1961 (FAOSTAT). Kenya's main export market is Europe, to which it supplies mainly the Fuerte variety avocado. In 2003, 92 percent of avocados produced by Kenya were of the Fuerte variety, while the other 8 percent were of the Hass variety (Deloitte Touche 2003). From the mid-1970s to the late 1990s, Kenya consistently ranked nineteenth among world producers, jumping to thirteenth in 1998. Kenya was able to maintain and even to improve its position based on natural market linkages to Europe and its ability to provide avocados during off-peak seasons. However, by 2000, a switch in European consumer tastes to the Hass variety, and other factors discussed below, pushed Kenya's market rank back to sixteenth (see figure 4.63). Unfortunately for Kenyan small growers, prices paid for the Fuerte avocado did not keep pace with other cash crops. The farmers, therefore, did not reinvest in avocado trees, and avocado quality declined.

By 2002, small Kenyan avocado farmers had no direct links with exporters for export-grade avocados. In late 2002, the government of Kenya (GoK) and USAID funded a project to improve market linkages between small avocado growers and exporters, while supporting a cluster initiative that strengthened the entire sector. A value chain analysis[2] (see figure 4.64) identified many important points,

Figure 4.63   Kenyan Avocado Production, 1994–2007

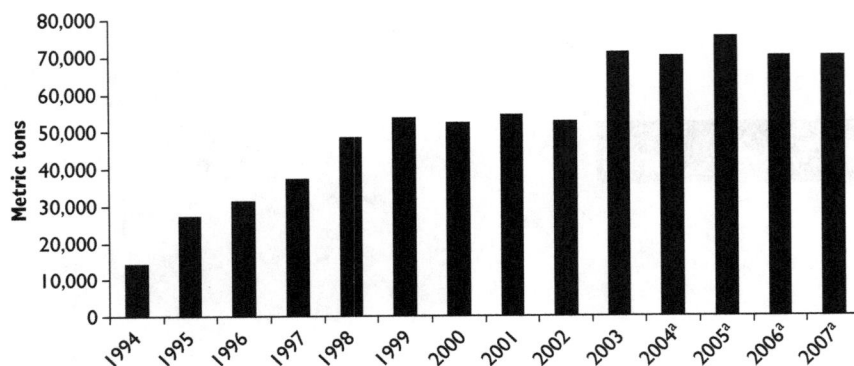

Source: FAOSTAT data.
a FAO estimate.

Figure 4.64   Kenyan Avocado Value Chain

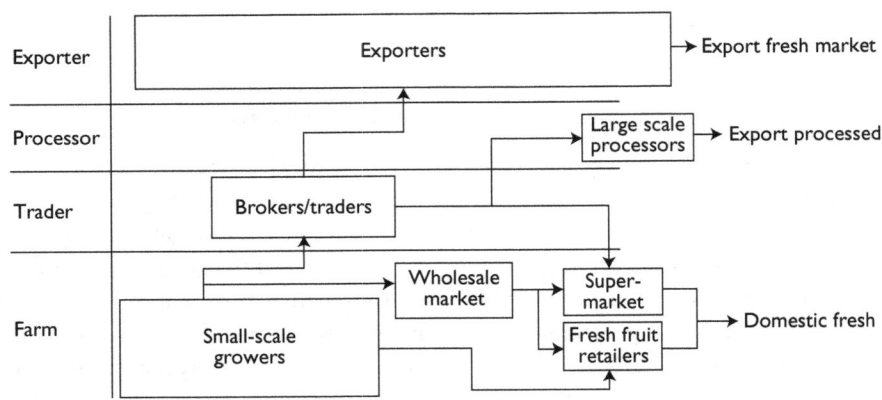

Sources: J. E. Austin Associates, Inc.; Kenya BDS.

such as the fact that the average avocado small grower had seven or fewer trees, and only 5 percent had more than 20 trees. The analysis also confirmed the predominance of indigenous Fuerte variety avocados, which were more susceptible to disease and were in declining demand in European markets. This analysis also showed that avocado small growers were very discouraged because of factors including rampant crop disease, little access to technical assistance, almost no access to finance, and dependence on poor-quality Fuerte avocados. With low grade-1 fruit yields, poor prices for the little grade-1 fruit harvested, and no market for grade-2 fruit, some farmers cut down their avocado trees to sell for firewood.

The goal of the Kenya Business Development Services[3] (Kenya BDS) Project was to improve access to markets and access to competitive skills by supporting lead firms in backward integration strategies, which provided extension services and supply contracts to small growers. In addition to supporting lead firms, the project helped to establish small outgrower producer groups. By supporting the avocado sector through these means, it was expected that a corresponding cluster initiative would take shape that would bolster the entire value chain, bring in other actors, and improve the relationship between exporters and small growers.

THE KENYAN AVOCADO VALUE CHAIN

The avocado value chain was a broker-dominated spot market whose value chain resulted in low prices and unreliable markets for growers (see figure 4.64). There were no standalone business services supporting the sector, nor was there a market for grade-2 "reject" avocados. Instead, almost all small-grower avocados were sold for domestic consumption. Constraints identified in this value chain included:

- Lack of information and knowledge of the markets
- Absence of farmer marketing groups
- Limited access to inputs
- Limited access to resources and weak incentives for upgrading
- Weak vertical and horizontal linkages within the value chain
- Lack of trust among producers, brokers, and exporters

After fruit was sold to brokers, those brokers then sourced it to various markets, local supermarkets, processors, and exporters. The little export-quality fruit that were produced were packed at one of seven packhouses situated within two hours of the production areas and, after pre-cooling, were loaded and transported to containers at Port Mombasa. Average transport time to Europe was 13–21 days.

As implementation of the Kenya BDS project began, lead firms were identified that were interested in participating in providing extension services to small-scale growers. The first such lead firm, East African Growers Association (EAGA), was very interested in participating in the project after realizing the benefits of integrating backward into the supply chain to improve EurepGAP eligibility. With the support of Kenya BDS, EAGA began providing farm extension services to producer groups (composed of 400 farmers) such as pruning,

manure application, spraying, grafting, grading, collection, and transport. Later, other exporters, like Indu-Farm Ltd., joined the market linkage activity. Indu-Farm signed memoranda of understanding to provide supply contracts to producer groups and committed an agronomist to work with farmers on good agricultural practices to prepare them for meeting EurepGAP certification. Supply contracts guaranteed the market and allowed growers to focus on improving quality. The result was a twofold and even threefold increase in prices over those previously received by growers who sold to brokers (figure 4.66).

THE KENYAN AVOCADO CLUSTER

As market linkages continued to form between exporters and small growers, other supporting industries were established, supported, and ultimately relied upon to provide services to the avocado sector. As the cluster map (figure 4.65) demonstrates, these services were provided by a variety of industries and input providers.

ROLE OF CLUSTER ACTORS

A variety of actors support the avocado cluster in Kenya. Some are existing businesses that seek to take advantage of market opportunities that exist in the newly revived avocado sector. Others are firms and entrepreneurs established through technical assistance. The cluster also includes institutions and associations that support the sector through

Figure 4.65   Kenyan Avocado Value Chain and Cluster

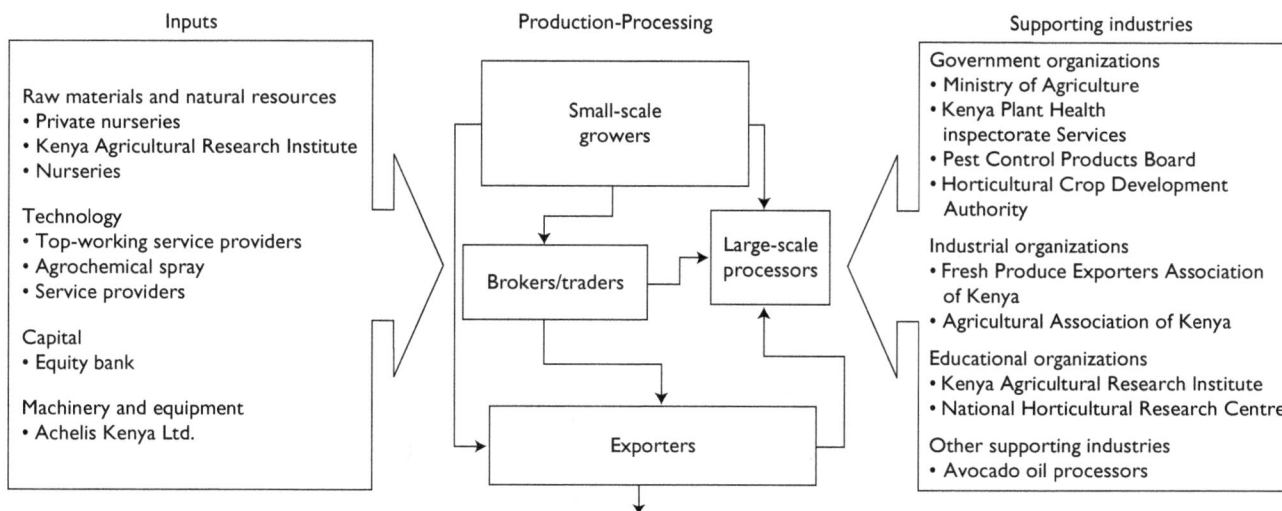

Sources: J. E. Austin Associates, Inc.; Kenya BDS.

research, certification, and advocacy. Each actor plays a useful role in the cluster and is presented in figure 4.65 in the categories of "supporting industries" and "inputs."

Supporting industries

To facilitate a market for the otherwise rejected grade-2 Fuerte avocados that most small growers produced, oil processors (Ruiru Natural Oils, All Green Ltd., and others) were funded by private investors, supported by the project, and linked to small growers. Other processors that already processed other fruits and nuts (Sunmango, Ltd., and Av-Oil Industries, Ltd.) purchased new equipment to retool their plants and enter the avocado sector. Through supply contracts, these processors provided a market for not only grade-2, but also grade-3 Fuerte avocados. Because processors required a steady supply of mature fruit for optimum operational efficiency in their plants (an average of 20 mt per processor, per day), Kenya BDS stepped in to facilitate additional producer-group supply contracts to ensure that supply was met. The oil processed by these facilities was shipped in crude form to South Africa to be refined for cosmetics. The introduction of these processors created an assured market for all grades of avocados produced on small-grower farms at a 25–50 percent higher price than previously received from brokers.

Educational organizations

The Kenya Agricultural Research Institute is Kenya's national organization for coordinating agricultural research. Its National Horticulture Research Centre (NHRC) focuses on horticultural research. KARI/NHRC continues to play a vital role in the avocado cluster by training producer groups and service providers on proper horticulture techniques. Many avocado technical assistance trainings also take place on KARI campuses.

Industrial organizations

The Fresh Produce Exporters Association of Kenya is a member-supported private association in the horticulture industry. It is Kenya's principal association representing growers and exporters. FPEAK's mission is to develop Kenyan horticulture in the global marketplace. In addition to marketing and technical support, it lobbies for its constituents' agendas, administers Kenya-GAP (a code of practice for Kenya's horticulture industry), and promotes member compliance in other international standards.

The Agricultural Association of Kenya (AAK) is the umbrella organization for manufacturers, formulators, repackers, importers, distributors, farmers, and users of pest-control products.[4] AAK assisted in the training of agrochemical service providers on the proper and safe application of pesticide on small-grower farms. Once properly trained, agrochemical service providers are then eligible for AAK certification.

Government organizations

The Kenya Plant Health Inspectorate Services organization emerged as a partner to help train newly formed private nursery service providers. KEPHIS is a regulatory agency for quality control of agricultural input and produce in Kenya. It coordinates all matters relating to crop pests and disease control and advises the Director of Agriculture on appropriate seeds and planting materials for export and import.[5]

A department in Kenya's Ministry of Agriculture, the Pest Control Products Board (PCPB), regulates the importation, manufacture, exportation, distribution, and use of pest-control products in Kenya. It ensures that only PCPB-assessed products are used in the country.

The Horticultural Crop Development Authority (HCDA) is a Kenyan parastatal organization tasked with promoting and regulating the horticulture sector. It helped train agrochemical service providers in regulatory compliance and in understanding the agronomic and physiological aspects of avocados.

Input suppliers/providers

Raw materials and natural resources. KARI nurseries and KEPHIS provided private nurseries with much-needed technical services to help convert and/or replenish avocado farms with Hass varieties. Services provided included top-working, pruning, planting, and providing root stock and scion materials for producer groups. Each participating nursery was inspected and registered with HCDA.

Technology. One identified service that avocado-producer groups needed was the introduction of agrochemicals to mitigate the risk of pest infestation and disease. Commercializing this service aspect was vital to ensuring the vitality of the avocado value chain. As such, service providers were identified, trained, and equipped through KARI/NHRC, KEPHIS, AAK, and PCPB so that the providers understood the complexities of safe and appropriate pesticide applications. The integrated pest-management program had two main components: developing and mentoring independent service providers and bringing in commercial financial arrangements that enabled farmers to access these services. The service providers came from varying backgrounds; some were drawn from within the farming community, while others were brokers who saw an opportunity to remain vitally linked to the changing avocado sector.

With a high percentage of Fuerte avocados on each small-grower farm, extension workers promoted on-farm diversification using Hass varieties. Serving as ecological insurance against variety specific pests and diseases, Hass avocados also showed a slight price preference on international markets. More importantly, the campaign served to mobilize economically marginal native trees, already common on farms, for export production. This mobilization relied on grafting, the technique of attaching fruit-producing branches of one tree to another. To facilitate this conversion, top-working commercial grafting services had to be introduced to the farmers. Awareness training provided for producer groups created demand for the service providers, and roughly 7,000 (Deloitte 2003) farmers preregistered for variety conversion. In some districts, the demand for variety conversion exceeded 100,000 trees, nearly twice the program's capacity. With the average price of top-working estimated at K Sh 250 per tree, conversion also presented a significant business opportunity for entrepreneurs willing to be trained in this intervention. As top-workers were trained, they were linked with producer groups to begin servicing trees. In as little as 12 months, the trees began to produce the new, higher-valued Hass avocados.

Capital. Addressing a major constraint in the avocado value chain, Equity Bank provided credit facilities that enabled avocado-producer groups to purchase agrochemical services on credit. Only producer groups with existing supply contracts and a history of buying and selling to a lead exporter were eligible to participate in this program. After applying for credit, eligible producers received their answer within 48 hours. The credit covered the labor for spraying, as well as the purchase and delivery of pesticides. All the costs were covered under a fixed-price-per-tree-sprayed plan, which is paid at the start of avocado season and then deducted by the bank on a draw-down basis every time spraying takes place or upon payment for the avocados delivered. Credit facilities were also established for service providers to buy and maintain mechanical spray-pump equipment, run agrochemical stores, and purchase fuel.

Machinery and equipment. Achelis Kenya Ltd., a subsidiary of a Taiwanese import/export company, played an integral role in the avocado cluster by selling and training service providers in its motorized agrochemical sprayer product line. Other machinery providers included Israeli firms that supplied pressing equipment used for grade-2 and grade-3 avocado processing.

Figure 4.66   Kenyan Avocado Exports, 1975–2005

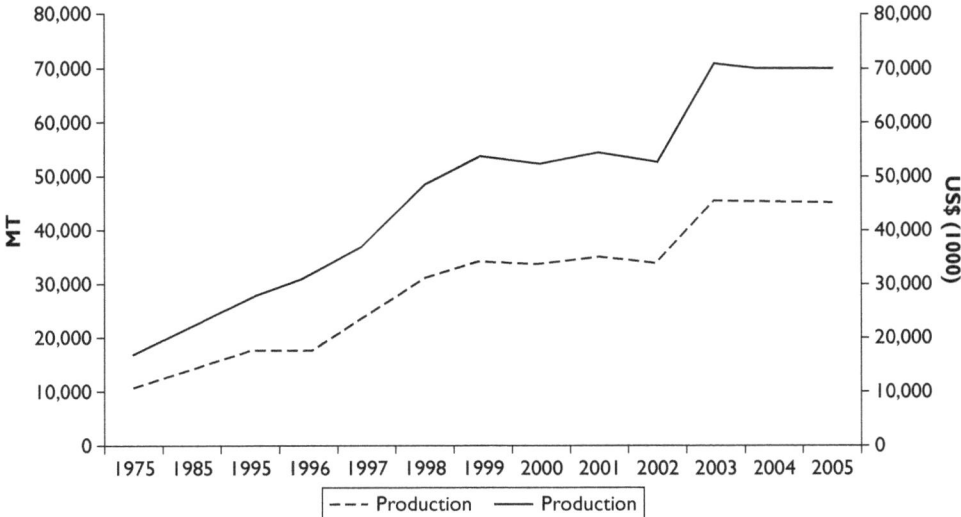

Source: FAOSTAT data.

RESULTS

Like many of this Guide's cases, the Kenyan avocado case is ongoing. By late 2006, the program had worked with 14,240 smallholder farmers organized into 475 producer groups.

Each small grower is accessing embedded services in extension, produce collection, transportation, and a guaranteed market whose prices average 3–4 times those of the brokers. Grade-1 fruit yields have increased from less than 15 percent to over 65 percent per tree. Participating farmers are collectively averaging between 30 and 40 mt of avocado production per day. In addition, the introduction of avocado processors has provided a stable market for all small-grower production grades and varieties, with crude oil exports reaching South Africa and Italy.

Other benefits from the backward linkages interventions and cluster initiatives include:

- Improved quality control
- A clear path of transition from Fuerte to Hass avocado production
- Faster and cheaper access to inputs
- Improved market linkages and information sharing

One of the program's most significant results is the commercial viability of the entire sector as demonstrated by the "replicated effect" that took place among exporters. Besides EAGA, four other lead firms have adopted the program and are working downstream with contract growers.

NOTES

1. Institute for Strategy and Competitiveness, Harvard Business School.

2. Conducted by Deloitte's Emerging Markets Group.

3. Kenya BDS is a five year, US$5 million project implemented by EMG with a period of performance from September 2002 to September 2007.

4. AAK, http://www.agrochem.co.ke/.

5. KEPHIS, http://www.kephis.org/.

Monitoring Achievements in Value Chain Performance

PURPOSE OF MONITORING

Monitoring and evaluation (M&E) methods can be used as a management tool that enables value chain participants and promoters to track implementation progress, evaluate value chain performance, and identify the impact of initiatives. In its most basic form, M&E uses indicators to identify progress toward achieving intermediate targets or ultimate goals. Monitoring systems comprise procedural arrangements for data collection, analysis, reporting, and feedback. In business, monitoring is used to measure the return on inputs as a means to verify an investment's success before returns are realized, as well as to receive guidance on prioritization and decision making for business programs.

M&E is, of course, already a well-developed field of practice with many established and effective implementation methods and processes. In private sector development, M&E methods have three principal modes: project monitoring, performance evaluation, and impact assessment. Effective impact assessment often depends on good program evaluation and, in turn, systematic project monitoring.

QUESTIONS TO ASK

When reviewing this case consider the following questions:

- What does the value chain really want to monitor?
- At what level does the value chain measure the impacts?

Project monitoring (PM) refers to the systematic collection and analysis of data and information about inputs, activities, and outputs. It is used for management purposes—to monitor progress against a plan, identify emerging issues and problems, and take corrective measures.

Performance evaluation (PE) is a periodic study at key points in a project cycle that examines a program or organization's performance more broadly (for example, looking at staff behavior, organizational structures and methodologies, and the efficient achievement of outputs). PEs should assess the effectiveness of different factors being used to create change and as opportunities for implementing organizations to learn about themselves.

Impact assessment (IA) measures outcomes and examines changes at higher levels of a program (that is, the goal and purpose level). IA effectiveness depends on having a baseline or control group with which to compare results so that changes can be properly attributed. IA should be able to identify which factors contributed to changes and in what fashion. Impact assessment exercises are also key opportunities for both program staff and beneficiaries to use in monitoring progress and affecting the evolution of program design.[1]

The focus of many M&E implementations has been on the "project" cycle of international development interventions. As such, the many insights gained from these studies have had many positive effects on increasing the efficacy and efficient implementation of projects and their goals. Unfortunately, the design and implementation of performance-monitoring methods useful for measuring the actual performance of a value chain and of its participants (rather than a project) have yet to be properly adapted for use in private sector development contexts.

Thus, for the purposes of implementing value chain improvements, the challenge is to provide methodologies that can be used by value chain participants to monitor the implementation of their own programs. Value chain participants will require monitoring to maintain focus, reach objectives, and track changes in value chain performance and development, including increases in productivity and other business measurements of success.

Monitoring activities should provide information about the current status of a project and general trends pertinent to the value chain. Some key points on monitoring (and related evaluation) include:

- Measurements are periodically carried out
- Monitoring is conducted for the specific purpose of checking the status of the agreed-upon process or initiative or evaluating progress toward a strategic or management objective
- The results of monitoring should be evaluated and should provide guidance for action

While there is often a great deal of anecdotal evidence of the impact of value chain initiatives and actions, formal measurements against a baseline or against a program of strategy implementation are frequently lacking. Some of the difficulties with the application of traditional monitoring approaches include:

- Systems that are not attuned to the industry's measuring vocabulary
- Difficulty in attributing changes to program interventions
- Monitoring that does not necessarily provide insights into better business practices to drive the industr forward
- Monitoring responsibility that is not clearly delegated or resources that are not allocated

IMPLEMENTING MONITORING IN VALUE CHAINS

Monitoring interventions require stakeholders to determine which indicators are most appropriate and useful for tracking program implementation and value chain performance. Traditionally, measurements of productivity or "value addition" are used to convey improvements in performance.

Three Different Perspectives on M&E

- Business perspective: monitor value chain performance and provide feedback to inform decision making
- Process perspective: provide guidance on value chain participants' focus as they reach their objectives
- Programmatic perspective: ensure that the money spent on implementation is achieving the intended results

Source: J. E. Austin Associates, Inc.

While measuring productivity is sufficient for measuring business performance, it does not necessarily provide measurement for implementation strategies, especially when the impact of implementation on value chain performance is seen only in the medium- or longer term. Therefore, process indicators are also needed.

The level at which an impact measurement should be taken will depend on the nature of the initiative. In various circumstances, measuring at the firm level, value chain aggregate level, country or national level, or individual level may all be appropriate.

Figure 4.67[2] illustrates an example of how value chain initiatives can begin to formulate effective monitoring and related evaluation programs. These require concerted actions by the various value chain participants. When assisting the value chain to develop its own monitoring and evaluation process, one must consider the following proposed steps.

- The value chain must be understood by expert analysis
- Key benchmarks must be determined
- Industry leaders must be consulted
- Program design must include M&E
- Different programs and initiatives must be linked to the value chain to take advantage of synergies
- Performance measurements inform effectiveness

In practice, the evaluation focus for value chains (and clusters) has been monitored in value-added increases as a measure of productivity improvement. However, single, quantitative measures can ignore the process side of a value chain initiative. One comprehensive evaluation approach is the PAID framework,[3] a measurement system for evaluating value chain initiatives that has been adapted from the approach to cluster evaluation.

The PAID M&E framework (see box 4.18) not only measures delivered results but also coinvestment by both the private and public sectors. This tool can be used in value chain projects on the basis of proper benchmarks being determined by participant organizations and institutions. For example, the *process indicators* measure the ability of value chain practitioners to engage the proper value chain–leading authorities and market players. The *action indicators* could track the value chain initiative's progress by looking at the changes that have occurred since the intervention. The *investment indicators* gauge the buy-in by value chain participants and those actors indirectly determining the health of the value chain's competitiveness. *Delivered results* measure the essential goal of any value chain initiative, which is to increase productivity, capture value, create jobs, and grow business.

Figure 4.67   M&E Value Chain Model

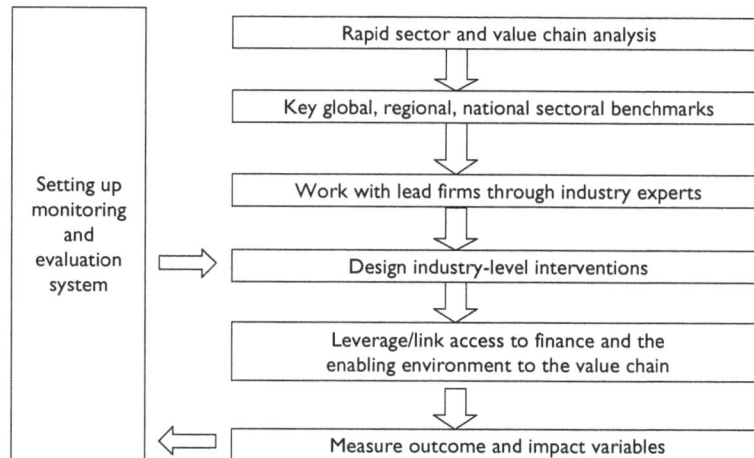

```
┌───────────┐      ┌──────────────────────────────────────────────┐
│           │      │        Rapid sector and value chain analysis  │
│           │      └──────────────────────────────────────────────┘
│           │                          ⇓
│           │      ┌──────────────────────────────────────────────┐
│           │      │  Key global, regional, national sectoral benchmarks │
│ Setting up│      └──────────────────────────────────────────────┘
│ monitoring│                          ⇓
│ and       │      ┌──────────────────────────────────────────────┐
│ evaluation│  ⇨   │   Work with lead firms through industry experts │
│ system    │      └──────────────────────────────────────────────┘
│           │                          ⇓
│           │      ┌──────────────────────────────────────────────┐
│           │      │        Design industry-level interventions     │
│           │      └──────────────────────────────────────────────┘
│           │                          ⇓
│           │      ┌──────────────────────────────────────────────┐
│           │      │  Leverage/link access to finance and the       │
│           │      │  enabling environment to the value chain       │
│           │      └──────────────────────────────────────────────┘
│           │                          ⇓
│           │  ⇦   ┌──────────────────────────────────────────────┐
└───────────┘      │       Measure outcome and impact variables     │
                   └──────────────────────────────────────────────┘
```

Source: Adapted from multiple FIAS-IFC presentations on value chains by Subramanian and Sur.

Box 4.17   Standards for Ghanaian Pineapples

Ghana's pineapple market has been built on strong entrepreneurship from the private sector and a demand for Ghanaian sea-freighted pineapples in Europe, especially outside the core French market. During the late 1980s and early 1990s, Ghana carved a niche in the EU market as a primary supplier of top-quality, airfreighted pineapples, controlling about 60 percent of the estimated annual 20,000 mt of pineapples airfreighted to Europe. Ghana also exported a small amount by sea-freight (2,710 mt), but the bulk were airfreighted (13,054 mt worth over US$400,000). To increase exports to EU markets, sea-freighting was explored. The Sea Freight Pineapple Exporters of Ghana is a consortium of 14 exporter firms supported

by USAID and the government of Ghana (GoG). SPEG was established to facilitate sea-freighting Ghanaian pineapple varieties by gaining the necessary scale to operate at competitive prices.

To ensure quality in its pineapple exports, SPEG worked with the Ghana Standards Board to develop a poster (see figure 4.68) that would be used by producers and packers alike as a simple guide to the minimal quality standards required for exporting. The easy-to-read poster was posted in strategic locations for exporters, traders, and farmers so that all actors within the Ghana pineapple chain consistently maintained the standards for color, shape, crown condition, and other pineapple characteristics.

Source: Carlton Jones, J. E. Austin Associates, Inc.

CONCLUSION

Methodologies such as the PAID framework can be effectively applied to value chain initiatives as long as they are designed to measure impacts experienced by the various value chain participants and the various segments of the value chain. Monitoring for value chains should focus on

two types of performance: 1) implementation of strategy and 2) increases of productivity. This Guide has presented 12 other tools and approaches that one can associate with implementing value chain programs. Most of these tools can be targets for monitoring, given measurement indicators before, during, and after an intervention.

Figure 4.68   Sample SPEG Poster Showing Desired Pineapple Qualities—USAID

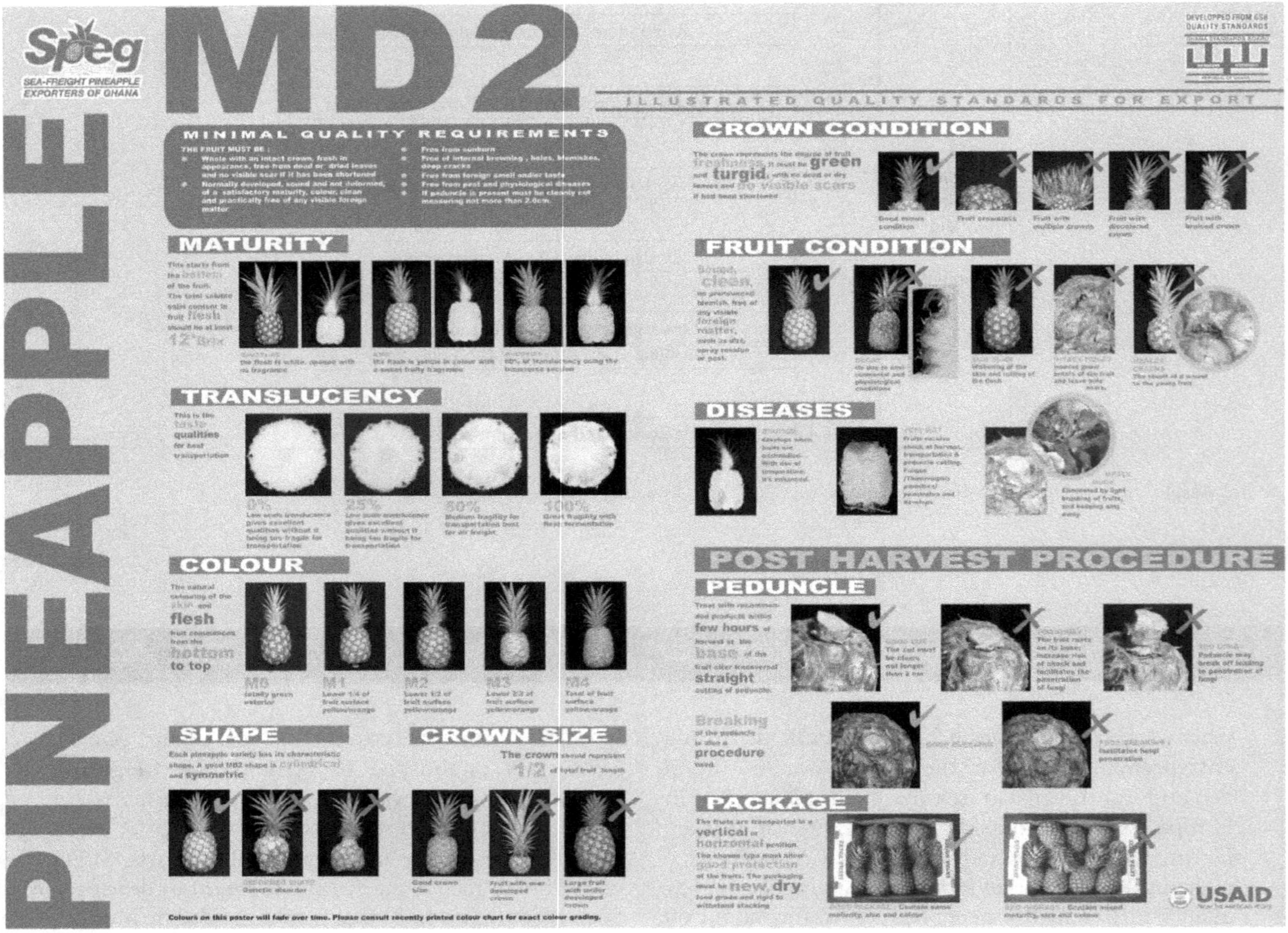

Source: USAID/Ghana Trade and Investment Program for a Competitive Export Economy implemented by Chemonics International.

Box 4.18   The PAID M&E Framework

Process indicators track the ability of the implementers to engage the leadership of the value chain, elicit a strong response, and structure a collaborative agreement. These indicators should be set at the project outset and are very important during the first year of activity.

Action indicators track whether progress is being made in implementing the strategic initiatives identified in the first phase of the project. These cannot be programmed at the outset.

Investment indicators track coinvestments by counterparts. Coinvestment typically begins modestly (through the contribution of cluster executives' time, provision of workshop venues, and so on) but then accelerates as the initiative moves to maturity. It may take time to prepare feasibility studies and projects and to secure financing. The most significant investments occur at the implementation stage of action initiatives.

(Box continues on the following page.)

Box 4.18   The PAID M&E Framework (continued)

Delivered results indicators focus on increases in productivity and value added but may also include export revenues, employment growth, new enterprise growth, average wages, and average profitability in the industry. It must also be demonstrated that the project contributed directly (wholly or partially) to delivering these results.

Source: Kevin X. Murphy, J. E. Austin Associates, Inc.

The results become measurable after some time, often years. However, there are delivered results that are more qualitative. The emergence of trust and cooperation within an industry, business-government and academic collaboration, changes of mindset, and spread effects can be observed but are not easily quantified.

A STEP-BY-STEP SUMMARY OF TOOL 13: MONITORING ACHIEVEMENTS IN VALUE CHAIN PERFORMANCE

- Analyze the present value chain to identify data points that may indicate future progress toward the value chain's goals.
- Identify process and results metrics that will demonstrate the progress of an intervention or initiative relative to the strategic goals. These will include a balance of process, action, investment, and delivered results indicators.
- The value chain stakeholders should agree on the M&E criteria. This will ensure that the actors monitor tracking indicators with clear relevance to the value chain stakeholders.
- Establish the monitoring sequence, sources of information, and responsibilities.

- Report the findings to the value chain stakeholders. This encourages continued buy-in and a continued sense of responsibility among implementers, and enables mid-course improvements and adjustments.

NOTES

1. Adapted from an online contribution from Mike Albu of Practical Action found at: "Impact Assessment: An Online Speaker's Corner Discussion Led by Gary Woller and Hosted by microLinks.org," September 26–28, 2006. More tools are available online at: http://www.enterprise-impact. org.uk/.

2. Taken from a presentation at the IFC on value chains.

3. Developed by J. E. Austin Associates, Inc., and applied in several countries.

BIBLIOGRAPHY

SECTIONS 1–4 AND GENERAL SOURCES

Altenburg, Tilman. 2006. "Donor Approaches to Supporting Pro-Poor Value Chains." German Development Institute, Report prepared for the Donor Committee for Enterprise Development Working Group on Linkages and Value Chains.

Asian Development Bank. 2005. "Agricultural Commercialization, Value Chains, and Poverty Reduction." Making Markets Work Better for the Poor, Discussion Paper No. 7.

Austin, James E. 1992. *Agroindustrial Project Analysis.* World Bank/Johns Hopkins Press, second edition.

———. 1998. *Strategic Management in Developing Countries.* The Free Press.

———. 2000. *The Collaboration Challenge.* Jossey-Bass.

———. 2002. *Managing in Developing Countries: Strategic Analysis and Operating Techniques.* Free Press.

Bernet, Thomas, André Devaux, Oscar Ortiz, and Graham Thiele. 2005. "Participatory Market Chain Approach." BeraterInnen News 1/2005. Agridea International.

Bolnick, Bruce, Andrea Camoens, and Julia Zislin, of Nathan Associates Inc. 2005. "Tanzania Economic Performance Assessment." USAID Country Analytical Support Report, p. 14.

Canadian International Development Agency. October 2004. "Programme de Développement des Marchés Agricoles (PDMAS)—AgMarkets Sénégal: Horticulture du Sénégal Cadre stratégique—Horizon 2010." GEOMAR.

Development Alternatives, Inc., for USAID. 2005. "Strengthening the Role of AIDS-Affected SMEs in Productive Markets: BDS on the Margins HIV/AIDS Paper." microREPORT No. 27, USAID, Washington, DC.

Dunn, Elizabeth. 2005. "AMAP BDS Knowledge and Practice Task Order Lexicon." microNOTE No. 6, USAID, Washington, DC.

The Economist. February 15, 2007. "Big Chains Enjoy a Buyer's Market."

English, P., S. Jaffee, and J. J. Okello. 2006. "Exporting Out of Africa: The Kenya Horticulture Success Story." In *Attacking Africa's Poverty: Experiences from the Ground,* ed. R. B. Liebenthal and M. L Fox. Washington, DC: World Bank.

Faivre, Dupaigre B., P. Baris, and L. Liagre. 2004. "Étude sur la Competitivité des Filières Agricoles dans l'Espace UEMOA." IRAM, UEMOA Commission-DDR.

FAO (Food and Agriculture Organization) of the United Nations, FAOSTAT located at: http://faostat.fao.org/default.aspx.

———. 2005. "The State of Food and Agriculture 2005: Agricultural Trade and Poverty: Can Trade Work for the Poor?" FAO Agriculture Series (SOFA) 36.

———. 2006. FAOSTAT Online Statistical Service. Rome: FAO. Available online at http://faostat.fao.org.

Feller, Andrew, Dan Shunk, and Tom Callarman. 2006. "Value Chains versus Supply Chains," BPTrends, March.

Fu, Hsin-Pin, Tien-Hsiang Chang, Wan-I Lee, and Cheng-Chin Lu. 2006. "A Study on the Value-Chain Strategies of Enterprises Adopting Electronic Marketplaces in Free and Controlled Markets." *Journal of Manufacturing Technology* 17(5): 621–32.

Gabre-Madhin, Eleni Z., and Nicholas Minot. 2004. "Successes and Challenges in Promoting Africa's Horticultural Exports." International Food Policy Research Institute, IFPRI and World Bank.

Gereffi, Gary, and Miguel Korzeniewicz. 1993. *Commodity Chains and Global Capitalism*. Greenwood Publishers.

Gibbon, Peter. 2003. "Commodities, Donors, Value-Chain Analysis and Upgrading." Danish Institute for International Studies, paper prepared for UNCTAD.

Gupta, S., and Y. Yang. 2006. "Unblocking Trade: To Underpin Growth, African Needs to Adopt a Comprehensive Approach to Boosting Trade." *Finance and Development* 43 (4).

Haggblade, Steven J., and Matthew Gamser. 1991. "A Field Manual for Subsector Practitioners: Tools for Microenterprise Programs: Nonfinancial Assistance Programs." Growth and Equity through Microenterprise Investments and Institutions (GEMINI) Program, funded through microLINKS, November, USAID.

Humphrey, John. 2004 revised. "Commodities, Diversification and Poverty Reduction." Paper presented at FAO symposium on the State of Agricultural Commodity Market Research, Rome, December 15–16, 2003.

———. 2005 "Shaping Value Chains for Development: Global Value Chains in Agribusiness." GTZ, Eschborn, Germany.

Humphrey, John, and Antje Oetero. 2000. "Strategies for Diversification and Adding Value to Food Exports: A Value Chain Perspective." UNCTAD, November 14.

Humphrey, John, and Hubert Schmitz. 2000. "Governance and Upgrading: Linking Industrial Cluster and Global Value Chain Research." University of Sussex, Institute of Development Studies, IDS Working Paper 120.

———. 2001. "Governance in Global Value Chains." University of Sussex, Institute of Development Studies. Published in IDS Bulletin, Vol. 32, No 3.

Ingram, Michael. 2005. "Summary of Kenya Value Chain Analysis." Note No. 8, September, World Bank.

ILO. 2006. PSD Reader, p. 43.

Janecka, Izabela. 2006. "Sourcing in Low-Cost Countries." Eye for Procurement.

J. E. Austin Associates, Inc. 2006. "Rwanda Export Promotion Action Plan." Submitted to the government of Rwanda, Rwanda Investment and Export Promotion Agency and Ministry of Finance and Economic Planning, with assistance from the World Bank.

Kaplinsky, Rafael. 2000. "Spreading the Gains from Globalization: What Can Be Learned From Value Chain Analysis?" Unpublished paper, Institute for Development Studies, University of Sussex.

Kaplinsky, Rafael, and Mike Morris. 2002. "A Handbook for Value Chain Research." IDRC. http://www.ids.ac.uk/ids/global/pdfs/VchNov01.pdf.

Kaplinsky, Rafael, and Jeff Readman. 2001. "Integrating SMEs in Global Value Chains: Toward Partnership for Development." UNIDO.

Kula, Olaf, Jeanne Downing, and Michael Field. 2006. "Globalization and the Small Firm: A Value Chain Approach to Economic Growth and Poverty Reduction." USAID microREPORT No. 42, prepared under the Accelerated Microenterprise Advancement Project Business Development Services Knowledge and Practice Task Order.

Lusby, Frank, and Henry Panlibuton. 2004. "Promotion of Commercially Viable Solutions to Subsector and Business Constraints." Office of Microenterprise Development, USAID.

McCormick, Dorothy, and Hubert Schmitz. 2001. "Manual for Value Chain Research on Homeworkers in the Garment Industry." IDS.

Miehlbradt, Alexandra O., and Mary McVay. 2006. "Implementing Sustainable Private Sector Development: Striving for Tangible Results for the Poor: The 2006 Reader." SDC, ILO.

Moran, Theodore H. 2001. "Parental Supervision: The New Paradigm for Foreign Direct Investment and Development." *Policy Analyses in International Economics*, No. 64.

Murphy, Kevin. 2003. "PAID Methodology: Monitoring and Evaluation of Cluster Competitiveness Initiatives." J. E. Austin Associates, Inc.

———. 2006. "Private Sector Contribution to Education Reform: 10 Bridges to a Competitive Workforce." J. E. Austin Associates, Inc.

Nugawela, Patrick, and Roland Oroch. 2005. "Cashew Subsector Strategic Framework." DfID.

Porter, Michael E. 1998a. *Competitive Advantage: Creating and Sustaining Superior Performance*. Free Press.

———. 1998b. *On Competition*. Boston: Harvard Business School Press.

———. 1998c. *The Competitive Advantage of Nations*. Free Press.

———. 2000a. "Attitudes, Values, Beliefs, and the Microeconomics of Prosperity." In *Culture Matters: How Values Shape Human Progress*, ed. L. E. Harrison and S. P. Huntington. New York: Basic Books.

———. 2000b. "Location, Competition and Economic Development: Local Clusters in a Global Economy." *Economic Development Quarterly* 14, No. 1, February: 15–34. Also reprinted in *Globalization and the Location of Firms*, ed. J. Cantwell. Cheltenham: Edward Elgar Publishing, 2004.

———. 2004. *Competitive Strategy*. Free Press.

Posthumus, Hans. 2004. "Capacitating Sector Analysis: A Practical Training Methodology to Analyze Value Chains." CAPSA, May 14, draft.

Raikes P., M. F. Jensen, and S. Ponte. 2000. "Global Commodity Chain Analysis and the French Filière Approach: Comparison and Critique." *Economy and Society,* August, 390–417.

Raney, Terri, et al. 2005. "The State of Food and Agriculture: Agricultural Trade and Poverty: Can Trade Work for the Poor?" FAO Agriculture Series (SOFA) 36.

Reardon, Thomas, and Luis Flores. "Customized Competitiveness Strategies for Horticultural Exporters: Central America Focus with Lessons from and for Other Regions." *Food Policy* 31: 6 December, 483–503.

Roduner, Daniel. 2004. "Draft Report on Value Chains: Analysis of Existing Theories, Methodologies and Discussions of Value Chain Approaches within the Development Cooperation Sector." Swiss Agency for Development and Cooperation.

Roduner, Daniel, Agridea Gerrits, and Andreas Gerrits. 2006. "Compilation of Insights on the Online Debate—Value Chains in Rural Development (VCRD): The Role of Donors in Value Chain Interventions." Swiss Agency for Development and Cooperation.

Salinger, B. L., and J. D. Stryker. November 2004. "Guide to Commodity-Based Export Diversification and Competitiveness Strategies for African Countries." Report prepared for UNCTAD/JITAP, Cambridge, MA: AIRD.

SNV. 2004. "Synthesis of the 1st Cycle of CVRD Debate."

Springer-Heinze, Andreas. 2004. "Info-Cadena: Instruments to Foster Value Chains." GTZ, draft.

Steen, Cynthia, Rich Magnani, and Lara Goldmark. June 2005. "Competitive Strategies for Agriculture-related MSES: From Seeds to Supermarket." USAID, prepared by Development Alternatives Inc., microREPORT No. 37.

Sturgeon, Timothy J. 2000. "How Do We Define Value Chains and Production Networks?" Background paper prepared for the Bellagio Value Chains Workshop, September 25 to October 1, 2000. Rockefeller Conference Center, Bellagio, Italy, Institute of Development Studies.

TechnoServe. 2004. "Partnerships for Agribusiness Development, Agricultural Trade, and Market Access: A Concept Note for NEPAD."

Temu, Andrew E., and Anna A. Temu. 2005. "High Value Agricultural Products for Smallholder Markets in Sub-Saharan Africa: Trends, Opportunities and Research Priorities." Prepared for an international workshop, "How Can the Poor Benefit from the Growing Markets for High Value Agricultural Products?" October 3–5, 2005, International Center for Tropical Agriculture, Cali, Colombia, ICTA.

van Roekel, Jan, Ronald Kopicki, Carry J. E. Broekmans, and Dave M. Boselie. 2001. "Building Agri-Supply Chains: Issues and Guidelines." World Bank, Washington, DC.

van Roekel, Jan, Sabine Willems, and Dave M. Boselie. 2002. "Agri-Supply Chain Management: To Stimulate Cross-Border Trade in Developing Countries and Emerging Economies." August 19, World Bank, Washington, DC.

Webber, C. Martin. 2006a. "Approaches to Economic Growth Value Chains and Competitiveness." Prepared for the workshop, "Nurturing the Sources of Economic Growth in Tanzania," held in Dar es Salaam, Tanzania, January 19–21, J. E. Austin Associates, Inc.

———. 2006b. "Enabling an Inclusive Private Sector: Opportunities and Key Constraints." J. E. Austin Associates, Inc.

———. 2006c. "Enabling an Inclusive Private Sector: Opportunities and Key Constraints in Burundi." PowerPoint presentation, J. E. Austin Associates, Inc.

———. 2006d. "Tanzania: Value Chain and Competitive Strategy—Current Approaches to Private Sector Development and Economic Growth." PowerPoint presentation, J. E. Austin Associates, Inc.

———. 2006e. "Uganda National Competitiveness Workshop: International Experience in Setting and Implementing Competitiveness Strategies." PowerPoint presentation, J. E. Austin Associates, Inc.

Westlake, Michael. 2005. "Addressing Marketing and Processing Constraints That Inhibit Agrifood Exports: A Guide for Policy Analysis and Planners." FAO Agricultural Services Bulletin 160, Rome.

World Bank. 2007. World Development Indicators.

———. 2008. World Development Report.

Tool 1: Choosing Priority Sectors for Value Chain Interventions

Norton, Roger, and Alvaro Balcazar. 2003. "A Study of Colombia's Agricultural Competitiveness." United Nations Food and Agriculture Organization, the World Bank, and United States Agency for International Development.

BOX CASE STUDY: THE EXAMPLE OF SENEGAL'S PROJET CROISSANCE ECONOMIQUE

J. E. Austin Associates, Inc. for IRG. 2006a. "Support for Accelerated Growth and Increased Competitiveness, Cashew Value Chain, Senegal: Analysis and Strategic Framework for Subsector Growth Initiatives." Washington, DC.

———. 2006b. "Support for Accelerated Growth and Increased Competitiveness, Mango Value Chain, Senegal: Analysis and Strategic Framework for Sub-Sector Growth Initiatives." Washington, DC.

September 2006c. "Support for Accelerated Growth and Increased Competitiveness, Bissap Value Chain, Senegal: Analysis and Strategic Framework for Sub-Sector Growth Initiatives." Washington, DC.

September 2006d. "Support for Accelerated Growth and Increased Competitiveness, Artisan Textile Value Chain, Senegal: Analysis and Strategic Framework for Sub-Sector Growth Initiatives." Washington, DC.

Nugawela, Patrick. 2007. "La Chaine de Valeurs de la Filière Cajou au Sénégal." Value Chain Presentation, February.

Sources interviewed
- Dr. Patrick Nugawela, J. E. Austin Associates, Inc., USAID Projet Croissance Economique au Sénégal
- C. Martin Webber, J. E. Austin Associates, Inc.

Case Study: Prioritizing Value Chains by Using Comparative Analysis—Value Chain Selection in Mozambique

Gergely, Nicolas. 2005. "Economic Analysis of Comparative Advantage for Major Agricultural Cash Crops in Mozambique." FAO.

Master, William A., and Alex Winter-Nelson. 1995. "Measuring the Comparative Advantage of Agricultural Activities: Domestic Recourse Costs and the Social Cost-Benefit Ratio." *American Journal of Agricultural Economics* 77(2) May: 243–250. http://links.jstor.org/sici?sici=0002-9092%28199505%2977%3A2%3C243%3AMTCAOA%3E2.0.CO%3B2-I.

O'Keefe, Thomas. 2001. "A Study of Revealed Comparative Advantage for AGOA-Eligible SADC Countries: Identifying Products Afforded Genuine Preferential Access to the U.S. Market under the African Growth and Opportunity Act." Mercosur Consulting Group, Ltd. Submitted by Chemonics International, Inc. Gaborone, Botswana.

World Bank. 2006. Mozambique Agricultural Development Strategy: Stimulating Smallholder Agricultural Growth. Report No. 32416-MZ. World Bank, Agriculture, Environment, and Social Development Unit, Africa Region.

Sources interviewed
- Nicolas Gergely, Independent Consultant
- Patrick Labaste, The World Bank

Case Study: A Structured Value Chain–Based Approach to Designing a Strategy of Agricultural Competitiveness and Diversification in Mali

Geomar International. 2006. "Profil Stratégique pour le Développement de la Compétitivité des Filières Agricoles du Mali : Identification des Opportunités Stratégiques de Valorization et de Diversification de l'Agriculture Malienne, Version Préliminaire." Montreal, QC.

World Bank. 2005. "Project Appraisal Document on a Proposed Credit in the Amount of SDR 30.7m to the Republic of Mali for an Agricultural Competitiveness and Diversification Project." Washington, DC.

Tool 2: Designing Informed Strategies Across the Value Chain

Case Study: Understanding the Value Chain and Integrating Information into Strategy: Nigerian Domestic Catfish

Dixie and Ohen. 2006. "The Market for Catfish and Other Aquaculture Products in Nigeria."

Engelmann and Swisscontact. 2005. "PLP Technical Note #4: An Inventory of BDS Market Assessment Methods for Programs Targeting Microenterprises." Swisscontact. http://www.seepnetwork.org/files/2991_file_Tech Note4_c.pdf.

EurekNews, and BBC News. http://news.bbc.co.uk/2/hi/science/nature/4187522.stm.

Moehl, John, Matthias Halwart, and Randall Brummet. 2005. "Report of the World Fish Center Workshop on Small-Scale Aquaculture in SSA." FAO.

NEPAD. 2005. "Hidden Harvests: Unlocking the Potential of Aquaculture in Africa." Technical Review Paper—Aquaculture. NEPAD "Fish for All" Summit, August 22–25. Abuja, Nigeria.

TechnoServe. 2004. "Partnerships for Agribusiness Development, Agricultural Trade, and Market Access: A Concept Note for NEPAD." Washington, DC.

Tool 3: Conducting Benchmarking and Gap Assessments of Value Chains

Box case study: Ugandan benchmarking constraints in the coffee industry

Chaffee, Ralph. 2002. "Enterprise-Linked Extension Services in Uganda." USAID Support for Private Enterprise Expansion and Development (SPEED) Project, Uganda.

Garcia Martinez, M., C. Skinner, N. Poole, J. Briz, I. de Felipe, P. Bandeiras, I. Yalcin, A. Koc, A. O. Akbay, L. Ababouch, and D. Messaho. 2003. Benchmarking Safety and Quality Management Practices in the Mediterranean Fresh Produce Sector. Working paper, EU INCO-MED research project: "The Impact of International Safety and Quality Standards on the Competitiveness of Mediterranean Fresh Produce." London, UK: Imperial College London.

Uganda Bureau of Statistics, http://www.ubos.org/.

170   BIBLIOGRAPHY

SOURCE INTERVIEWED
■ Mark Wood, USAID APEP Project

Case Study: Ugandan Floriculture—Benchmarking and Gap Analysis

de Vette, Hans, and Eleni Z. Gabre-Madhin. 2004. "Uganda Hortifloriculture Sector Development Study." Prepared for ESSDN and PSD, Africa Region of the World Bank, February.

Gabre-Madhin, Eleni, IFPRI, and V. E. K. Vette. 2004. Adviesgrouep B.V. for the World Bank. "Uganda Horti-Floriculture Sector Technical Note 2." Prepared for ESSD and PSD Departments, Africa Region, World Bank, in the framework of the Uganda Export Growth and Competitiveness Project.

Tool 4: Upgrading and Deepening the Value Chain

BOX CASE STUDY: MONGOLIAN MEAT INDUSTRY— UPGRADING THE VALUE CHAIN
Written by C. Martin Webber with information from J. E. Austin Associates, Inc., and Nathan Associates.

BOX CASE STUDY: DEEPENING THE VALUE CHAIN: GLASS JAR PRODUCTION IN ARMENIA
C. Martin Webber, with information from secondary sources from the field

Sevak Hovhannisyan, USAID/CAPS Project, Armenia, e-mail correspondence

Case Study: Kenyan Green Beans and Other Fresh Vegetable Exports

Hallam, David, Pascal Liu, Gill Lavers, Paul Pilkauskas, George Rapsomanikis, Julie Claro. 2004. "The Market for Non-Traditional Agricultural Exports." FAO.

Knopp, David. 2005. "From Seed to Shelf: Value Chain Dynamics in Kenyan Horticulture." Value Chain Presentation. Emerging Markets Group. Arlington, VA.

Jaffee, Steven. 2003. "From Challenge to Opportunity: Transforming Kenya's Fresh Vegetable Trade in the Context of Emerging Food Safety and Other Standards in Europe." Agriculture and Rural Development Discussion Paper, World Bank, Washington, DC.

Irwin, Bronwyn, Bill Grant, Joan Parker, and Mary Morgan. 2005. "Strengthening the Role of AIDS-Affected MSEs in Productive Markets" BDS on the Margins HIV/AIDS Paper, microREPORT No. 27, USAID, Washington, DC.

Minot, Nicholas, and Margaret Ngigi. 2004. "Are Horticultural Exports a Replicable Success Story? Evidence from Kenya and Côte d'Ivoire." International Food Policy Research Institute and Egerton University, paper presented at the InWEnt, IFPRI, NEPAD, CTA conference, "Successes in African Agriculture," Pretoria December 1–3, 2003.

Okado, Mark. 1999. "Background Paper on Kenya Off-Season and Specialty Fresh Vegetables and Fruits: Lessons of Experience from the Kenya Horticulture Industry." UN Conference on Trade and Development.

TechnoServe. 2004. "Partnerships for Agribusiness Development, Agricultural Trade, and Market Access: A Concept Note for NEPAD." Draft.

SOURCE INTERVIEWED
■ David Knopp, COP-USAID Kenya BDS Program, Emerging Markets Group

Tool 5: Identifying Business Models for Replication

Deloitte Touche. 1997. "Cashew Marketing Liberalization Impact Study: Mozambique." Deloitte & Touche ILA, final report, Maputo, Mozambique.

BOX CASE STUDY: REPLICABLE BUSINESS MODELS— RWANDAN COFFEE WASHING STATIONS
Associated Press. 2006. "Rwandan Coffee in Your Cup: Starbucks Introduces Product in N. America." *Montreal Gazette*, March 3.

Bureau pour le Developpement de la Production Agricole (BDPA). 2005. "Analyse Economique et Financière de la Filière Café." France.

Chemonics International, Inc. 2001. "Assistance a la Dynamisation de l'Agribusiness au Rwanda: ADAR, Year 1 Work Plan." Washington, DC.

———. 2002. "Considerations for Initiating a Specialty Coffee Industry in Rwanda." Washington, DC.

———. 2004. "ADAR Agribusiness Development Assistance 2004: 2nd Quarter Progress Report, April 1 to June 30, 2004." Washington, DC.

———. 2005. "Assessing USAID's Investments in Rwanda's Coffee Sector: Best Practices and Lessons Learned to Consolidate Results and Expand Impact." Washington, DC.

J. E. Austin Associates, Inc. May 2006. "Rwanda Export Promotion Action Plan." Submitted to the government of Rwanda, Rwanda Investment and Export Promotion Agency and Ministry of Finance and Economic Planning, with assistance from the World Bank.

Lecraw, Donald. 2005. "The Coffee, Tea, Tourism, and Handicrafts Sectors: Export Potential and Contribution to Growth and Poverty Reduction," draft version. Integrated Framework, Diagnostic Trade Integration Study.

On the Frontier. 2002. "Rwanda Coffee Strategy and Action Priorities, Rwanda Competitiveness and Innovation Program." Work Group on Coffee, presentation.

——. 2004. "The Rwandan National Competitiveness and Innovation Project: A National Transformation Process." Washington, DC.

Rwanda Coffee Development Authority (OCIR CAFÉ). 2006. "New Action Plan 2006–2008, for the Development of the Rwanda Coffee Sector."

BOX CASE STUDY: DAIRY PAKISTAN—IDENTIFYING AND REPLICATING BUSINESS MODELS WITHIN THE VALUE CHAIN

Arocha, Marcos. 2006. "The PISDAC II Evaluation Report." J. E. Austin Associates, Inc.

Stokes, Justin. 2006. "The White Revolution." J. E. Austin Associates, Inc.

Case Study: Identifying and Implementing Replicable Business Models—Mozambican Cashews

AfricanCashew.com. 2006. General Country Statistics: Mozambique. http://www.africancashew.com/countries/facts.php?id=30.

Artur, Luis, and Nazneen Kanji. 2005. "Satellites and Subsidies: Learning from Experience in Cashew Processing in Northern Mozambique." IIED, London. http://www.iied.org/NR/agbioliv/documents/SatellitesandSubsidiesKanji.pdf.

Deloitte Touche ILA (Africa) 1997. "Cashew Marketing Liberalization Impact Study: Mozambique." Final report, Maputo, Mozambique.

Frey, Sharon. 2006. "Leading Firms in the Value Chain: The Development of a Globally Competitive Cashew Industry in Mozambique." Presentation given during the workshop, "Role of Lead Firms in the Value Chain: Benefits to Micro- and Small Enterprises." SEEP Network Annual Meeting. October 2005.

Harilal, K. N., Nazneen Kanji, J. Jeyaranjan, Mridul Eapen, and Padmini Swaminathan. 2006. "Power in Global Value Chains: Implications for Employment and Livelihoods in the Cashew Nut Industry in India." http://www.iied.org/pubs/pdf/full/14514IIED.pdf.

Kanji, Nazneen. 2004. "Corporate Responsibility and Women's Employment: The Cashew Nut Case." IIED. London. http://www.iied.org/pubs/pdf/full/16005IIED.pdf.

Kanji, Nazneen, Carin Vijfhuizen, Luis Artur, and Carla Braga. 2004. "Liberalization, Gender, and Livelihoods: The Mozambique Cashew Nut Case Summary Report." http://www.iied.org/pubs/pdf/full/9554IIED.pdf.

KIT, Faida MaLi, and IIRR. 2006. "Chain Empowerment: Supporting African Farmers to Develop Markets." Ch. 3: Chain Actors. Royal Tropical Institute, Amsterdam; Faida Market Link, Arusha; and International Institute of Rural Reconstruction, Nairobi.

Labaste, Patrick, ed. 2005. "The European Horticulture Market: Opportunities for Sub-Saharan African Exporters." World Bank Working Paper No. 63. World Bank, Washington, DC.

Londner, Steve. 2005. "Expanding Economic Opportunities for Smallholder Farmers through Development of a Globally Competitive Cashew Industry in Mozambique." IAMA's USAID/World Bank Post-Conference Workshop. http://www.globalfoodchainpartnerships.org/chicago/presentations/SteveLondnerCashewMozambique.pdf.

McMillan, Margaret, Karen Horn Welch, and Dani Rodrik. 2003. "When Economic Reform Goes Wrong: Cashew in Mozambique." Brookings Trade Forum 97–165.

Michigan State University. 2007. "Strengthening Mozambique's Capacity for Agricultural Policy Analysis, Productivity, Growth and Poverty Reduction." Agricultural Economics Department, Lansing, Michigan. http://www.aec.msu.edu/fs2/mozambique/index.htm.

Pearce, Douglas, and Myka Reinsch. 2005. "Small Farmers in Mozambique Access Credit and Markets by Forming Associations with Assistance from CLUSA CGAP Agricultural Microfinance." Case Study No. 5. http://www.cgap.org/portal/binary/com.epicentric.contentmanagement.servlet.ContentDeliveryServlet/Publications/html_pubs/AMCaseStudy_05.html.

Piper, Tim. 2007. "Choosing Between Strategies: Adapting Industry Approaches to Specific Value Chain Analysis Using Three Comparative Commodities." TechnoServe, Inc., Washington, DC. http://www.technoserve.org/news/SEDWorkshop2007.pdf.

Southern African Regional Poverty Network (SARPN). 2006. "Agricultural Intensification in Mozambique: Infrastructure, Policy, and Institutional Framework—When Do Problems Signal Opportunities?" www.sarpn.org.za/documents/d0002233/index.php.

Swennenhuis, Joss. 2003. "CASCA Support Programme for Cashew Processing, Sub-Sector Case Study for BDS Reference Guide of SNV (Stichting Nederlandse Vrijwilligers)." SNV Mozambique.

TechnoServe, Inc. 2003. "Cashew in Eastern and Southern Africa." TechnoServe, Inc., for the East Africa Fine Coffee Association, November, Washington, DC.

——. 2004. "Enhancing the Global Competitiveness of Mozambique's Cashew Industry." Washington, DC. http://www.technoserve.org/news/TNSCashewBrief.pdf.

————. 2005. "New Trade and Enterprise Development (NEW TREND) Program Final Performance Report." Washington, DC.

USAID. 2006. "USAID: Telling Our Story: Simple Technology Revitalizes Mozambique." Washington, DC. http://www.usaid.gov/stories/mozambique/ss_mozambique_nuts.html.

Vijfhuizen, Carin, Luis Artur, Nazneen Kanji, and Carla Braga. 2003. "Liberalization, Gender, and Livelihoods: The Cashew Nut Case." Working Paper 2: Mozambique Phase 2, The South, January–December 2003. http://www.poptel.org.uk/iied/docs/sarl/WP2e_moz_phase2_cashew_eng.pdf.

Walter, Jake. 2006a. "Note from the Field: Quality Pricing for Cashews Pays Off." TechnoServe, Inc., Washington, DC. http://www.microlinks.org/ev_en.php?ID=13537_201&ID2=DO_TOPIC.

————. 2006b. "What Drives Competitiveness in the Mozambique Cashew Value Chain?" PowerPoint presentation, TechnoServe, Inc., Washington, DC.

Wilson, John S. 2003. "Standards and Global Trade: A Voice for Africa." World Bank, Washington, DC. http://siteresources.worldbank.org/INTRANETTRADE/Resources/Topics/StandardsTradeAfrica_DFID_SeminarAugust03.pdf.

Wilson, John S., and Victor O. Abiola, eds. 2003. "Standards and Global Trade: A Voice for Africa." World Bank, Washington, DC. http://www1.worldbank.org/publications/pdfs/15473frontmat.pdf.

World Bank. 2006. "Project Brief on a Proposed Credit in the Amount of SDR 14.0 Million (US$20.0 Million Equivalent) and Proposed Grant from the Global Environment Facility Trust Fund in the Amount of US$6.2 Million to the Government of Mozambique for a Market-Led Smallholder Development in the Zambezi Valley Project." Environment, Rural and Social Development Unit, AFTS1 Country Department 2, Mozambique Africa Region. http://www.gefweb.org/documents/Council_Documents/GEF_C28/documents/288905-17-06 Revised-MzBriefWPEntry.pdf.

SOURCES INTERVIEWED
- Antonio Miranda, Miranda Caju
- Shakti Pal and Jake Walter, TechnoServe Mozambique

Tool 6: Capturing Value through Forward and Backward Integration

Austin, James E. 1992. *Agroindustrial Project Analysis*. World Bank/Johns Hopkins Press, second edition.

BOX CASE STUDY: BENEFITS OF VERTICAL INTEGRATION—ZEGA AND ZAMBIA'S HORTICULTURAL VALUE CHAIN

Cassidy, Dermot. 2006. "Annex 2: Working Paper on Review of Zambia's Current System of Phytosanitary Management." World Bank, Washington, DC. http://siteresources.worldbank.org/INTRANETTRADE/Resources/Topics/Standards/Zambia_annexes.pdf.

Sergeant, Andrew, and Mirvat Dewadeh. 2006. "Annex 6: Working Paper on Current Status of Zambia's Agricultural Exports." World Bank, Washington, DC. http://siteresources.worldbank.org/INTRANETTRADE/Resources/Topics/Standards/Zambia_annexes.pdf.

Wijnands, J. "Sustainable Industrial Networks in the Flower Industry." International Society for Horticulture Science, *Scripta Horticulturae* No. 2. http://www.actahort.org/chronica/pdf/sh_2.pdf.

SOURCES INTERVIEWED
- Steve Humphreys, FinTrac
- C. Martin Webber, J. E. Austin Associates, Inc.

BOX CASE STUDY: BULGARIAN WINE—INTEGRATING OPERATIONS TO SECURE SOURCING OF RAW MATERIAL

Vinzavod-Assenovgrad, http://www.mavrud.com/en/index.htm.

SOURCES INTERVIEWED
- Borislav Georgiev, Independent Consultant
- Krassen Stanchev, IME

Case Study: Capturing Value through Integration—The Ghanaian Pineapple Industry and Blue Skies Holdings Ltd.

Blue Skies, http://www.bsholdings.com/.

Danielou, Morgane, and Christophe Ravry. 2005. "The Rise of Ghana's Pineapple Industry." World Bank, Africa Region Working Paper Series No. 93.

Ghana Export Promotion Center News, http://www.gepcghana.com/news.php?item=4&n.

Hallam, David, Pascal Liu, Gill Lavers, Paul Pilkauskas, George Rapsomanikis, and Julie Claro. 2005. "The Market for Non-Traditional Agricultural Exports." Commodities and Trade Division, FAO.

Imbert, Eric. 2003. "The World Pineapple Market: When Growth Goes Hand in Hand with Diversity." Prepared for the Food and Agricultural Organization (FAO) conference, "Committee on Commodity Problems, Intergovernmental Group on Bananas and on Tropical Fruits," Third Session, Puerto de la Cruz, Spain, December 11–15.

Rougé, B., and M. N'Goan. 1997. "L'Ananas en Afrique de l'Ouest et du Centre." *Acta Horticulturae* 425: 75–82.

Sea Freight Pineapple Exporters of Ghana (SPEG). http://www.ghana-exporter.org/speg/.

SOURCES INTERVIEWED
- Nick Railstor, TechnoServe Ghana
- Susan Bornstein, TechnoServe, Washington, DC
- Jean Michel Voisard, TIPCEE Ghana
- Emmanuel Owusu, GHANA SPEG

Tool 7: Creating and Taking Advantage of Economies of Scale

The Economist. February 15, 2007. "Big Chains Enjoy a Buyer's Market."

Vagneron I., G. Faure, and D. Loeillet. 2005. "Is There a Pilot in the Chain? Identifying the Key Drivers of Change in the Fresh Pineapple Sector." CIRAD.

Case Study: Creating and Taking Advantage of Economies of Scale—The Ghana and Côte d'Ivoire Experiences in Fresh Pineapple Exports

Danielou, Morgane, and Christophe Ravry. 2005. "The Rise of Ghana's Pineapple Industry." World Bank, Africa Region Working Paper Series No. 93.

Ghana Export Promotion Center News, http://www.gepcghana.com/news.php?item=4&n.

Hallam, David, Pascal Liu, Gill Lavers, Paul Pilkauskas, George Rapsomanikis, and Julie Claro. 2005. "The Market for Non-Traditional Agricultural Exports." Commodities and Trade Division, FAO.

Loeillet, D. 2003. "The World Pineapple Market: When Growth Goes Hand in Hand with Diversity." Prepared for the Food and Agricultural Organization (FAO) conference, "Committee on Commodity Problems, Intergovernmental Group on Bananas and on Tropical Fruits," Third Session, Puerto de la Cruz, Spain, December 11–15.

Minot, N., and M. Ngigi. 2003. "Are Horticultural Exports a Replicable Success Story? Evidence from Kenya and Côte d'Ivoire." International Food Policy Research Institute and Egerton University, paper presented at the InWEnt, IFPRI, NEPAD, CTA conference "Successes in African Agriculture," Pretoria, December 1–3.

Rougé, B., and M. N'Goan. 1997. "L'Ananas en Afrique de l'Ouest et du Centre." *Acta Horticulturae* 425: 75–82.

Sea Freight Pineapple Exporters of Ghana (SPEG). http://www.ghana-exporter.org/speg/.

TechnoServe. 2004. "Partnerships for Agribusiness Development, Agricultural Trade, and Market Access: A Concept Note for NEPAD."

Ti, T.C. 2000. "The Global Pineapple Economy." *Acta Horticulturae*.

Voisard, Jean-Michel, and Peter Jaeger. 2003. "Ghana Horticulture Study."

SOURCES INTERVIEWED
- Nick Railstor, TechnoServe Ghana
- Susan Bornstein, TechnoServe, Washington, DC
- Jean Michel Voisard, TIPCEE Ghana
- Emmanuel Owusu, GHANA SPEG

Case Study: Creating and Taking Advantage of Economies of Scale within the Mozambican Cashew Value Chain

AfricanCashew.com. 2006. General Country Statistics: Mozambique. http://www.africancashew.com/countries/facts.php?id=30.

Artur, Luis, and Nazneen Kanji. 2005. "Satellites and Subsidies: Learning from Experience in Cashew Processing in Northern Mozambique." IIED, London. http://www.iied.org/NR/agbioliv/documents/SatellitesandSubsidiesKanji.pdf.

Frey, Sharon. 2006. "Leading Firms in the Value Chain: The Development of a Globally Competitive Cashew Industry in Mozambique." Presentation given during the workshop, "Role of Lead Firms in the Value Chain: Benefits to Micro- and Small Enterprises." SEEP Network Annual Meeting. October 2005.

Harilal, K. N., Nazneen Kanji, J. Jeyaranjan, Mridul Eapen, and Padmini Swaminathan. 2006. "Power in Global Value Chains: Implications for Employment and Livelihoods in the Cashew Nut Industry in India." http://www.iied.org/pubs/pdf/full/14514IIED.pdf.

Kanji, Nazneen. 2004. "Corporate Responsibility and Women's Employment: The Cashew Nut Case." IIED, March, London. http://www.iied.org/pubs/pdf/full/16005IIED.pdf.

Kanji, Nazneen, Carin Vijfhuizen, Luis Artur, and Carla Braga. 2004. "Liberalization, Gender, and Livelihoods: The Mozambique Cashew Nut Case Summary Report." http://www.iied.org/pubs/pdf/full/9554IIED.pdf.

KIT, Faida MaLi, and IIRR. 2006. "Chain Empowerment: Supporting African Farmers to Develop Markets." Ch. 3: Chain Actors. Royal Tropical Institute, Amsterdam; Faida Market Link, Arusha; and International Institute of Rural Reconstruction, Nairobi.

Labaste, Patrick, ed. 2005. "The European Horticulture Market: Opportunities for Sub-Saharan African Exporters." World Bank Working Paper No. 63. World Bank, Washington, DC.

Londner, Steve. 2005. "Expanding Economic Opportunities for Smallholder Farmers through Development of a Globally Competitive Cashew Industry in Mozambique."

IAMA's USAID/World Bank Post-Conference Workshop. http://www.globalfoodchainpartnerships.org/chicago/presentations/SteveLondnerCashewMozambique.pdf.

McMillan, Margaret, Karen Horn Welch, and Dani Rodrik. 2003. "When Economic Reform Goes Wrong: Cashew in Mozambique." *Brookings Trade Forum* 97–165.

Michigan State University. 2007. "Strengthening Mozambique's Capacity for Agricultural Policy Analysis, Productivity, Growth and Poverty Reduction." Agricultural Economics Department, Lansing, Michigan. http://www.aec.msu.edu/fs2/mozambique/index.htm.

Pearce, Douglas, and Myka Reinsch. 2005. "Small Farmers in Mozambique Access Credit and Markets by Forming Associations with Assistance from CLUSA CGAP Agricultural Microfinance." Case Study No. 5. http://www.cgap.org/portal/binary/com.epicentric.contentmanagement.servlet.ContentDeliveryServlet/Publications/html_pubs/AMCaseStudy_05.html.

Piper, Tim. 2007. "Choosing Between Strategies: Adapting Industry Approaches to Specific Value Chain Analysis Using Three Comparative Commodities." TechnoServe, Inc., Washington, DC. http://www.technoserve.org/news/SEDWorkshop2007.pdf.

Southern African Regional Poverty Network (SARPN). 2006. "Agricultural Intensification in Mozambique: Infrastructure, Policy, and Institutional Framework—When Do Problems Signal Opportunities?" www.sarpn.org.za/documents/d0002233/index.php.

Swennenhuis, Joss. 2003. "CASCA Support Programme for Cashew Processing, Sub-Sector Case Study for BDS Reference Guide of SNV (Stichting Nederlandse Vrijwilligers)." SNV Mozambique.

TechnoServe, Inc. 2003. "Cashew in Eastern and Southern Africa." TechnoServe, Inc., for the East Africa Fine Coffee Association, November, Washington, DC.

———. 2004. "Enhancing the Global Competitiveness of Mozambique's Cashew Industry." Washington, DC. http://www.technoserve.org/news/TNSCashewBrief.pdf.

———. 2005. "New Trade and Enterprise Development (NEW TREND) Program Final Performance Report." Washington, DC.

USAID. 2006. "USAID: Telling Our Story: Simple Technology Revitalizes Mozambique." Washington, DC. http://www.usaid.gov/stories/mozambique/ss_mozambique_nuts.html.

Vijfhuizen, Carin, Luis Artur, Nazneen Kanji, and Carla Braga. 2003. "Liberalization, Gender, and Livelihoods: The Cashew Nut Case." Working Paper 2: Mozambique Phase 2, The South, January–December 2003. http://www.poptel.org.uk/iied/docs/sarl/WP2e_moz_phase2_cashew_eng.pdf.

Walter, Jake. 2006a. "Note from the Field: Quality Pricing for Cashews Pays Off." TechnoServe, Inc., Washington, DC. http://www.microlinks.org/ev_en.php?ID=13537_201&ID2=DO_TOPIC.

———. 2006b. "What Drives Competitiveness in the Mozambique Cashew Value Chain?" PowerPoint presentation, TechnoServe, Inc., Washington, DC.

Wilson, John S. 2003. "Standards and Global Trade: A Voice for Africa." World Bank, Washington, DC. http://siteresources.worldbank.org/INTRANETTRADE/Resources/Topics/StandardsTradeAfrica_DFID_SeminarAugust03.pdf.

Wilson, John S., and Victor O. Abiola, eds. 2003. "Standards and Global Trade: A Voice for Africa." World Bank, Washington, DC. http://www1.worldbank.org/publications/pdfs/15473frontmat.pdf.

World Bank. 2006. "Project Brief on a Proposed Credit in the Amount of SDR 14.0 Million (US$20.0 Million Equivalent) and Proposed Grant from the Global Environment Facility Trust Fund in the Amount of US$6.2 Million to the Government of Mozambique for a Market-Led Smallholder Development in the Zambezi Valley Project." Environment, Rural and Social Development Unit, AFTS1 Country Department 2, Mozambique Africa Region. http://www.gefweb.org/documents/Council_Documents/GEF_C28/documents/288905-17-06 Revised-MzBriefWPEntry.pdf.

SOURCES INTERVIEWED
- Antonio Miranda, Miranda Caju
- Shakti Pal and Jake Walter, TechnoServe Mozambique

Tool 8: Positioning Products and Value Chains for Greater Value and Competitiveness

BOX CASE STUDY: ECUADORIAN CACAO—POSITIONING THE VALUE CHAIN FOR GREATER VALUE AND COMPETITIVENESS

ARD. "Ecuador Northern Border Income and Employment Project." http://www.ardinc.com/projects/detail_region.php?id=118.

InfoComm. "Cocoa: Quality." Market Information in the Commodities Area. UNCTAD. http://www.unctad.org/infocomm/anglais/cocoa/quality.htm.

SOURCE INTERVIEWED
- Karl Walk, Purchaser, Blommer's Chocolate

BOX CASE STUDY: THAILAND GAP CLUSTER—POSITIONING PRODUCTS (AND THE VALUE CHAIN) FOR GREATER VALUE AND COMPETITIVENESS

Arocha, Marcos. 2004. Monitoring and Evaluation Report of the USAID-funded Southeast Asia Competitiveness Initiative (SEACI). J. E. Austin Associates, Inc.

SOURCE INTERVIEWED
■ Anan Patannathanes, KIAsia

Case Study: Value Chain Strategies for Market Repositioning—Rwandan Coffee

Associated Press. "Rwandan Coffee in Your Cup: Starbucks Introduces Product in N. America." *Montreal Gazette*, March 3, 2006.

Bureau pour le Developpement de la Production Agricole (BDPA). 2005. "Analyse Economique et Financière de la Filière Café." France.

Chemonics International, Inc. 2001. "Assistance a la Dynamisation de l'Agribusiness au Rwanda: ADAR, Year 1 Work Plan." Washington, DC.

———. 2002. "Considerations for Initiating a Specialty Coffee Industry in Rwanda." Washington, DC.

———. 2004. "ADAR Agribusiness Development Assistance 2004: 2nd Quarter Progress Report, April 1 to June 30, 2004." Washington, DC.

———. 2005. "Assessing USAID's Investments in Rwanda's Coffee Sector: Best Practices and Lessons Learned to Consolidate Results and Expand Impact." Washington, DC.

J. E. Austin Associates, Inc. 2006. "Rwanda Export Promotion Action Plan." Submitted to the government of Rwanda, Rwanda Investment and Export Promotion Agency and Ministry of Finance and Economic Planning, May, with assistance from the World Bank.

Lecraw, Donald. 2005. "The Coffee, Tea, Tourism, and Handicrafts Sectors: Export Potential and Contribution to Growth and Poverty Reduction," Draft version, Integrated Framework, Diagnostic Trade Integration Study.

On the Frontier. 2002. "Rwanda Coffee Strategy and Action Priorities, Rwanda Competitiveness and Innovation Program." Work Group on Coffee, presentation.

———. 2004. "The Rwandan National Competitiveness and Innovation Project: A National Transformation Process." Washington, DC.

Rwanda Coffee Development Authority (OCIR CAFÉ). November 2005. "New Action Plan 2006–2008, for the Development of the Rwanda Coffee Sector."

SOURCES INTERVIEWED
■ Rob Henning, On the Frontier, Washington, DC
■ Patrick Nugawela, J. E. Austin Associates, Inc.
■ C. Martin Webber, J. E. Austin Associates, Inc.
■ Warren Weinstein, J. E. Austin Associates, Inc.
■ Maurice Wiener, Chemonics, Inc., former Chief of Party, USAID/ADAR Project

Tool 9: Applying Standards and Certifications to Achieve Greater Quality

BOX CASE STUDY: THAILAND GAP CLUSTER—USE OF STANDARDS AND CERTIFICATIONS TO UPGRADE VALUE
Arocha, Marcos. 2004. Monitoring and Evaluation Report of the USAID-funded Southeast Asia Competitiveness Initiative (SEACI). J. E. Austin Associates, Inc.

SOURCE INTERVIEWED
■ Anan Patannathanes, KIAsia

BOX CASE STUDY: ECUADOR CACAO—IMPROVING QUALITY AT THE PRODUCER LEVEL TO ACHIEVE HIGHER MARKET PRICES
ARD. "Ecuador Northern Border Income and Employment Project." http://www.ardinc.com/projects/detail_region.php?id=118.

InfoComm. "Cocoa: Quality." Market Information in the Commodities Area, UNCTAD. http://www.unctad.org/infocomm/anglais/cocoa/quality.htm.

SOURCE INTERVIEWED
■ Karl Walk, Purchaser, Blommer's Chocolate

Case Study: Ugandan Nile Perch Quality Management and Certification

Ponte, Stefano. 2005. "Bans, Tests and Alchemy: Food Safety Standards and the Ugandan Fish Export Industry." Danish Institute for International Studies, DIIS Working Paper No. 2005/19. http://www.isn.ethz.ch/pubs/ph/details.cfm?lng=en&id=18423.

World Bank. 2006. "Uganda, Standards and Trade: Experience, Capacities, and Priorities." http://siteresources.worldbank.org/INTRANETTRADE/Resources/Topics/Standards/Uganda_Standards_final.pdf.

SOURCES INTERVIEWED
■ Patrick Nugawela, J. E. Austin Associates, Inc.
■ Philip Borel de Bitche, GreenFields Uganda LTD.
■ C. Martin Webber, J. E. Austin Associates, Inc.

Tool 10: Identifying Needed Support Services for the Value Chain

BOX CASE STUDY: UGANDAN COTTON—ENTERPRISE-LINKED EXTENSION SERVICES MODEL
Support for Private Enterprise Expansion and Development (SPEED). 2003. "Support for Private Enterprise Expansion

and Development, Private Sector Takes on Development Role." SPEED Bulletin, June.

BOX CASE STUDY: SRI LANKAN CINNAMON

Bolnick, Bruce. 2003. "The Economic Impact of Cluster Initiatives Under the Competitiveness Initiative Project Interim Assessment and Recommendations." Nathan Associates Inc.

Iqbal, Mohammad. 1993. "International Trade in Non-Wood Forest Products: An Overview." Food and Agriculture Organization (FAO), Rome, Italy. http://www.fao.org/docrep/x5326e/x5326e00.htm#Contents.

Nathan Associates, Inc. 2002. "A Competitiveness Strategy for Sri Lanka's Spices Industry." Developed by the Spices Industry Cluster, supported and funded by the Competitiveness Initiative, a joint project of the United States Agency for International Development (USAID), Nathan Associates Inc., and J. E. Austin Associates, Inc. Colombo, Sri Lanka.

USAID. 2005. "Helping restore the legacy of 'Ceylon cinnamon.'" http://www.usaid.gov/lk/news/tos/july05-cinnamon.html.

USAID. 2007. "Request for Proposal: Connecting Rural Economies (CORE) for Sri Lanka."

Case Study: Identifying Needed Support Services for the Value Chain—Zambian Cotton

Food Security Research Project. 2000. "Improving Smallholder and Agri-Business Opportunities in Zambia's Cotton Sector: Key Challenges and Options." Lusaka, Zambia.

Regional Agricultural Trade Expansion Support (RATES) Program. 2003. "Cotton-Textile-Apparel Value Chain Report: Zambia." USAID.

Tschirley, David, Colin Poulton, and Duncan Boughton. 2006. "The Many Paths of Cotton Sector Reform in Eastern and Southern Africa: Lessons from a Decade of Experience." Working Paper No. 18. Food Security Research Project, Lusaka, Zambia.

Tschirley, David, Ballard Zulu, and James Shaffer. 2004. "Cotton in Zambia: An Assessment of Its Organization, Performance, Current Policy Initiatives, and Challenges for the Future." Working Paper No. 10. Food Security Research Project, Lusaka, Zambia.

SOURCE INTERVIEWED
- Ben Sekamatte, Dunavant Cotton, Zambia

Tool 11: Improving the Operating Environment by Promoting Public-Private Dialogue

BOX CASE STUDY: TANZANIAN COFFEE AND KILICAFE: PRODUCTIVE PUBLIC-PRIVATE DIALOGUE

TechnoServe, Inc. 2006. Case Study on Coffee in Tanzania. Washington, DC.

Tschirley, David. 2004. "Cotton in Zambia: An Assessment of Its Organization, Performance, Current Policy Initiatives, and Challenges for the Future."

SOURCES INTERVIEWED
- Thom Dixon, TechnoServe Tanzania
- Susan Bornstein, TechnoServe

Case Study: Improving the Operating Environment by Promoting Public-Private Dialogue—Botswana Cattle Producers Association

Botswana Meat Association. 2006. "Maun Abattoir Fate to Be Decided Soon." Daily News, September 22. http://www.gov.bw/cgi-bin/news.cgi?d=20060922&i=Maun_abattoir_fate_to_be_decided_soon.

"Advocating for Cattle Policy Reform." http://www.satradehub.org/CXA_html/ss_case_study.html.

"Cattle Farmers Get Higher Prices." USAID. http://www.usaid.gov/stories/botswana/ss_bw_meat.pdf.

Food Chain Center. "Cutting Costs—Adding Value in Red Meat." http://www.foodchaincentre.com/cir.asp?type=1&subtype=6&cir=117.

"f) Concept—What does Value in Red Meat mean to Consumers?" September 2003.

"g) Concept—Where to find Savings in the Red Meat Chain?" September 2003.

Jefferis, Keith. n.d. "How Trade Can Help to Revitalize Botswana's Beef and Cattle Sector." http://www.satradehub.org/CXA_html/docs/reports/How%20Trade%20Can%20Help%20to%20Revitalise%20Botswana%20Final.pdf.

———. 2005. "How Trade Liberalization Can Contribute to Solving the Crisis in the Cattle and Beef Sector." USAID.

Monnane, M. "Experience on Competition Policy: The Case of Botswana." Botswana Institute for Development Policy Analysis.

"Presidential Initiatives 2005: Global Action, Focused Results." http://pdf.usaid.gov/pdf_docs/PDACG999.pdf.

"Trade Hub Happenings." Issue No. 45. http://www.satradehub.org/CXA_html/docs/HH-Dec2006%20-%20Jan2007.pdf/http://www.satradehub.org/CXA_html/hh_issue45.html.

SOURCES INTERVIEWED

■ Keith Jefferis, Southern Africa Global Competitiveness Hub Consultant

■ Martin Norman, Hub Manager, Southern Africa Global Competitiveness Hub

■ Philip Fischer, President, Botswana Cattle Producer's Association

Tool 12: Achieving Synergies through Clustering

Porter, Michael E. 2007. "Creating a Competitive South Africa." Institute for Strategy and Competitiveness, Harvard Business School. Johannesburg, South Africa. 3 July 2007.

Graphic Sources:

Harvard Business School student team research. (2007). Hornberger, K, N. Ndiritu, L. Ponce-Brito, M. Tashu, and T. Watt. 2007. "Kenya's Cut-Flower Cluster." Final Paper for Microeconomics of Competitiveness.

Case Study: Achieving Synergies through Clustering—Kenyan Avocados

Deloitte Touche. 2003. "Development of the Kenyan Avocado Value Chain." Kenya BDS Activity Brief.

Emerging Markets Group. 2006. "Marketing News: Kenya Horticulture Development Program." Kenya BDS, November/December. Arlington, VA.

Hallam, David, and Pascal Liu. 2004. "The Market of Non-Traditional Agricultural Exports." FAO.

Jaffee, Steven. 2003. "From Challenge to Opportunity: Transforming Kenya's Fresh Vegetable Trade in the Context of Emerging Food Safety and Other Standards in Europe." Agriculture and Rural Development Discussion Paper, World Bank, Washington, DC.

Minot, N., and M. Ngigi. 2003. "Are Horticultural Exports a Replicable Success Story? Evidence from Kenya and Côte d'Ivoire." International Food Policy Research Institute and Egerton University. Paper presented at the InWEnt, IFPRI, NEPAD, CTA Conference "Successes in African Agriculture." December 1–3, Pretoria.

Okado, Mark. 1999. "Background Paper on Kenya Off-Season and Specialty Fresh Vegetables and Fruits: Lessons of Experience from the Kenya Horticulture Industry." UN Conference on Trade and Development.

Shah, Tiku. 2003. "Kenya Avocados." Presentation on the market, November, Fresh Produce Exporters Association of Kenya (FPEAK).

SOURCE INTERVIEWED

■ David Knopp, Chief of Party, USAID/BDS Project

Tool 13: Monitoring Achievements in Value Chain Performance

BOX CASE STUDY: STANDARDS FOR GHANAIAN PINEAPPLES

Danielou, Morgane, and Christophe Ravry. 2005. "The Rise of Ghana's Pineapple Industry: From Successful Takeoff to Sustainable Expansion." World Bank, Washington, DC.

"Ghana: European Tastes Affect Country's Pineapple Exports." All Africa. http://allafrica.com/stories/printable/200612110733.html.

Ghana News Agency. 2004. "GEPC Orders Pineapple Plantlets." 11 October. http://www.ghanaweb.com/GhanaHomePage/NewsArchive/artikel.php?ID=67530.

Yawson, David, and Luis Kluwe Aguiar. 2006. "Agility in the Ghanaian International Pineapple Supply Chain." Presentation to the International Symposium on Fresh Produce Supply Chain Management, December 6-10, Chiang Mai, Thailand.

SOURCE INTERVIEWED

■ Malick Antoine, ESSD Africa, World Bank

BOX CASE STUDY: THE PAID M&E FRAMEWORK

Adapted from the model developed by Kevin X. Murphy, J. E. Austin Associates, Inc.

INDEX

Boxes, figures, notes, and tables are indicated by *b*, *f*, *n*, and *t*, respectively.

Holland. *See* Netherlands
Homegrown (Kenyan horticultural exporter), 75–76
Honduras, 91
horizontal collaboration and linkages. *See also* vertical integration and linkages
  in avocado industry, 157
  cashew processors and, 102–103
  in clusters, 9
  economies of scale and, 95–96, 100
  integration and, 69
  market supply and, 25
  in value chains, 9, 16, 19
Horticultural Association of Ghana (HAG), 92
Horticulture Crops Development Agency (HCDA, Kenya), 73, 158
human resources assessments, 46, 47

I

Illy-cafe (coffee company), 141*b*
impact assessment (IA), 161
India, 3, 81, 83*n*3, 91, 101
Indonesia, 91
Indu-Farm Ltd. (avocado exporter), 157
information and information sharing
  in avocado industry, 157, 160
  in cashew industry, 102–103
  in literature review, 22
  in Nigerian domestic catfish market, 52
  public-private dialogue and, 142
  quality standards and certification and, 116–117
  value chain analysis and, 11
infrastructure, 47, 142
innovations, 8, 13, 15, 22
institutional alignment, 139–140
Integral Ghana Ltd. (pineapple company), 98
integration, 25, 85–90. *See also* horizontal collaboration and linkages; vertical integration and linkages
  backward, 22, 88*b*
  considerations for, 87
  forward integration, 85, 90*n*1
  Ghanaian pineapple industry and, 91–94
  national value chain perspective on, 85–87, 86*f*
  summary of tool, 87, 90
Inter-American Development Bank, 106*b*
International Development Association (IDA), 33
International Finance Corporation (IFC), 7, 142
International Food Policy Research Institute (IFPRI), 2
investment
  FDI, 10, 69, 72, 152
  indicators, 162, 164*b*
  TIP, 99*n*1
ISO 9001 certification, 124–125, 125*f*, 126
Israel, 159
Italy, 105, 122, 160

J

J.E. Austin Associates, Inc.
  PAID approach to cluster evaluation, 153
  "10 Bridges Approach," 48*n*5

Jefferis, Keith, 146, 147
Jei River Farms (Ghanaian pineapple exporter), 92, 98
John Lawrence Farms (Ghanaian pineapple export company), 98
joint ventures, 69, 72, 95

K

Kaesetsart University, 118*b*
Kenya
  airfreight tonnage in, 88*b*
  benchmarking of floriculture in, 61, 62–64, 67*t*
  coffee production in, 109, 111, 141*b*
  cut flowers in, 152, 153*f*
  diversification of exports in, 3
  FPEAK, 74, 158
  Fresh Produce Terminal, Nairobi airport, 74
  map of, 74*f*
  Nile perch production in, 122
Kenya Agricultural Research Institute (KARI), 158
Kenya-GAP (code of practice for horticulture industry), 158
Kenyan avocados, 155–160. *See also* avocados
  background on, 155–156
  cluster actors' roles for, 157–159
  cluster for, 157, 157*f*, 160
  educational organizations and, 158
  government organizations and, 158
  increase in export of, 157, 159*f*
  industrial organizations and, 158
  industry results for, 160
  input suppliers/providers for, 158–159
  points to consider, 155
  supporting industries for, 158
  value chain for, 156–157, 156*f*, 157*f*
Kenyan Business Development Services (Kenya BDS) Project, 156–157, 158
Kenyan green beans, 73–76
  added operations and, 73, 76
  background on, 73–74
  timeline of horticultural development in Kenya, 74
  value chain for, 74–76, 75*f*
Kenya Plant Health Inspectorate Services (KEPHIS), 158
KILICAFE (Association of Kilimanjaro Specialty Coffee Growers), 141*b*
Koranco Farms (Ghanaian pineapple exporter), 92

L

lead firms, 20, 22, 81, 117, 121
Liberia, agricultural production decline in, 4
linkages. *See* horizontal collaboration and linkages; vertical integration and linkages
Lint Company of Zambia (LINTCO), 134
literature review of value chains. *See* value chains, literature review of
Lonrho Cotton (cotton company), 134, 135

M

Madagascar, aquaculture in, 50
maize, 130*b*
Mali

Thai exports to, 118*b*
Ugandan Nile perch market in, 125
University of Moratuwa, 72
upgrading. *See* value chains, upgrading and deepening
U.S. African Growth and Opportunity Act of 2000 (AGOA), 31*b*
U.S. Agency for International Development (USAID)
  avocado industry and, 155
  cashew sector and, 80, 81, 100
  cattle producers and, 145
  Ecuadorian cacao and, 119*b*
  Mongolian meat industry and, 70*b*
  Projet Croissance Economique support by, 31*b*
  Rwandan coffee and, 112
  SPEG and, 99*n*1, 163*b*, 164*f*
  Ugandan cotton and, 129*b*, 130*b*
  Ugandan Nile perch and, 125
  value chain analysis and, 7
U.S. Department of Agriculture (USDA), 70*b*

V
value chains, 9–13
  Africa's development agenda and, 1–2
  analysis of, 10–12
  benchmarking. *See* benchmarking and gap assessments of value chains
  for Blue Skies Holdings Ltd., 93
  for Botswana cattle, 146, 149
  buyer-driven, 21, 92
  case studies. *See individual case studies, e.g. Ugandan Nile perch*
  clustering and, 151–152, 155
  competitiveness and, 10, 12, 23, 26, 105–108.
    See also competitiveness
  definition of concepts, 9–10
  gap assessments. *See* benchmarking and gap assessments of value chains
  for Ghanaian pineapples, 98–99, 98*f*
  horizontal collaboration and, 95
  for Kenyan avocados, 156–157, 156*f*, 157*f*
  for Kenyan green beans, 74–76, 75*f*
  monitoring results in development, 26
  for Mozambican cashews, 82, 82*f*, 102–103
  Nigerian domestic catfish and, 49–53, 51*f*, 53*f*
  operating environment implications for, 12–13
  for pineapple exports, 98–99
  producer-driven, 21
  public-private dialogue and, 139, 140, 142
  quality and, 12, 115, 115*f*, 117, 121
  support services for, 129–137
  tools for implementation. *See* tools for value chain implementation
  Ugandan floriculture analysis of, 62–64, 62*f*, 64*f*
  for Ugandan Nile perch, 122–123, 124*f*, 126–127
  vertical and horizontal linkages in, 9, 16, 19, 85–87
  for Zambian cotton, 135, 135*f*, 136*f*, 137
value chain interventions, priority sectors for, 25, 29–32.
    See also interventions
  domestic capacity and economic impact and, 30–31

initial list of products for, 29–30, 31*b*
  market analysis and, 30
  summary of tool, 32
  testing commitment and, 31–32
value chain performance monitoring, 8, 26, 161–165
  Ghanaian pineapple standards and, 163*b*
  implementation of, 162–163, 163*f*
  purpose of monitoring, 161
  questions to ask about, 161–162
  summary of tool, 165
value chains, literature review of, 15–23, 17–18*t*
  creating trust and, 15, 16–20
  governance and, 15, 20
  innovation, information, and knowledge and, 15, 22
  intervention points and, 15, 22
  market power and, 15, 20–22
  power relations in value chains, 20, 21*f*
  works of particular interest from, 15–16
value chains, upgrading and deepening, 25, 69–72
  adding operations for, 69, 72
  categories of, 22
  commercial joint ventures and, 72
  domestic and foreign direct investment and, 69, 72
  domestic capacity and, 30
  Kenyan green beans and, 73, 76
  methods for deepening value chain, 69–72
  new entrants/entrepreneurs and, 69
  specialization and, 69, 129
  summary of tool, 72
  testing commitment and, 32
  vertical integration and, 71, 72
value chain strategies, 25, 41–48.
    See also Rwandan coffee
  business environment assessment and, 46–47, 48*n*7
  Competitiveness Diamond and, 42–44, 47
  human resources assessment and, 46, 47
  mapping and, 132
  operational productivity assessment and, 44–45, 47
  productivity and, 41–47, 41*f*
  status assessment of value chains, 41–42, 42*f*
  strategic productivity assessment and, 44, 47
  summary of tool, 47
  supply chain quality assessment and, 45–46, 47
  SWOT analysis of, 42, 47
value chain support services, 26, 129–137
  extension services model for, 129, 129*b*
  mapping of business and financial services, 132, 132*f*
  Sri Lankan cinnamon and, 131*b*
  summary of tool, 132–133
  Ugandan cotton and, 129–130*b*
  Zambian cotton and, 134–137
Value Chain Wiki, 7
vertical integration and linkages. *See also* horizontal collaboration and linkages
  in avocado industry, 157
  in floriculture industry, 61–62
  Ghanaian pineapple industry and, 91, 97

governance and, 20
from national value chain perspective, 85–87, 88b, 89t
value chain deepening and, 69, 71, 72
in value chains, 6, 16, 19
Vietnam, 56b, 110
Vinzavod-Assenovgrad (VA), 89b

W

washing stations for coffee, 78b
"weaner" system of cattle production, 147, 148, 149
West African Economic Monetary Union, 3
Wienco (agrochemical supplier), 99
wine industry, 89–90b
workforce quality, 46, 48n5
World Bank
  agricultural trade facilitation by, 5, 7
  Doing Business Report, 48n7, 56
  IDA loan funds from, 33
  Mali and, 37
  Mozambique and, 34, 36, 81, 101
  public-private dialogue and, 142

Sustainable Development Department of the Africa Region (AFR-SDN), 7
Ugandan floriculture sector and, 61, 62
World Development Report, 1
World Customs Organization (WCO), 131b
World Development Indicators, 56
World Development Report (World Bank), 1
World Economic Forum, 48n6, 56

Z

Zambia, 3, 4, 88b
Zambia Airways, 88b
Zambian cotton, 134–137
  background on, 134–135, 135f
  Dunavant's distributor model, 135–137, 136f, 137t
  increase in exports of, 137, 137f
  points to consider, 134
  sector growth for, 137
Zambian Export Growers Association (ZEGA), 88b
Zambia Privatization Agency (ZPA), 134
"Zambique" (cashew brand name), 102, 103
Zimbabwe, 4, 8n3, 88b

ECO-AUDIT
Environmental Benefits Statement

The World Bank is committed to preserving endangered forests and natural resources. The Office of the Publisher has chosen to print **Building Competitiveness in Africa's Agriculture** on recycled paper with 30 percent post-consumer waste, in accordance with the recommended standards for paper usage set by the Green Press Initiative, a nonprofit program supporting publishers in using fiber that is not sourced from endangered forests. For more information, visit www.greenpressinitiative.org.

Saved:
- 10 trees
- 3 million British thermal units of total energy
- 981 pounds of net greenhouse gases (CO_2 equivalent)
- 4,727 gallons of waste water
- 287 pounds of solid waste

green
press
INITIATIVE

www.ingramcontent.com/pod-product-compliance
Lightning Source LLC
Chambersburg PA
CBHW080545220326
41599CB00032B/6372